"This book is exceptional in that it has practical benefits for both obsessive-compulsive disorder (OCD) sufferers and for clinicians. For sufferers, it serves as a self-help treatment guide for understanding the disorder and using proven treatment techniques to bring about symptom reduction. For clinicians, it serves as a treatment manual that can assist in making the initial diagnosis, identifying the particular OCD subtype, and developing a successful treatment plan."

—Paul R. Munford, Ph.D., director of the intensive outpatient treatment program at the Cognitive Behavior Therapy Center for OCD and Anxiety in San Rafael, CA, author of *Overcoming Compulsive Washing*

"A wealth of information and real help for people with OCD and their families! *The OCD Workbook* is a great resource that is practical and easy to understand, with the latest updates and effective step-by-step strategies."

—Aureen Pinto Wagner, Ph.D., author of *Up and Down the Worry Hill: A Children's Book About OCD*, *What to Do When Your Child Has OCD*, and *Treatment of OCD in Children and Adolescents*

"While there are many self-help books for OCD sufferers, there are few that are of the same caliber, in terms of completeness and usefulness, as Hyman and Pedrick's *The OCD Workbook*. This is a first-rate resource for those seeking to recover their lives from this torturous disorder."

—Fred Penzel, Ph.D., licensed psychologist and executive director of Western Suffolk Psychological Services in Huntington, NY, and author of *Obsessive-Compulsive Disorders*

"Bruce Hyman and Cherry Pedrick's updated and expanded version of their classic, *The OCD Workbook*, is one of the best self-help books on OCD. Many sections have been expanded and new ones added. Readers will find up-to-date information on their own particular OCD concerns and how to conquer them."

—Bruce Mansbridge, Ph.D., author of *The Complete Idiot's Guide to Conquering Obsessive-Compulsive Behavior* and clinical assistant professor of psychology at the University of Texas, Austin

"The third edition of *The OCD Workbook* expands on the already comprehensive second edition by adding new insights in areas including mindfulness meditation, responsibility modification techniques, and acceptance and commitment therapy. Here the reader finds the most comprehensive survey of cognitive behavioral treatment for OCD that is accessible to the layman. All is clearly written, easily grasped, and laid out in a very user-friendly manner. Every OCD sufferer should read this book!"

—Ian Osborn, MD, psychiatrist, assistant professor of psychiatry at the University of New Mexico Health Science Center, and author of *Tormenting Thoughts and Secret Rituals: The Hidden Epidemic of Obsessive-Compulsive Disorder*

"This book is an extremely helpful step-by-step guide to overcoming OCD. The authors are experienced in the treatment of this debilitating disorder and provide an easy formula for understanding and treating the symptoms of OCD and some spectrum disorders, such as health anxiety and body dysmorphic disorder. It is a very thorough book explaining the need to engage in therapy and how to apply specific strategies for specific symptoms. Some helpful hints are also provided for family members. I strongly recommend the book for those combating OCD."

—Fugen Neziroglu, Ph.D., board-certified behavior and cognitive therapist, director of the Bio-Behavioral Institute in Great Neck, NY, and author of *Body Dysmorphic Disorder*

"This is an excellently organized, self-directed program to assist sufferers of OCD. The examples of cognitive behavioral treatment components for adults and children with OCD are very comprehensive. Parents and family will find support and assistance in breaking the patterns of enabling, and therapists will be able to implement behavioral assignments that will decrease OCD suffering."

—Blanche Freund, adjunct professor of psychology and psychiatry at the University of Miami School of Medicine

"There has long been a need for a workbook that puts concrete instructions for doing therapy directly into the hands of people with OCD and their families. Hyman and Pedrick have admirably filled that need in this book. *The OCD Workbook* provides critically important practical information on how to overcome a wide variety of OCD symptoms."

—Jeffrey M. Schwartz, MD, research professor of psychology at the University of California, Los Angeles, and author of *Brain Lock* and *The Mind and the Brain*

"This book offers a clear explanation of the modern treatment of OCD. I personally expect to recommend it to many of my OCD patients. It contains clear, step-by-step procedures for exposure and ritual prevention that are fundamental parts of what we know to be the most powerful treatment for OCD. In addition, I was pleased to find step-by-step procedures and examples of how to use cutting-edge cognitive techniques. The book offers clear suggestions for working with a variety of forms of OCD, including scrupulosity, hit and run, and hoarding problems. This book should be helpful to people who need to do self-directed treatment as well as to therapists who can use the examples and steps to treat OCD effectively."

—James M. Claiborn, Ph.D., ABPP, psychologist and member of the Scientific Advisory Board of the Obsessive-Compulsive Foundation

"More than just a workbook, this work by Hyman and Pedrick defines and demystifies obsessive-compulsive disorder. In addition, it offers therapists and patients a highly specific and useful treatment program. *The OCD Workbook* should be an important addition to your collection of OCD treatment literature."

—Robert H. Ackerman, MSW, clinical assistant professor in the Department of Psychiatry at the State University of New York, Health Science Center at Brooklyn

"What a delight to read *The OCD Workbook!* In my twenty years of clinical practice and research involving people suffering from obsessive-compulsive disorder, this is the best self-help resource I have come across. Hyman, a clinical social worker, and Pedrick, a registered nurse, have written a terrific resource for persons with OCD and their families. Plus, this book should be on every therapist's bookshelf. Thoroughly grounded in the principles of evidence-based practice, *The OCD Workbook* is a very readable, interesting, and easy-to-understand manual. I highly recommend it!"

—Bruce A. Thyer, Ph.D., dean of the School of Social Work at Florida State University in Tallahassee, FL

"The authors of this wonderful manual are to be congratulated for creating a comprehensive, balanced, and highly readable book. It should be a boon to patients and their family members and anyone else who wants to know about OCD and related disorders. The book provides detailed instructions for self-treatment that are about the best I have seen. I urge therapists to get a hold of this book and study it. Not only will they learn to be better therapists, but they will also understand their patients better."

—Donald W. Black, MD, professor of psychiatry at the University of Iowa College of Medicine

"The OCD Workbook is a must for anyone affected by OCD. This comprehensive, easy-to-read, informative book presents a sensitively written self-guided program for exposure and response prevention (ERP) and covers many of the issues related to OCD. Hyman and Pedrick also include cognitive strategies aimed to identify faulty beliefs and challenge them, a strong addition to any treatment plan. Thousands of people have already benefited from this workbook!"

—Barbara Van Noppen, Ph.D., assistant professor and assistant chair of education at the Keck School of Medicine at the University of Southern California

"The OCD Workbook is readable and informative. I would encourage my patients to read it to learn more about OCD, its symptoms, and how we can be partners in its treatment."

—Roberto A. Domiguez, MD, former professor of psychiatry at the University of Miami School of Medicine

"The OCD Workbook is an amazing resource. It includes everything you need to conduct self-directed treatment for OCD. It is thorough, practical, and well-organized. It is an invaluable resource for clinicians as well."

—Bradley C. Riemann, Ph.D., director of the OCD Center at Rogers Memorial Hospital in Oconomowoc, WI

"The OCD Workbook was already a useful tool for OCD sufferers. However, new sections on topics like mindfulness and health anxiety, an expanded list of resources, and other updates make the third edition better than ever."

—C. Alec Pollard, Ph.D., director of the Anxiety Disorders Center at the Saint Louis Behavioral Medicine Institute and professor of family and community medicine at Saint Louis University

"In The OCD Workbook, Hyman and Pedrick have crafted an excellent self-help guide that details proven methods of addressing obsessive-compulsive symptoms. Readers will find this book to be clearly written, easy to understand, and, most importantly, very user-friendly. Given the demonstrated powerful effects of behavioral therapy for OCD, this book promises to spread information about effective strategies for this problem and holds great potential for improving individuals' quality of life."

—Eric A. Storch, Ph.D., associate professor at the University of South Florida and director of the University of South Florida OCD Program

THE OCD WORKBOOK

THIRD EDITION

Your Guide to

Breaking Free from

Obsessive-

Compulsive

Disorder

BRUCE M. HYMAN, PH.D.

CHERRY PEDRICK, RN

NEW HARBINGER PUBLICATIONS, INC.

Publisher's Note

This publication is designed to provide accurate and authoritative information in regard to the subject matter covered. It is sold with the understanding that the publisher is not engaged in rendering psychological, financial, legal, or other professional services. If expert assistance or counseling is needed, the services of a competent professional should be sought.

Distributed in Canada by Raincoast Books

New Harbinger Publications, Inc.
5674 Shattuck Avenue
Oakland, CA 94609
www.newharbinger.com

FSC
www.fsc.org
MIX
Paper from responsible sources
FSC® C011935

Cover design by Amy Shoup
Text design by Tracy Marie Carlson
Acquired by Catharine Sutker
Edited by Jasmine Star

Library of Congress Cataloging-in-Publication Data

Hyman, Bruce M.
The OCD workbook : your guide to breaking free from obsessive-compulsive disorder / Bruce M. Hyman and Cherry Pedrick. -- 3rd ed.
p. cm.
Includes bibliographical references.
ISBN 978-1-57224-921-9 (printed book) -- ISBN 978-1-57224-922-6 (pdf ebook) 1. Obsessive-compulsive disorder--Treatment--Popular works. 2. Obsessive-compulsive disorder--Treatment--Handbooks, manuals, etc. I. Pedrick, Cherry. II. Title.
RC533.H95 2010
616.85'227--dc22

2010028481

14 13 12

10 9 8 7 6 5 4

Contents

PART 2

The Self-Directed Program

PART 3

Using the Self-Directed Program for Specific Forms of OCD

The OCD Workbook is dedicated to the millions of people who struggle daily with OCD; their families, whose lives are deeply affected by the presence of OCD in their loved ones; the clinicians who dedicate their lives to helping lessen the burden of OCD in their patients; and the researchers and scientists who work to increase our understanding of OCD and discover breakthroughs in its treatment.

Acknowledgments

This book has been made possible with the help of many people. Thank you to Blanche Freund, Ph.D., who served as a teacher and mentor through my years of learning about cognitive behavioral treatment for OCD; to my late mother, Mildred Hyman, who instilled the values that made me who I am; to my late father, Louis Hyman, from whom I learned kindness and the love of science and art; to Cherry Pedrick, who continues to be a fine collaborator; to Robin, my life partner, who provided quiet support and gentle encouragement for this project; and to my patients, who teach me every day about gratitude, courage, and hope.

—Bruce M. Hyman, Ph.D., LCSW

Bruce Hyman made coauthoring *The OCD Workbook* a wonderful experience. I am grateful to my husband, Jim, and my son, James, for their support and encouragement throughout the process of writing this book. I thank Michael Jenike, MD, for his insight and vast knowledge about the brain. Thank you to my cats, Melody, Spunky, Little Kitty, and Andy, for the entertainment and cuddles during the lonely days of writing. Most of all, I thank my God for making it all possible.

—Cherry Pedrick, RN

We would both like to thank the many people at New Harbinger Publications who have made this revision a reality with their encouragement and patience. We especially thank Jasmine Star for her patience and fine editing work.

—Bruce and Cherry

Introduction

The great thing in this world is not so much where we are, but in what direction we are moving.

—Oliver Wendell Holmes

The OCD Workbook has been a valuable resource for people with OCD, their families, and clinicians for over a decade. This third edition discusses even more variants of the OCD spectrum and has been updated to reflect some of the latest trends in cognitive behavioral treatment. We've also added more help and guidance for family members struggling with OCD in a loved one. If you are seeking a greater understanding of OCD and how to overcome it, this book can help.

WHO WE ARE

"I have to go back. I have to go back and see if I locked the door." I stared at the door of our house. I had to check it again. Turning off the ignition, I jumped out of the car.

"I saw you lock it, Mom," my son, James, called after me, obviously annoyed. He didn't want to be late for school again. "You checked it twice."

I knew I had locked the door. I always locked it, so why did I need to check it again? I couldn't explain. I just had to check again. This happened more and more often until I was regularly returning home just to see if the doors were locked. In the middle of the day, without warning, my fears would hit me. Did I lock the door? Did I turn off the coffeepot, the lights? Soon I was checking and rechecking appliances, locks, car brakes, and paperwork. When the constant checking began to interfere with my job as a home health nurse, I sought treatment.

I was diagnosed with obsessive-compulsive disorder (OCD). As a nurse, I was somewhat familiar with obsessive-compulsive disorder, but I wasn't prepared for the struggle ahead. My need to recover motivated me to read every book and article about OCD I could find. This led to writing several magazine articles and a continuing education home study course for nurses. The research and writing helped me apply cognitive behavioral therapy principles to my own illness.

As my OCD improved, I reached out to others who were struggling with OCD, and I met many people who were suffering from a lack of knowledge and support. I discovered support systems on the Internet and through the Obsessive-Compulsive Foundation (now the International OCD Foundation). Help is available for people struggling with OCD, but there is a great need to get information to the people who need it.

My brilliant computer nerd son offered to make a website for me. A website! What would I do with a website? I soon found out. He made a beautiful home page dedicated to educating others about OCD. Thousands of people have stopped by my website at http://CherryPedrick.com on their educational journey. From there, links lead to the best OCD sites on the Internet.

Today, after applying what I've learned about cognitive behavioral therapy, my OCD seems to be gone. However, I remain on guard for fleeting urges to needlessly check on something or wash my hands. Giving in once too often could unleash an OCD monster once again.

I met Dr. Bruce Hyman, a psychotherapist specializing in OCD, at the 1997 Obsessive-Compulsive Foundation conference. He was writing a book—a workbook designed to give people with OCD the tools to work on their problem. For the previous two years, he had been seeking a medical professional with OCD who could write about the experience of having OCD from the patient's point of view. We discovered we could each fill a need in writing a book about OCD. Together, the two of us bring important expertise to this project. My nursing background helps me understand the medical aspects of OCD and its treatment. Having the disorder myself helps me relate the information with compassion and understanding. We believe that this combined expertise is one reason why this book has been so successful. I'm thankful for the opportunity to update the workbook so that it can continue to assist people in recovering from OCD.

—Cherlene (Cherry) Pedrick, RN

No, I don't have OCD, but in 1987, after I'd been conducting a general clinical psychotherapy practice for seven years, a middle-aged male was referred to me for treatment of severe washing and checking rituals. He took two-hour showers, obsessively avoided touching unfamiliar objects, feared dirt and germs, and washed his hands seventy-five times a day.

Having never been consulted previously by a person with OCD, I was baffled by his strange behavior and moved by his profound suffering. When I realized that my traditional training was ill-suited to truly helping him, I embarked upon a mission to learn everything I could about OCD and to seek guidance from whomever in the country might have specialized knowledge of it. In 1988, this led me to the Anxiety Disorders Unit at the former Medical College of Pennsylvania (now the Drexel University College of Medicine), directed by Dr. Edna Foa (who is presently on the faculty of the University of Pennsylvania School of Medicine and in 2010 was voted among the top one hundred most influential people in the world by *Time* magazine).

There I observed the successful use of intensive behavioral treatment methods with OCD patients. Having a previous foundation in cognitive behavioral treatment methods, in time I was able to adopt the methods for use with my own OCD patients. Subsequently, I received several years of ongoing clinical case consultation from Dr. Blanche Freund. In 1992 I established the OCD Resource Center of Florida with offices in Fort Lauderdale (Hollywood), Miami, and Boca Raton, Florida. Presently, approximately 90 percent of my busy practice is devoted to the treatment of adults and children with OCD and related disorders.

The idea of writing a book on OCD grew out of my awareness that very few people with OCD are receiving the proper help. Although our culture has come a long way toward greater understanding and destigmatization of psychiatric disorders, including OCD, much fear and ignorance persists. Far too many people struggling with OCD fear the embarrassment and discomfort of seeking help and confronting the disorder. Those who do seek help for OCD are often disappointed by the results. Many of my patients report having sought help from several well-intentioned but misinformed health care professionals before finding someone truly knowledgeable about OCD. Due to the often desperate nature of the disease, people will seek help from almost any source that offers the remotest hope for relief. Frequently, these disappointing encounters with the health care system result in further emotional pain, guilt, discouragement, and mistrust. Many give up hope and lose confidence in their ability to break free from the power OCD has over their lives.

There is still no medical cure. You will probably still have OCD after reading this book, but you also will have the weapons you need to fight against the disorder. My goal in writing this book is to help people with OCD get on track in their battle with OCD by guiding them step-by-step through the process of change.

Most of the treatment techniques in this book are not new. They have been presented in other self-help books, as well as in clinical texts for professional psychologists. *The OCD Workbook* brings the best and most effective of these techniques together in one book, and also presents current theories about behavioral change processes in clear and understandable language. It is the product of more than twenty years of experience treating over one thousand people with every conceivable type of OCD.

—Bruce M. Hyman, Ph.D., LCSW

HOW THIS BOOK CAN HELP YOU

The workbook format could appear as an obstacle to some people. You may not like to write in your books, or you may have checked this book out from your local library. Or you could be reading *The OCD Workbook* in digital form. In this edition of the book, we've addressed these concerns by providing instructions for doing the exercises in a journal or notebook.

The OCD Workbook isn't intended as a substitute for psychiatric or psychological treatment by a qualified mental health professional. Rather, it should be used in the following ways:

- **In conjunction with ongoing psychiatric or psychological treatment.** For example, you may be seeing a professional who is highly qualified but who doesn't specialize in treating OCD. In addition to being helpful to you as you work through the steps toward gaining control of your OCD, this book can assist your therapist in coaching, guiding, or advising you.

- **By people reluctant to seek professional help.** People with OCD are often reluctant to seek professional help, even if it's available to them. There are often feelings of shame and embarrassment at the notion of seeking the services of a mental health professional. You may be inhibited by the notion that seeking help would be an admission that you might be "crazy." Many people with OCD obsess that they may be crazy and fear that the doctor will only confirm their worst nightmare. This can make seeking help unthinkable. We hope that this book will help you shed many of the myths and misconceptions about what OCD is and how it's treated. Its aim is to start you down the road toward self-directed treatment or, if necessary, to help you seek out qualified help without shame or embarrassment.

- **By people with OCD who want to help themselves but don't know how to go about doing it, or those who don't have access to qualified treatment.** You may have a desire to learn as much about OCD as possible and wish to use this book as a guide for self-directed intervention. If you think you have OCD, we urge you to seek out the services of a mental health professional who is experienced in the diagnosis and treatment of OCD. Chapter 19 provides guidance on finding a qualified mental health professional. A psychiatrist or psychologist can verify the diagnosis of OCD and help you decide if self-directed cognitive behavioral therapy is appropriate for you. As discussed in chapter 16, certain other illnesses sometimes co-occur with OCD and can complicate recovery. With some of these illnesses, it may be important to develop a comprehensive treatment strategy that addresses each diagnosis.

- **By family members seeking a greater understanding of OCD.** Just as it is not recommended that a doctor treat his or her own family for diseases, we recommend that family members not try to take on the role of psychotherapist to a loved one using this book, even if trained as therapists. However, family members can provide valuable support as the person with OCD works through the self-help process outlined in this book. Chapter 4 describes how a trusted friend or family member can play the role of behavioral assistant, and chapter 18 is devoted to how family members can help. In addition, each chapter includes a section specifically aimed at family and friends.

ABOUT THIS BOOK

The OCD Workbook is divided into four parts. After reading part 1 (chapters 1 through 3), you will understand what OCD is, how it is diagnosed, what the symptoms are, and how the disorder is currently treated. These chapters discuss the most commonly accepted theories about the causes of OCD. Chapter 3 contains a review of the most effective treatments for OCD: medication and cognitive behavioral therapy.

Part 2 (chapters 4 through 9) is the heart of this book, providing step-by-step instructions to guide you through the self-directed program for combating OCD. These chapters discuss attitudes that can help or hinder recovery. They also address realistic expectations regarding progress, especially the need for tolerance and patience with yourself. When you commit to the self-directed program, you'll need to set aside a period of three to six weeks during which the program will be a top priority in your life. The reward of freedom from the distress of OCD will make this sacrifice worthwhile. Note that we don't say freedom from OCD, but freedom from the distress. You'll find that you can live a more productive and fulfilling life with a little bit of OCD in your life than you can with a lot of OCD.

Part 2 includes instructions for using *The OCD Workbook* alone or with a therapist functioning as a coach. It also discusses how to determine whether you need professional counseling. If you don't have a therapist available for support, a trusted friend or family member can take on the role of behavioral assistant. In this edition, part 2 also includes a new chapter 9, Acceptance and Mindfulness Approaches to OCD. This chapter presents material on the "third wave" of cognitive behavioral therapy, including the use of acceptance and commitment therapy (ACT) for OCD, an approach that is gaining increasing recognition within the mental health field.

Part 3 (chapters 10 through 17) offers an introduction to specific symptoms and disorders within the OCD spectrum. It isn't necessary for you to read through all of part 3; feel free to skip to whatever chapter or chapters are most relevant to you. In this part of the book you'll learn powerful strategies for coping with less common but debilitating OCD symptoms and disorders related to OCD. These include primarily obsessional OCD, scrupulosity, "hit-and-run" OCD, health-related anxiety, and hoarding.

Part 4 (chapters 16 through 19) includes valuable information on disorders related to OCD, family issues, and gives detailed information that will assist you in reaching out to others for help. Chapter 16 discusses some of the so-called spectrum disorders related to OCD, including body dysmorphic disorder and trichotillomania (hair pulling). Because OCD happens to children too, chapter 17 provides information on how to apply the principles in this book to OCD in children. Your family can play an important role in your recovery, so chapter 18 is devoted to this important topic. In addition, in this revised edition of the book we've included a new section entitled "Help for Family and Friends" at the end of each chapter. We encourage you to share this information with your closest friends and family members. Depending on your situation, you may also need professional help. Chapter 19 offers guidance in selecting a qualified mental health professional. And because support groups can also be quite helpful in overcoming the shame and isolation that often accompany OCD, chapter 19 outlines resources that can assist you in locating OCD support groups in your area.

The appendix also contains valuable resources. Certain people in your life may be clueless when it comes to OCD and wonder why you act strangely. Or maybe you've kept your OCD secret, so "coming out" will be a surprise to the people in your life. Therefore the appendix contains a concise description of the disorder that you may copy and give to teachers, school counselors, family members, spiritual advisors, and other people who might benefit from this information. The appendix also contains the Yale-Brown Obsessive Compulsive Scale (Y-BOCS), a self-administered rating scale that helps determine the degree of severity of OCD symptoms. Each item asks about some dimension of how symptoms interfere with day-to-day life. The range of scores is from 0 to 40, with 40 representing the most severe level of OCD symptoms. Consider the Y-BOCS to be something like a snapshot of your present level of symptoms. It's a good idea to take the Y-BOCS at the beginning of the self-directed program, midway through, and at a point when you've completed a significant amount of work on your OCD. It can give you a good idea of how far you've come, and how far you still need to go in reducing the interference of symptoms in your daily life.

PART I

Learning About OCD

CHAPTER 1

What Is OCD? Its Many Faces

There is perhaps nothing so bad and so dangerous in life as fear.

—Jawaharlal Nehru

The people you will meet in this chapter are representative of the millions of people who have obsessive-compulsive disorder, or OCD. They struggle with a neurobehavioral disorder that fills their minds with unwanted thoughts and threatens them with doom if they don't perform repetitive, senseless rituals. They are not a rare group. About one in forty people has OCD.

In the *Diagnostic and Statistical Manual of Mental Disorders* (American Psychiatric Association 2000), *obsessive-compulsive disorder* is placed within the class of psychiatric disorders known as *anxiety disorders*. Other anxiety disorders include panic disorder, social phobia, simple phobia, generalized anxiety disorder, and post-traumatic stress disorder. OCD is characterized by obsessions and/or compulsions that are time-consuming, distressing, and/or interfere with normal routines, relationships, or daily functioning. *Obsessions* are persistent, unwanted thoughts, images, or urges that intrude into a person's thinking and cause excessive worry and anxiety. *Compulsions* are covert mental acts or overt behaviors performed repetitively to relieve or prevent the worry or anxiety generated by the obsession. They often have the intent of magically preventing or avoiding some dreaded event, such as death, illness, or some other perceived misfortune.

FORMS OF OCD

OCD has many faces, but the patterns of thoughts and behaviors of people with the disorder are remarkably and unmistakably consistent. The most common symptoms associated with OCD are checking, washing and cleaning, ordering and repeating, hoarding, and scrupulosity. Some people who suffer from OCD don't seem to engage in these behaviors, at least not overtly. This is known as primarily obsessional OCD.

Checking. Those who engage in checking live with an excessive, irrational sense of being held responsible for possible dangers and catastrophes that may befall themselves or others as a result of their "imperfect, " "incomplete," or "careless" actions. They feel compelled to repeatedly check that, for example, doors and windows are locked, the stove and iron are turned off, the coffee maker is unplugged, or the garage door is down. They will check over and over until they get a "just right" feeling or a sense of assurance that disaster will be averted. They might also repeatedly check on loved ones to make sure they haven't caused harm to them. Checking compulsions also occur within the context of health-related obsessions; for example, repeatedly checking one's heart rate or blood pressure for evidence of abnormalities that could signify the presence of a catastrophic illness. Checking relieves the anxiety brought on by the obsessive thoughts, but the relief is short-lived. The worries often return or are replaced by similar obsessive thoughts, calling for more checking. A vicious cycle is thus created: anxiety followed by checking, which results in limited relief, then a return of the anxiety, followed by even more checking, and on and on.

Washing and cleaning. People who wash and clean excessively have obsessions about the possibility of contamination by dirt, germs, viruses, or foreign substances. They live with a near-constant dread of either causing harm to others or to themselves, or failing to prevent it. In response to their fear-provoking thoughts, they excessively wash their hands, shower, or clean their homes for hours on end. Over time, fears compound as they perceive more possibilities for harm. The washing and cleaning become more and more elaborate and yet bring less and less relief.

Ordering and repeating. Those who engage in ordering and cleaning might feel they must arrange certain items in a particular, exact, "perfect" way, or they might repeat particular actions over and over until they feel "just right." Many demand that particular objects, such as their shoelaces, hair, or personal belongings, be perfectly even or symmetrical. They become extremely distressed if their things are moved, touched, or rearranged even slightly. Obsessive thoughts or fears of harm coming to them or a loved one can lead to a frenzy of ordering or repeating certain behaviors over and over. They might cross over a room threshold repeatedly, count or repeat words silently, rearrange items, or turn light switches on and off until it feels "just right." Only then will the obsessive thoughts or fears subside, if only for a few moments.

Scrupulosity. People with scrupulosity obsess about religious, ethical, or moral issues. They demand a code of conduct from themselves that goes well beyond that of most people who subscribe to their beliefs. Their compulsions may involve excessive praying and repeatedly, needlessly seeking reassurance of their moral purity from others, usually priests, ministers, or rabbis. Rather than providing peace and freedom from the anxiety, these compulsions actually bring on even more anxiety as the OCD demands more "perfect" adherence to religious rules and practices, triggers even more reassurance seeking, and leads to other rituals to relieve the doubts.

Hoarding. Those with hoarding collect insignificant items and have difficulty throwing away things that most people would consider junk. They develop a strong attachment to their hoarded items and overvalue their importance. Often they are afraid they might need the items at some vague time in the distant future. For these people, letting go of things can cause so much distress that it's easier just to keep them. This results in chaotic and unbearable living conditions in which there is little usable space in the house that isn't taken up with junk.

Primarily obsessional OCD. Those with primarily obsessional OCD experience unwanted, intrusive, horrific thoughts and images of causing danger or harm to others and sometimes even themselves. The themes are almost always of a violent or sexual nature. Or they may have unwanted thoughts of acting upon a sexual impulse toward others in a manner that is clearly disgusting and repulsive even to them. The term "primarily obsessional OCD" implies the presence of obsessive thoughts without accompanying *overtly* performed compulsions. Research over the past twenty years has revealed that most people with primarily obsessional OCD do indeed perform compulsions, but they are subtle, covert behaviors, such as mental compulsions or rituals (Steketee 1993; Freeston and Ladouceur 1997). For example, many engage in repetitive thoughts, such as counting, praying, or repeating certain words, to counteract their anxious thoughts. They may also mentally review situations obsessively to ward off doubt and relieve anxiety. Or they may excessively monitor and scrutinize the feelings in their genitals for any feelings of arousal in unwanted circumstances. They often repeatedly ask others for reassurance that they aren't going to harm someone. As with checkers, washers, orderers, and repeaters, these mental rituals offer only temporary relief from the anxiety brought on by intrusive thoughts. With time, the relief lessens, anxiety mounts, and mental rituals may become more elaborate and time-consuming.

Many people can identify with all these forms of OCD to some extent. Who hasn't checked to see whether the door is locked a second time or shuddered from a disturbing or frightening thought that occurs out of the blue? One person's prized, dusty old newspaper collection may be a pile of worthless junk to another. When these thoughts, feelings, and behaviors cause significant distress or result in marked interference with one's daily living, OCD could be the problem.

Maybe you have a few of the symptoms described above but they don't seem to interfere significantly with your life. Read on. You may realize that your habits do indeed interfere with your life way more than you realized. But even if your symptoms aren't severe enough to warrant a diagnosis of OCD, you may benefit from the same cognitive behavioral therapy principles used to help people with full-blown OCD.

It's common for people with OCD to suffer from a variety of OCD symptoms. For example, Cherry Pedrick had problems with checking, mental rituals, and hand washing. Many people with OCD may have one predominant symptom for years, only to have it go away and then have another one begin. For example, someone who has been a washer for many years may lose the fear of contamination and become a checker, or vice versa. There is no typical pattern; however, a change in the form of the OCD symptoms over time does appear to be the norm.

THE FACE OF OCD

Now we'd like to introduce you to people with OCD so you can see how these symptoms affect people in their daily lives. Except for Cherry, these people are composites of many people with OCD. You may observe similarities between yourself and one or more of the people described, but this is only coincidental.

Cherry's Story: "What If?"—An Unwanted Companion

My struggle with OCD began with the fear that I hadn't locked the door when I left the house. After some time passed, my need to check and worry increased until it invaded my entire life. I frequently and repeatedly returned to the house to check the door, coffeepot, or stove. Away from home, I often stopped what I was doing and returned to my car to make sure the emergency brake was set and the door was locked. What-if scenarios became my constant companions: "What if I left the car door unlocked, and a child got inside the car and then got hurt?" "What if I didn't set the brake, and the car was bumped from behind and rolled forward and hurt someone?" My obsessions revolved around the fear that I had done something—or hadn't done something—that could result in harm to others. I also had a problem with hand washing when I prepared meals, fearing that I might contaminate the food.

Now, over fifteen years after OCD became my constant unwanted companion, I can say that I've broken free from OCD. As I used the techniques Dr. Hyman and I have written about, my OCD became more and more bearable, and then gradually faded. In addition, I've used spiritual techniques and practices to help me let go of obsessive thoughts and resist compulsions.

Mary's Story

Obsessive fears of becoming gravely ill from a disease took over Mary's life when her oldest son contracted a life-threatening virus. She began to avoid blood, dirt, germs, and red spots for fear of the possibility—no matter how remote—of getting sick and not being able to take care of her son. Her fears grew for five years before she sought treatment. By that time, Mary was washing her hands about one hundred times a day, and her daily showering ritual took about one full hour.

She avoided going near hospitals, clinics, and doctors' offices because she considered them contaminated. Certain streets were off-limits too—streets where homeless people were likely to hang out, because she felt that homeless people were more likely to have open sores than people with homes. She avoided anything that might have a red spot on it in case the spot might be camouflaging a bloodstain.

Mary only felt truly comfortable in certain sections of her own home that she considered safe and clean. These areas were off-limits to other family members, especially her husband. Because he worked for a delivery company and made daily deliveries to local hospitals, Mary considered him to be contaminated. When he came home from work, he had to shower immediately and put his clothes in the washing machine so Mary wouldn't have to touch them.

Melody's Story

Melody couldn't remember a time when she didn't check excessively. She didn't consider her checking behavior to be a problem until she went to college and moved out of her parents' home into a small apartment with a roommate. At first her roommate was thankful for Melody's concern. It made her feel safe to see Melody check the door, stove, and appliances every night. However, Melody's nightly rituals grew longer as more and more items were added to the list of things that had to be checked every night.

Her roommate grew alarmed when she saw that Melody was checking the windows, which were always locked, and looking in the backs of closets and under the beds. Also, everything had to be checked in a certain order. If Melody was interrupted or her concentration was broken, she started over. And sometimes she started over just because "it didn't feel right."

Melody also made copies of her course work and kept them in a box. In the evenings, she checked these copies over and over, afraid she had missed a crucial point or had written something offensive. She called home three or four times a day to check on her parents and little brother. She also checked on her friends and others she had associated with during the day. Had she said the wrong thing? Had she harmed someone by coughing with her mouth uncovered? Entire evenings were often spent reviewing the day's events, looking for mistakes she might have made and ways she might have harmed someone.

Robert's Story

Checking was a problem for Robert, too, but most of his checking compulsions revolved around driving. One night he saw a man standing in the median between the lanes. Robert glanced in the rearview mirror and saw the man dart across the road behind his car. Had he hit him? He looked back and didn't see him on the other side of the street.

Robert made a U-turn at the next intersection and went back. He drove slowly by the spot where he had seen the man. Although he didn't see a dead or injured body, he still wasn't sure, so he turned around and drove by again. An hour later, he was late for his appointment and still unsure. He went home and waited anxiously for the evening television news. Surely they would report an accident if someone had been injured.

A week later, Robert drove by a woman riding a bicycle in the bike lane. Again, he was jolted by the thought that he might have hit her. He looked in the rearview mirror. She was still there, riding calmly, oblivious to his fears. Soon he was looking back and checking his mirror whenever he passed pedestrians and bicyclists. He got into the habit of watching the eleven o'clock news each night to check for accidents in areas where he had driven.

Ben's Story

As a child, Ben had organized the toys in his room very carefully. Toy soldiers went in a box. Puzzles had their own place on the bookshelf. His books were sorted on the shelves according to their size: short ones on the right, taller ones on the left. At school, the other children had whispered about Ben's rituals. He had placed his books under his chair in the same spot every day. His pencil always had a sharp point and was positioned at the top of his desk, exactly in the middle. He kept an eraser on the upper right corner, not too close to the edge. His papers always were arranged carefully in the middle of his desk.

As an adult, Ben rarely had visitors in his home. It was too much effort to put things back in order after they left. He couldn't enjoy the few visits family members made because of the anxiety he experienced when something was moved out of its place.

Jack's Story

Going through the thresholds of doors was Jack's difficulty. If he had a "bad" thought or "something just didn't feel right," he had to go back and walk through the door again. When he passed through a doorway, he had to touch the right side, then the left, then the top of the doorway. If he felt okay, he walked through the door. If it didn't feel right, he took a step back, then a step forward, and then he repeated his touching ritual.

Sitting in a chair or standing up from a chair also involved a ritual. First, Jack touched the floor, then both sides of the chair, then he stood. Writing took a lot of effort and time. He had to retrace each letter twice. Consequently, everything took Jack much longer than most people. He set his alarm for three in the morning so he could leave the house by seven. Every minute task involved in getting dressed and groomed had to be done "just right."

Mark's Story

Guilt plagued Mark constantly. When "bad" thoughts—usually of a blasphemous or sexual nature—came to his mind, he prayed. But the prayer had to be right, or it wouldn't work. So the prayers had to be repeated over and over until they felt just right. It was particularly painful to Mark that his bad thoughts invaded his mind most often while he was in church. As a result, he was tempted to stay away from church and to give up his belief in God completely. But he also feared that if he left the church, that would make him feel even guiltier.

Liz's Story

"One person's trash is another person's treasure." For years, Liz justified her collection of stuff by repeating this phrase. But most of the items stashed in the boxes that lined her apartment were no one's treasures, and over time the boxes became a burden. Liz tried to solve the problem by moving. She put the boxes in storage and started over, but her new apartment quickly filled with boxes too.

Liz saved newspapers, magazines, receipts, and mail—even the years-old advertisements and catalogs that filled her mailbox. She wasn't sure why she saved things. But the thought of throwing anything away made her feel extremely anxious. Liz was deeply embarrassed and hadn't had a visitor to her home in many years, which strained her friendships, as she made up excuses for never inviting her friends over.

Angelita's Story

Angelita, a thirty-three-year-old mother with a two-year-old daughter, was preparing lunch. She picked up a knife to cut a tomato and suddenly, out of the blue, the thought of plunging the knife into her daughter popped into her mind. Horrified by such a thought, she was overwhelmed by intense feelings of guilt. The thought returned the next day, again while she was in the kitchen. That evening, while bathing her daughter, the thought "What if I drown my baby?" popped into her head. Again, the thought deeply disturbed her.

For the next several days, over and over again she thought, "I must be a horrible mother to think such terrible thoughts! I'd better do whatever I can to stop these thoughts." To keep herself from thinking such disturbing thoughts, she distracted herself by repeating, "I'm a good mother and I'd never do that," over and over in her mind. But still the thoughts recurred, growing stronger and stronger. Whenever she was alone with her daughter, she felt anxious. She began to avoid touching knives or anything sharp in the presence of her little girl, and she made sure that her mother (who didn't know about the distressing thoughts), was present whenever she bathed her daughter.

Ron's Story

Ron was also plagued by unwanted thoughts. In his mind, certain images played over and over like a continuous movie. They scared him because he feared they would come true. In these thoughts, he was harming someone violently, usually his wife, but also his coworkers and even his closest friends—whomever he was with at the time. He knew in his heart that he didn't have any desire to harm anyone, so he was baffled as to why these thoughts played so strongly in his mind. He could be enjoying a movie or a meal with his family or friends, or just talking to a coworker, and the thoughts would burst into his mind. He developed a strategy of clenching his hands together tightly when the thoughts occurred, which caused severe muscle and joint soreness. He worried constantly that he was losing his mind or going crazy.

The Story of Your Struggle with OCD

You have just read some typical stories of people with OCD. Now, in this exercise, you'll write your own story. Write it as if you are talking to someone safe, like your closest friend, someone you feel confident would never reject, judge, or criticize you for what you write. Permit yourself to express all of your thoughts and feelings about your life with OCD. You may wish to use more space than is available here. If so, feel free to use as much paper as you like. If you prefer not to write in this book, or if you only have it in digital form, purchase a notebook to use as a journal and write your story there as your first entry. If you're afraid someone will read your story, write it in your journal or on a separate sheet of paper, and after completing the exercise, place what you've written in an envelope and store it safely away. One day, when you are truly free from OCD, you'll see this exercise as one of the first important milestones on your road to recovery.

Briefly describe the story of your struggle with OCD:

____

____

____

____

Describe some of your worst OCD symptoms:

____

____

____

____

Describe the progression of these symptoms from when they first started until the present. How have they changed over the months or years?

____

____

____

____

How have the symptoms impacted your life: work, career, family, friends, relationships, and so on?

____

____

____

____

How might your life be different if you were free from OCD?

____

____

OCD THROUGH THE AGES

In the first half of the twentieth century, OCD was known by such names as "compulsion neurosis" and "obsessional neurosis." Obsessive-compulsive disorder was once thought to be a rare disease. In 1964, researchers estimated OCD affected only 0.05 percent of the population (1 out of 2,000 people). In 1977, the estimate was 0.32 percent (3 out of 1,000 people). Major studies now estimate a lifetime prevalence of 2.5 percent (Yaryura-Tobias and Neziroglu 1997b). Much of the reason for the previously low estimates of OCD prevalence lies in the secrecy of people who have the disorder.

Sigmund Freud, the founder of psychoanalysis, believed OCD was a psychological disorder caused by internal conflict and used the psychoanalytic technique of "the talking cure" to treat it. Over the decades, the results from this form of treatment generally weren't good, and OCD became known as a disorder that was difficult to treat. Freud admitted being puzzled by OCD. And even as he continued to promulgate his psychological theories, he looked toward a future when a more thorough understanding of the brain's chemistry and anatomy would play an important role in understanding psychiatric illnesses.

That future is here. Psychology has moved from theories of the mind to research on the brain. Modern technological advances include techniques like positron-emission tomography (PET), single photon emission computed tomography (SPECT), and magnetic resonance imaging (MRI). With these techniques, scientists can look at the deep structures and chemical reactions within the brain. We now know that OCD isn't caused by unconscious conflicts, but by abnormalities in the structure, chemistry, and circuitry of the brain.

Recent discoveries in neurochemistry and pharmacology have helped scientists link OCD with problems in the regulation of the brain chemical *serotonin*, which plays a vital role in the control of our moods and behavior. Today, we have seven medications that help correct such a chemical imbalance: clomipramine (Anafranil), fluoxetine (Prozac), fluvoxamine (Luvox), paroxetine (Paxil), citalopram (Celexa), escitalopram (Lexapro), and sertraline (Zoloft). Most people with OCD will see a reduction of their symptoms with any of these medications. For others, these medications offer only minimal relief, and still other medications may be required to enhance the effectiveness of the first-line drugs. This tells us that serotonin imbalance isn't the only cause. Clearly, there is still a lot more to be learned about brain chemistry and pharmacology as it relates to OCD.

Until the 1960s, psychoanalysis was routinely used to treat OCD. As medications began to prove useful in treating OCD, therapy was changing too. In 1966, British psychologist Victor Meyer began using behavior therapy to treat hospitalized OCD patients with severe contamination fears. Meyer and his colleagues combined intensive exposure to feared objects, such as bathroom doorknobs and faucets, with strict restrictions on showering and washing. In fact, he had the water shut off in the hospital unit except to areas used exclusively for toileting. This new, innovative therapy worked, and it worked quickly.

After several days of intensive treatment, fourteen of his fifteen patients had a marked reduction of their OCD symptoms. Ten were greatly improved or symptom free, and four showed moderate improvement. Since then, numerous studies around the world have demonstrated improvement of OCD symptoms using these behavior therapy techniques, known as *exposure and response prevention* (Steketee 1993).

Unlike psychoanalytic therapy, which emphasizes the role of hidden, unconscious forces in directing our behavior—forces that are out of our control—behavior therapy emphasizes the role of learning in human behavior and focuses on changing behavior by learning new ways of responding.

In the 1980s, researchers such as Paul Salkovskis and Paul Emmelkamp began to recognize the role of faulty beliefs and attitudes in maintaining OCD symptoms. They applied ideas of cognitive therapy originally developed in the 1960s and 1970s (Ellis 1962; Beck, Emery, and Greenberg 1985) to understanding OCD. *Cognitive therapy* involves recognizing and disputing the irrational beliefs and faulty thought patterns that result in abnormal behavior. Cognitive therapy was then applied as an adjunct to behavior therapy in the treatment of OCD (Yaryura-Tobias and Neziroglu 1997b). Together, this is called *cognitive behavioral therapy* (CBT). It is the cornerstone of this book and a powerful tool in breaking free from OCD.

BREAKING FREE FROM OCD

After reviewing your struggle with OCD, it wouldn't be abnormal to feel confused, despairing, uncertain, or anxious about your future, and about bearing the burden of OCD in your life. In its most severe forms, it can be a truly wretched existence. However, with the advances in the scientific understanding of psychiatric disorders in general, and OCD in particular, there is more reason for optimism than ever before. The increasing availability of effective medications and more widespread recognition and use of cognitive behavioral therapy in the treatment of OCD offer an unprecedented level of hope for those with OCD. Obsessive-compulsive disorder has begun to receive a great deal of attention in the media, reflecting an increased acceptance by our culture. People with OCD no longer need to feel ashamed and embarrassed by their problem.

Cognitive behavioral therapy has been established as the most effective treatment for OCD. Cherry applied the principles of *The OCD Workbook* and broke free from her OCD. She's not cured. Indeed, there is no cure for OCD as of yet. But her life is no longer ruled by obsessive thoughts and compulsions. At one time, she was seldom free of anxiety and intrusive thoughts during her waking hours. When intrusive thoughts invade, she can dismiss them. Yes, sometimes she checks the door a second time or washes her hands unnecessarily, but she doesn't feel compelled to perform the ritual over and over. It is our firm belief that you too can achieve significant relief from the stranglehold of OCD. The information in this book will provide you with the tools necessary to make this a reality.

We have just one caveat: If you also suffer from other mental health disorders, including clinical depression, this can complicate the treatment of OCD. If you suspect your OCD is complicated by another disorder, consult a mental health professional. A comprehensive treatment strategy that addresses each diagnosis will be more successful than focusing only on your OCD.

HELP FOR FAMILY AND FRIENDS

Obsessive-compulsive disorder isn't just a personal matter. It also affects family and personal relationships, often in profound ways. This new edition of *The OCD Workbook* will place additional emphasis on the issues that confront family members and partners of the person with OCD by including a "Help for Family and Friends" section at the end of each chapter. We've also listed books for family members, friends, and teachers of those with OCD in the resources section, found at the end of the book. In our experience, family members who are open to growing in their understanding of this mysterious and baffling disorder often play a key role in successful recovery.

Take a few moments to talk with your loved one about how his or her OCD has impacted your life. As you read through this book, you will undoubtedly discover ways that your interactions with your loved one have been less than helpful. This is normal and to be expected. Find the humility to own up to and acknowledge the mistakes you've made, and find the resolve to learn everything you can to be an effective catalyst in your loved one's recovery.

CHAPTER 2

A Closer Look at OCD: Symptoms and Causes

Although the world is full of suffering, it is full also of the overcoming of it.

—Helen Keller

In the United States, obsessive-compulsive disorder is the fourth most common psychiatric diagnosis, with a lifetime prevalence rate of up to 2.5 percent. This means one out of every forty people in this country—over 7.6 million men, women, and children—may suffer from OCD. As mentioned in chapter 1, previous estimates were much lower: 0.05 to 0.32 percent. Estimates today are as much as fifty times greater than in 1964 and 1967 (Yaryura-Tobias and Neziroglu 1997a). About 65 percent of people with OCD develop the disorder before the age of twenty-five, and only 15 percent develop it after the age of thirty-five. There is a slightly higher incidence of OCD in women. However, among children with OCD, boys outnumber girls by about two to one. Obsessive-compulsive disorder exists in every culture and on every continent (Niehous and Stein 1997).

What do these statistics mean to the average person with OCD? They provide confirmation that you are not alone. People with OCD tend to keep the illness a secret. As a result, you may not realize how many people have similar problems. Look around you next time you're amidst a large number of people—at a baseball game, concert, or mall, or even waiting in line at the department of motor vehicles. On average, it's likely that one out of forty people surrounding you has OCD.

The onset of OCD symptoms is usually gradual, although though some children suffer sudden onset in a form of OCD known as PANDAS (see chapter 17). It isn't uncommon for OCD symptoms to flare up during times of emotional stress at work or at home. Major life transitions such as leaving home for the first time, pregnancy, the birth of a child, the termination of a pregnancy, increased levels of responsibility, health problems, and bereavement may be linked to the onset or worsening of OCD symptoms.

The *Diagnostic and Statistical Manual of Mental Disorders* (*DSM*; American Psychiatric Association 2000) is the diagnostic bible for mental health professionals. In its criteria for a diagnosis of OCD, it states, "The essential features of obsessive-compulsive disorder are recurrent obsessions or compulsions... that are severe enough to be time-consuming (i.e., they take more than one hour a day) or cause marked distress or significant impairment... At some point during the course of the disorder, the person has recognized that the obsessions or compulsions are excessive or unreasonable" (American Psychiatric Association 2000, 456-457).

As explained in chapter 1, obsessions are persistent ideas, images, thoughts, or urges experienced as inappropriate and intrusive, and that cause marked anxiety. People with OCD have the sense that these thoughts aren't within their control and that they aren't the kind of thought that they would expect to have. They are also aware that the thoughts are a product of their own minds, versus externally imposed, which would be indicative of a psychotic disorder, not OCD.

In OCD, the discomfort of an obsessive thought or urge results in attempts to contain or neutralize the discomfort through some repetitive action, performed either covertly with thoughts, or overtly with behaviors. Repetitive overt behaviors include ordering, checking, or hand washing, while mental acts may include repeating words silently, praying, or counting. The function of a compulsive ritual or behavior is to reduce the distress that accompanies an obsessive worry or fear. It has the effect of containing, controlling, or neutralizing anxiety. People with OCD don't derive gratification or pleasure from performing their compulsions. They often feel driven to do them to prevent some dreaded situation—usually harm to others or themselves. Compulsions may be related to the content of the obsession but are clearly excessive, or they may not even be connected in a realistic way with what they are designed to neutralize or prevent.

WHAT OCD IS NOT

In order to understand what OCD is, it's important to know what OCD is not. Almost everyone worries, at times excessively. The worries resulting from OCD differ in that they are usually senseless and irrational, and ignoring them makes the person feel anxious and nervous. It is important to distinguish this from worrying that is excessive but rational, which may be a symptom of depression.

Similarly, many people are compulsive without having OCD. They give careful attention to details and procedures and are overly concerned with rules, regulations, and doing things the "right" way. In contrast, the compulsions of people with OCD are senseless and repetitive and are performed to dispel anxiety. Most often, those with OCD consider their compulsions silly, pointless, and troublesome, and even embarrassing and shameful. People aren't always aware of these distinctions, so many forms of repetitive behavior may be mistakenly labeled as OCD, including superstition, ritual, and prayer; substance abuse and compulsive gambling; eating disorders; and obsessive-compulsive personality disorder.

Superstition, Rituals, and Prayer

It is important to recognize that certain repetitive or ritualistic behaviors may be due to cultural or religious influences, not OCD. The *DSM* addresses this point:

> Culturally prescribed ritual behavior is not in itself indicative of obsessive-compulsive disorder unless it exceeds cultural norms, occurs at times and places judged inappropriate by others of the same culture, and interferes with social role functioning... Important life transitions and mourning may lead to an intensification of ritual behavior that may appear to be an obsession to a clinician who is not familiar with the cultural context...
>
> Superstitions and repetitive checking behaviors are commonly encountered in everyday life. A diagnosis of obsessive-compulsive disorder should be considered only if they are particularly time-consuming or result in clinically significant impairment or distress. (American Psychiatric Association 2000, 459)

Rituals and repetitive behaviors are part of the normal repertoire of behaviors we all possess. Prayer, for example, can be an important part of our daily lives. Most people perform some ritualistic and repetitive behavior in the normal course of daily life, and many people are superstitious. But when these behaviors take over, resulting in significant impairment, distress, or anxiety, or are excessively time-consuming, OCD could be responsible. In his workshops, OCD expert Robert Ackerman, MSW, aptly described OCD as a "cult of one."

Substance Abuse and Compulsive Gambling

Although many problem behaviors are considered compulsive, they don't necessarily fit the clinical definition of OCD, and therefore aren't considered OCD. This is the case with pathological gambling and substance addictions, including addictions to drugs and alcohol. The main difference between OCD and these addictive or impulse control disorders is that the obsessive thoughts and compulsive behaviors of OCD are, for the most part, unwanted and unpleasant. Unlike addictions, OCD brings no anticipation of pleasure or satiation. Again, these behaviors are done to reduce discomfort and worry, not for pleasure.

Obsessive-Compulsive Personality Disorder

When we hear the word "personality," we generally think of phrases describing people's overall behavior: "She has a nice, caring personality," "He has a strong, tenacious, domineering personality," and so on. Personality is a consistent, enduring, lifelong set of learned and inherited responses to a multitude of situations and challenges in life. It encompasses characteristics that don't change much throughout the life span.

When a personality style or a set of features fundamental to a personality causes an excess of stress or difficulty in life, the person is said to have a personality disorder. According to the *DSM* (American Psychiatric Association 2000), people with obsessive-compulsive personality disorder (OCPD) are characterized by a preoccupation with details, rules, lists, orderliness, perfectionism, and mental and interpersonal control at the expense of flexibility, openness, and efficiency. They tend to view the world in black-and-white, all-or-nothing terms. There are no gray areas. They often adopt a "my way or the highway" approach to coworkers and family members, often referred to as "truth ownership," that damages and sours these relationships. For these people, it is unacceptable for their performance in any area of life to fall short of "perfection."

This pattern begins by early adulthood and is present in a variety of contexts in the person's life. In the area of work, people with this disorder tend to be highly efficient, reliable, and organized, but often excessively so. They may get overinvolved with the details of a task and lose the forest for the trees. In their personal lives, they spurn change and spontaneity, instead preferring predictability, repetition, and a highly routinized way of life. They tend to keep their emotions and behavior highly controlled and may appear rather cold and aloof to others.

Although people with OCD often have features of OCPD, only a small percentage of people with OCD (6 to 25 percent) actually have full-blown OCPD (Baer and Jenike 1998). The main difference between OCD and OCPD lies in the degree of life impairment. People with OCD suffer substantially from their problem and they wish to be rid of it. People with OCPD, on the other hand, are rarely uncomfortable about it and seldom feel the need for help for their problems. In fact, they are often unaware of the problem their behavior may be causing until these difficulties are brought to their attention by coworkers or family members who have been adversely affected by their behavior.

When a person with OCD also has OCPD, characteristics such as rigidity, perfectionism, and the need for control make it more difficult to change the OCD behaviors. This is mostly due to the reluctance of people with OCPD to accept guidance and intervention from outside themselves, as it implies that they are less than perfect. Unfortunately, when they do reach a point where they are ready to wholeheartedly face their problems, all may seem lost. However, hitting rock bottom often provides the opportunity and motivation to change. Elements of the self-directed program can be useful for people with OCPD. For example, they can use cognitive restructuring (covered in chapter 8) for perfectionism and "truth ownership," and exposure and response prevention to increase their behavioral flexibility in carrying out daily routines.

THE SYMPTOMS OF OCD

Although OCD can manifest in a wide variety of ways, the most common symptoms are checking compulsions and washing or cleaning compulsions. Other symptoms include compulsive counting, the need for symmetry, unwanted sexual or aggressive thoughts, the need to constantly seek reassurance, ordering rituals, and hoarding. As discussed in chapter 1, some people have primarily obsessional OCD, meaning that they have obsessions but no overt compulsions. They are likely to have repetitive, unwanted, and intrusive thoughts of aggressive or sexual acts that are reprehensible to them. Others exhibit *primary obsessional slowness*, wherein their compulsive rituals and need to perform even the simplest daily tasks "just right" results in spending hours every day getting washed, dressed, and groomed.

The pattern of symptoms in OCD is extremely varied. While many people with OCD have one symptom throughout their lives, others have multiple obsessions and compulsions. For example, a checker may also be a washer. In addition, the symptoms may alternate and transform over the years.

For example, a person with intrusive thoughts in adolescence may get over that problem only to become a washer in early adulthood, and then become a checker later in life.

Identifying Your OCD Symptoms

Below, you'll find a lengthy, detailed list of OCD symptoms related to obsessions, and another related to compulsions. Recognizing these symptoms can help the person with OCD come out of a self-imposed closet and seek treatment. Read through the lists and check off all of the symptoms that apply to you, or if you prefer, list your symptoms in your journal—just be sure to record them one way or the other. You'll use this list as you work your way through the self-directed program in this book. Recognizing that you have these symptoms is an important first step in understanding your OCD and developing a treatment plan. (And remember, having these symptoms is not sufficient to diagnose a person with OCD. OCD is diagnosed only when these behaviors result in significant impairment, distress, or anxiety, or are too time-consuming.)

Identifying Your Obsessions

CONTAMINATION OBSESSIONS

Excessive fear or disgust in regard to, and preoccupation with avoiding...

- ☐ Bodily waste or secretions, such as urine, feces, saliva, or blood
- ☐ Dirt or germs
- ☐ Sticky substances or residues
- ☐ Household cleansing agents or chemicals
- ☐ Environmental contaminants, such as radon, asbestos, radiation, or toxic waste
- ☐ Touching animals
- ☐ Insects
- ☑ Becoming ill from contamination
- ☐ Making others ill by contaminating them
- ☐ Diseases, such as AIDS, hepatitis, herpes, or other sexually transmitted diseases

HOARDING, SAVING, AND COLLECTING OBSESSIONS

- ☐ Worry about throwing things away, even seemingly useless items

- ☐ Urge to collect useless things
- ☐ Feeling uncomfortable with empty space in the home and having a need to fill it
- ☐ Urge to purchase multiples of the same item
- ☐ Urge to maintain purchased items in pristine condition, resulting in not using them
- ☐ Urge to pick up useless items from the ground

ORDERING OBSESSIONS

- ☐ Preoccupation with symmetry, exactness, or order
- ☐ Excessive concern that handwriting be perfect or "just right"
- ☐ Concern with aligning papers, books, and other items a certain "perfect" way

RELIGIOUS OBSESSIONS AND SCRUPULOSITY

Excessive fear, worry, and preoccupation with...

- ☐ Having blasphemous thoughts and being punished for them
- ☐ Praying "perfectly"
- ☐ Violating, even slightly, religious rules or precepts
- ☐ The possibility of losing control and shouting expletives in a church or synagogue

BODY IMAGE OBSESSIONS

Excessive fear, worry, and preoccupation with...

- ☐ Having a physical defect that makes you look ugly
- ☐ The possibility that others easily notice your perceived defect and consider it ugly

HEALTH OBSESSIONS

Excessive fear, worry, and preoccupation with...

- ☐ The possibility of having a catastrophic illness despite being told you are healthy
- ☐ The possibility that you may be responsible for causing or not preventing a potentially catastrophic illness in yourself or a loved one

AGGRESSIVE OBSESSIONS

Preoccupation with and excessive, irrational fear of...

- ☐ Losing control and harming yourself or others
- ☐ Acting on unwanted impulses, such as running over someone with your car
- ☐ Choking or stabbing someone
- ☐ Responsibility for some terrible accident, fire, or burglary due to personal carelessness
- ☐ Blurting out insults, obscenities, or racial epithets
- ☐ Doing something embarrassing or looking foolish

SEXUAL OBSESSIONS

Unwanted, worrisome, and intrusive...

- ☐ Sexual thoughts, images, or impulses of "snapping" or losing control
- ☐ Thoughts of molesting your own children or other children
- ☐ Thoughts of groping others
- ☐ Thoughts of being or becoming a homosexual
- ☐ Preoccupation with the idea of committing violent, sexual acts toward others without knowing that you are doing it

MISCELLANEOUS OBSESSIONS

- ☐ An unwanted urge to know, seek out, or remember useless information, such as slogans, license plate numbers, names, words, or historical events
- ☐ Fear of saying something wrong, not saying something just right, or leaving out details
- ☐ Worry about losing things
- ☐ Worry about making mistakes
- ☐ Worry that you didn't perfectly understand something you read
- ☐ Worry that you wrote imperfectly
- ☐ Worry that you wrote an expletive or racial epithet without knowing it

- ☐ Being easily bothered by certain sounds and noises, such as clocks ticking, loud noises, or buzzing
- ☐ Being easily bothered by the feel of clothing or other textures on the skin
- ☐ Intrusive nonsense sounds, music, or words
- ☐ Fear of saying certain words because of superstitious beliefs about those words
- ☐ Fear of using certain colors for superstitious reasons
- ☐ Excessive superstitious fears and rigid adherence to them
- ☐ Excessive concern with lucky and unlucky numbers

Identifying Your Compulsions

CLEANING AND WASHING COMPULSIONS

Excessive, illogical, and uncontrollable…

- ☐ Hand washing, often performed in a ritualistic way
- ☐ Showering or bathing, often performed in a ritualistic way
- ☐ Ritualistic tooth brushing, grooming, or shaving
- ☐ Cleaning of the house, certain rooms, the yard, sidewalks, or cars
- ☐ Cleaning of objects or household items
- ☐ Use of special cleansers or cleaning techniques
- ☐ Avoidance of objects considered contaminated
- ☐ Avoidance of specific places considered contaminated, such as cities, towns, or buildings
- ☐ Concern with wearing gloves or other protection to avoid "contamination"

CHECKING COMPULSIONS

Checking over and over (despite repeated confirmation)…

- ☐ That you didn't harm others without knowing it
- ☐ That you didn't harm yourself
- ☐ That others didn't harm you

- ☐ That you didn't make a mistake
- ☐ That nothing terrible happened
- ☐ That you didn't do something that could cause future harm
- ☐ Some aspect of physical condition, such as appearance, or of health, such as pulse or blood pressure
- ☐ Physical surroundings, such as locks, windows, appliances, or stoves
- ☐ That jars are closed by excessive tightening
- ☐ That doors are closed by excessive, repeated shutting

HOARDING, SAVING, AND COLLECTING COMPULSIONS

- ☐ Saving or collecting seemingly useless items
- ☐ Picking up useless items from the ground
- ☐ Difficulty throwing seemingly useless items away, as they might someday be useful

REPEATING, COUNTING, AND ORDERING COMPULSIONS

- ☐ Reading and rereading things excessively
- ☐ Excessively writing and rewriting things
- ☐ Repeating routine activities, such as going in and out of doorways, getting up and down from a chair, combing hair, tying shoes, or dressing and undressing over and over
- ☐ Doing certain activities a particular number of times
- ☐ Counting items, such as books on a shelf, ceiling tiles, or cars going by
- ☐ Counting during compulsive activities, such as checking or washing
- ☐ Arranging items in a certain order, such as books, pencils, or objects in cupboards

BODY IMAGE COMPULSIONS

- ☐ Excessively checking your body for signs of a physical defect
- ☐ Making extensive efforts to hide perceived defects from others
- ☐ Changing your appearance to hide or "fix" perceived physical defects

HEALTH-RELATED COMPULSIONS

- ☐ Requiring repeated reassurance that you don't have a catastrophic illness
- ☐ Getting repeated medical tests
- ☐ Excessively checking your body (for example, your blood pressure or heart rate) for signs of disease
- ☐ Spending excessive time on the Internet researching symptoms of catastrophic disease

MISCELLANEOUS COMPULSIONS

- ☐ Mental rituals, such as prayers or repeating "good" thoughts to counteract "bad" thoughts (with the intention of reducing or neutralizing anxiety)
- ☐ Reassuring self-talk or mantras stated over and over (with the intention of reducing or neutralizing anxiety)
- ☐ Excessive need to repetitively ask others for reassurance when ample assurance is evident to others and has already been provided
- ☐ Excessive need to confess "wrong" behavior, even the slightest insignificant infractions or perceived infractions against others
- ☐ Superstitious behavior that takes excessive amounts of time
- ☐ Need to touch, tap, or rub certain items or people
- ☐ Measures, other than checking, to prevent harm to self or others, such as avoidance of certain objects or extreme precautions to prevent highly unlikely harm or danger
- ☐ Eating ritualistically according to specific rules, such as arranging food or utensils, eating at certain times, or eating foods in a particular order

OCD-RELATED COMPULSIONS

- ☐ Pulling hair from your scalp, eyebrows, eyelashes, or pubic area
- ☐ Acts of self-damage or self-mutilation, such as picking skin
- ☐ Compulsive shopping (often related to hoarding; for example, buying a number of things for fear of running out)

HOW IS OCD DIAGNOSED?

The journey of recovery from OCD begins with an accurate diagnosis. If you suspect that you have OCD, you will find the following pages to be quite helpful in determining whether this is actually the case. If you aren't sure if you have OCD, it is possible that your uncertainty is actually a symptom of OCD. In any case, it's a good idea to obtain an accurate diagnosis from a qualified mental health professional if you haven't already done so.

A diagnosis of OCD is made on the basis of a psychiatric or psychological examination, a history of the person's symptoms and complaints, and the degree to which the symptoms interfere with daily functioning. Based on the nature, length, and frequency of the symptoms presented, the mental health professional will differentiate OCD from other conditions with similar symptoms. These include schizophrenia, phobias, panic disorder, and generalized anxiety disorder. A physical exam may be recommended to rule out other possible causes of the symptoms. There is no blood test available to reliably diagnose OCD. So how do mental health professionals distinguish between OCD and those people who just worry a great deal?

Studies have shown that 80 to 99 percent of people experience unwanted thoughts (Niehous and Stein 1997). But most people can hold unpleasant thoughts in their mind without too much discomfort, or they can easily dismiss the thoughts entirely. Their thoughts are shorter in duration, less intense, and less frequent than the intrusive thoughts of people who have OCD. The obsessive thoughts of OCD, on the other hand, usually have a specific onset, produce significant discomfort, and result in a powerful, overwhelming urge to neutralize or lessen them. The obsessions and compulsions of OCD significantly interfere with life. People with OCD recognize that they are excessive or unreasonable—at least most of the time.

There are several assessment tools that mental health professionals can use to aid in the diagnosis of OCD. The Yale-Brown Obsessive Compulsive Scale (Y-BOCS) is a questionnaire that can help target obsessive-compulsive symptoms and assess their severity. (We've included the Y-BOCS in the appendix to this book.) The Y-BOCS is also used to monitor the person's response to treatment. There is also a children's version of this scale. Other assessment tools include the Compulsive Activity Checklist (CAC), the Leyton Obsessional Inventory (LOI), the Maudsley Obsessive Compulsive Inventory (MOCI), the Padua Inventory (PI), and the National Institute of Mental Health Global Obsessive-Compulsive Scale (NIMH Global OC).

OCD AND SHAME

People with OCD are typically secretive and shameful about their obsessive thoughts and compulsive behaviors. Many are successful in hiding their illness for years. Unlike people with many other mental illnesses, those with OCD are aware, at least at times, of their inappropriate behaviors and thoughts. However, they are often unaware that their symptoms are part of a recognizable condition that can be treated. Or they may fear that they'd be scorned, perhaps even locked up, if they were to reveal their obsessions and compulsions to others.

Because of this secretiveness, many people wait years, even decades, to seek help. Meanwhile, the obsessive thoughts and compulsive behaviors become more deeply ingrained in their lives. The average time between the onset of symptoms and seeking treatment is over seven years (Yaryura-Tobias and Neziroglu 1997b). Hopefully, further advances in scientific knowledge and understanding of OCD will narrow this time period.

Due to the shame people with OCD often feel, many won't consult a mental health professional. They may prefer to seek help for their symptoms from another type of health professional. Alert medical doctors can detect symptoms of OCD in people who come to see them for seemingly unrelated problems, and the family doctor may be the first professional to see signs of OCD in a person. Parents and family members may mention their concern about the person's frequent washing, counting, or checking. Excessive worry about having AIDS or other serious illnesses, resulting in repeated unnecessary tests and consultations, may also alert physicians.

Other doctors likely to detect signs of OCD include dermatologists, plastic surgeons, dentists, obstetricians, neurologists, neurosurgeons, orthopedic surgeons, pediatricians, infectious disease internists, and even oncologists. Dermatologists may notice chapped hands and eczema-type conditions due to excessive hand washing. People with perfectly normal appearances may present themselves to plastic surgeons requesting surgery for what they feel are noticeable deformities. A dentist may be alerted by gum lesions from excessive teeth cleaning. An orthopedic surgeon may be consulted for musculoskeletal or joint problems arising from repetitive motion activities, such as repeatedly pressing the refrigerator door to make sure it's shut. Signs of OCD may intensify during pregnancy and postpartum and therefore be noticed by obstetricians. Neurologists and neurosurgeons see signs of OCD associated with Tourette syndrome, head injury, epilepsy, and other disorders of the nervous system (discussed later in this chapter). The informed physician with a keen eye will detect OCD and make the appropriate referral to a psychiatrist or other mental health professional, rather than dismissing the person as odd or crazy.

OCD AND DEPRESSION

Many people with OCD suffer from some degree of depressive symptoms, ranging from mild ("the blues") to severe, life-threatening depressive illness characterized by strong, persistent feelings of sadness, hopelessness, helplessness, loss of interest in normal activities and pursuits, lack of energy, impaired sleep and appetite, and suicidal thoughts. At the time they seek treatment, approximately one-third have major clinical depression—the most severely disabling form of depression—and about two-thirds of people with OCD have had at least one episode of major clinical depression in their lifetime (Jenike 1996). Many others suffer from a lesser form of depression known as *dysthymia*—a kind of low-grade depressed mood. Most people with OCD who also have dysthymia are depressed because OCD imposes severe limits on quality of life. For these people, successful treatment of OCD often results in a lifting of the dysthymia.

There is some controversy about whether depression is a separate disease, independent from OCD, or a secondary disease caused by the OCD. In one study, 56.9 percent of people with OCD were diagnosed with a major depressive episode first. Some OCD experts estimate that 90 percent of people with OCD have depression secondary to their OCD (Yaryura-Tobias and Neziroglu 1997b).

Interestingly, many of the medications used to treat depression also work well for OCD, which may indicate that similar issues in regard to brain structure and neurochemical abnormalities are at work in the two disorders. Undoubtedly, further research will reveal more about the connection between OCD and depression. Perhaps depression is a natural outgrowth of having a devastating disease such as OCD. Indeed, it can be depressing to suffer from OCD.

If OCD is an issue for you, it's important to be on the lookout for the warning signs of major clinical depression, since those with major depression often lack the perspective to see what's happening to them. For the same reason, it's also important for doctors and family members to watch for warning signs of major clinical depression. The presence of major clinical depression complicates the treatment of OCD. If you are severely depressed, you may not benefit fully from the self-directed program presented in this book due to the learning and memory deficits typical of major clinical depression. The diagnosis of depression is best made by a licensed mental health professional, who may use a variety of clinical tools to assess the likelihood and severity of depression.

To help you determine whether you may be depressed and therefore should consult with a mental health professional about this, we've provided a couple of assessments. The first is a list of the signs of major clinical depression. Check off all that apply to you (or write them on a separate sheet of paper):

- ☐ Depressed mood most of the day, nearly every day
- ☐ Markedly diminished interest or pleasure in all, or almost all, activities
- ☐ Significant weight loss or gain, or decrease or increase in appetite nearly every day
- ☐ Insomnia or excessive sleep nearly every day
- ☐ Feelings of extreme restlessness or being slowed down
- ☐ Fatigue or loss of energy nearly every day
- ☐ Feelings of worthlessness or excessive or inappropriate guilt nearly every day
- ☐ Diminished ability to think or concentrate, or indecisiveness, nearly every day
- ☐ Recurrent thoughts of death or of suicide (without a specific plan), or a plan for committing suicide or an actual attempt

The diagnosis of major clinical depression requires that you have at least five of the symptoms above, that they are present for two weeks, and that there is a marked change in your previous functioning. In addition, one of the symptoms must be either depressed mood or diminished interest or pleasure in activities (American Psychiatric Association 2000).

A second way of assessing whether you may be depressed is a self-rating measuring instrument like the Zung Self-Rating Depression Scale (Zung 1965), which follows. For every statement in the left column, check the response that describes how you *presently* feel.

Zung Self-Rating Depression Scale				
	Never	Sometimes	Most of the time	All the time
I feel downhearted and blue.		M	Z	
Morning is when I feel the best.		Z		M
I have crying spells or feel like it.	M	Z		
I have trouble sleeping at night.		M	Z	
I eat as much as I used to.				Z/M
I still enjoy sex.				
I notice that I am losing weight.	Z/M			
I have trouble with constipation.		M Z		
My heart beats faster than usual.	M	Z		
I get tired for no reason.		Z M		
My mind is as clear as it used to be.			M Z	
I find it easy to do the things I used to do.		Z	M	
I am restless and can't keep still.	Z M			
I feel hopeful about the future.		Z	M	
I am more irritable than usual.		Z M		
I find it easy to make decisions.			Z	M
I feel that I am useful and needed.		Z		M
My life is pretty full.		M Z		
I feel that others would be better off if I were dead.	M Z			
I still enjoy the things I used to do.		Z	M	

Scoring

For questions 1, 3, 4, 7, 8, 9, 10, 13, 15, and 19, give yourself 1 for never; 2 for sometimes, 3 for most of the time; and 4 for all the time. For questions 2, 5, 6, 11, 12, 14, 16, 17, 18, and 20, give yourself 4 for never; 3 for sometimes; 2 for most of the time; and 1 for all the time. Then total your score. Calculate your rating as follows: Divide your score by 80, then multiply by 100. This number is your depression rating. Here's a key to what the ratings mean:

Below 50	=	Within the normal range
50 to 59	=	Minimal to mild depression
60 to 79	=	Moderate to marked depression
70 or more	=	Severe to extreme depression

Use this scale to determine where you might stand. If you find that you're moderately to severely depressed, tell your doctor about your score on this test immediately and discuss it together. Effective treatment for depression is widely available. Improving depression can pave the way for you to break free from OCD.

If you have major clinical depression, especially with accompanying suicidal thoughts, even if those thoughts occur only occasionally, we urge you to seek help from a qualified mental health professional now. Most cities and states have a suicide hotline that can help you find and obtain the help you need. Whether the person who is thinking of or talking about suicide is you, a family member, or a friend, don't hesitate. *Get help immediately.*

WHAT CAUSES OCD?

No one knows exactly what causes OCD, but researchers are piecing together the puzzle. It appears that OCD results from a combination of genetically inherited tendencies or predispositions, together with significant environmental factors. Inherited tendencies include subtle variations in brain structure, neurochemistry, and circuitry. Environmental factors include psychological and physical trauma, childhood neglect, abuse, family stress, illness, death, and divorce, plus major life transitions, such as adolescence, moving out to live on one's own, marriage, parenthood, and retirement. Inherited biological predispositions serve as a kind of tinderbox, which, when combined with environmental lightning bolts, can ignite and activate OCD symptoms.

Does OCD Run in Families?

OCD appears to be, at least in part, a genetically inherited disorder. One indication is that OCD is more prevalent among identical than fraternal twins (Billett, Richter, and Kennedy 1998). Studies going back as far as 1930 have found OCD traits in blood relatives at rates of 20 to 40 percent (Yaryura-Tobias and Neziroglu 1997b). In addition, there may be higher rates of subclinical OCD, tics, and Tourette syndrome among relatives of people with OCD (Alsobrook and Pauls 1998), and those with childhood-onset OCD are more likely to have a blood relative with OCD (Geller 1998).

Yet while OCD often appears to run in families, the exact mechanism by which it is transmitted from generation to generation isn't well understood. Genetics probably plays a role, but as of yet, researchers believe there is no specific gene that causes OCD. Rather, it is suspected that several genes may work in concert to contribute to a vulnerability to OCD. Genetics seems to play more of a role in childhood-onset OCD than in OCD that occurs initially in adulthood (Abramowitz, Taylor, and McKay 2009). More research is needed, and more is presently being done.

Neurological Factors

The most widely held biological theory of OCD is that it is related to abnormal functioning of one of the brain's vital chemical messengers: serotonin. Serotonin plays a role in many biological processes, including sleep, appetite, body temperature, pain, mood, aggression, and impulse control. Serotonin dysregulation has also been implicated in other mental illnesses, including depression, eating disorders, self-mutilation, and schizophrenia (Yaryura-Tobias and Neziroglu 1997b).

Serotonin is in the class of chemicals known as *neurotransmitters*, compounds that nerve cells use to communicate with one another. Neurotransmitters do their work in the small space between two nerve cells, called the *synaptic cleft*. The transmission ends when the neurotransmitters are absorbed back up into the transmitting cell, a process known as *reuptake*. Certain medications can increase the amount of serotonin available, apparently by causing changes in the receptors in some of the membranes of the nerves. It is believed that these receptors may be abnormal in people with OCD (Jenike 1996).

More recent studies indicate that the brain chemical glutamate may play a role in OCD (Lafleur et al. 2005; Coric et al. 2005). Like serotonin, glutamate is a brain neurotransmitter that is vital to optimal brain function. Recently, drugs that improve the regulation of glutamate in the brain, such as riluzole (Rilutek) have been found to improve OCD symptoms in people who don't respond to other treatments.

In addition to dysregulation of neurotransmitters, structural problems in the brain may play a role. Brain-imaging studies have demonstrated abnormalities in several parts of the brain in people with OCD. These include the thalamus, caudate nucleus, orbital cortex, and cingulate gyrus.

The *thalamus* processes sensory messages coming to the brain from the rest of the body. The *caudate nucleus* is part of the *basal ganglia*, located deep in the center of the brain. The caudate nucleus controls the filtering of thoughts. Sensory information is sorted here. Normally, unnecessary information is disregarded. In people with OCD, the caudate nucleus isn't as effective at filtering, so they become overwhelmed with intrusive thoughts and urges. The caudate nucleus of a person with OCD is like a doorman who does a poor job keeping out the undesirables.

The *orbital cortex* is in the front part of the brain, above the eyes. This is where thoughts and emotions combine. The orbital cortex tells us when something is wrong and when we should avoid something. It's like an early warning system in the brain, and it seems to work overtime in people with OCD. When the caudate nucleus lets unnecessary thoughts and impulses through, this makes the orbital cortex's job much more difficult.

The *cingulate gyrus*, located in the center of the brain, helps shift attention from one thought or behavior to another. When it's overactive, we get stuck in certain behaviors, thoughts, or ideas. The cingulate gyrus is also the part of the brain that signals danger, and as such, it's the part that says something horrible will happen if you don't carry out your compulsions.

Imagine all of these parts of your brain screaming at you when your OCD symptoms are at their worst:

- The thalamus sends messages from other parts of the body, making you hyperaware of everything going on around you.
- The caudate nucleus opens the gate and lets in unwanted intrusive thoughts.
- The orbital cortex mixes thoughts with emotions, then tells you, "Something is wrong here! Take cover!"
- The cingulate gyrus tells you to perform compulsions to relieve the anxiety the rest of your brain has heaped on you.

By now you're probably thinking, "No wonder I have problems!" Hopefully, you're also starting to realize that your OCD isn't your fault. It's your brain! Of course we have simplified this greatly, and experts still aren't even sure exactly what different parts of the brain do. As we said, the puzzle is still being pieced together.

Other Physiological Factors

Research has found that certain autoimmune diseases, such as rheumatic fever, pediatric streptococcal infections, lupus, and Sydenham's chorea, also may be related to some instances of OCD (Mell, Davis, and Owens 2005; Pavone et al. 2006; Huey et al. 2008). In addition, some studies have shown an association between OCD and head trauma, brain tumors, epilepsy, hypothalamic lesions, and von Economo's encephalitis (encephalitis lethargica). However, most cases of OCD don't have such dramatic causes (Jenike 1998; Yaryura-Tobias and Neziroglu 1997b). In chapter 17, we'll further discuss pediatric autoimmune neuropsychiatric disorder associated with streptococci (PANDAS), a rare autoimmune reaction that sometimes causes OCD symptoms in children.

THERE IS HOPE!

Although many processes remain unclear, there is increasing evidence that problems with the neurochemistry, circuitry, and structure of the brain play a significant role in OCD. In addition, environmental or developmental events are likely to affect the onset, expression, and severity of the symptoms. One thing that is clear is that parents, spouses, and other family members are not to blame for OCD. Regardless of the role any specific factors—genetic, biological, or environmental—play in the appearance of OCD in any one individual, there is hope. Medication can help correct serotonin dysregulation. And studies have found that cognitive behavioral therapy can bring about positive changes in brain function (Nakatani et al. 2003). Together, these powerful treatment strategies can help you break free from the grip of OCD.

HELP FOR FAMILY AND FRIENDS

This chapter defines OCD: what it is, the symptoms, how it's diagnosed, and potential causes. Read this chapter carefully. It will give you a better understanding of your loved one's illness. As we noted, people with OCD often feel ashamed and are secretive about their obsessive thoughts and compulsive behaviors. Your loved one may be hiding symptoms from you. As both of you gain a better understanding of OCD, your loved one will be more open, especially if you show that you're willing to learn and try to understand. Notice that we say *try* to understand. No one can fully understand what someone else is going through.

Learning what you and your loved one are dealing with is a beginning. Both of you will probably experience a host of feelings as you embark on this journey toward recovery: relief at finding hope, fear of the unknown, acceptance, a release of shame and embarrassment, uneasiness about trying cognitive behavioral therapy, and more. Discuss these feelings, both positive and negative, with your loved one.

CHAPTER 3

What Can Be Done? Treatment Options

Do the thing we fear, and the death of fear is certain.

—Ralph Waldo Emerson

OCD was once considered a hopeless, untreatable psychiatric illness, but the last three decades have brought huge progress in the effective treatment of OCD. Considerable clinical and scientific evidence has demonstrated that cognitive behavioral therapy combined with medications can be an effective treatment. Thanks to these developments, many people with OCD now live productive and useful lives.

The word "cognitive" in cognitive behavioral therapy refers to specific methods and techniques that help change faulty ideas and beliefs, including those prevalent in OCD. The word "behavior" refers to specific methods for changing behavior or the actions, such as the compulsive rituals of OCD. Cognitive behavioral therapy includes many approaches and techniques. The one considered most effective in the treatment of OCD is exposure and response prevention (ERP), also referred to at times as exposure and ritual prevention. The self-directed program presented in this book employs many cognitive behavioral therapy techniques, including exposure and response prevention.

In this chapter, we'll take a closer look at cognitive behavioral therapy. We'll also summarize how medications are currently used in treating OCD. While the latter information may be helpful to you, it is vitally important that you consult with your prescribing physician to determine the specific OCD medication that is right for you.

This chapter also addresses talk therapy and its limitations with OCD, and neurosurgery—an extreme and invasive approach generally appropriate in only the most disabling and resistant cases. We'll also touch upon so-called alternative treatments, none of which have been proven effective for OCD. We want you to be well informed about all of these choices, because the wrong treatment can be harmful.

MEDICATION TREATMENTS

The most effective medications for treating OCD are in the class of drugs known as antidepressants, specifically, the *selective serotonin reuptake inhibitors* (SSRIs). The most commonly used SSRIs are fluvoxamine (Luvox), fluoxetine (Prozac), sertraline (Zoloft), paroxetine (Paxil), citalopram (Celexa), and escitalopram (Lexapro). Venlafaxine (Effexor), duloxetine (Cymbalta), and other antidepressants may also be useful, but more study is needed.

Clomipramine (Anafranil), the first successful medication for OCD, belongs to an older family of drugs known as tricyclic antidepressants. It has been used all over the world since the 1970s and was approved for use in the United States in 1990. It was considered the first breakthrough drug in the treatment of OCD. It has a powerful effect on serotonin levels but also has effects on dopamine and other chemical messengers in the brain. The next generation of drugs target serotonin specifically and have fewer adverse side effects, hence the term "selective serotonin reuptake inhibitors," because they are selective in their action on the brain chemical serotonin. They seem to work by making more serotonin available in the brain.

Here is a brief overview of how these medications help with OCD. Let's start by reviewing the information from chapter 2 about the role of serotonin. Serotonin is one of the neurotransmitters, or chemical messengers, that nerve cells in the brain use to communicate with each other. These neurotransmitters are active when they are present in the small space between two nerve cells, called the synaptic cleft. For one nerve cell to communicate with another, various neurotransmitters must be released into the synaptic cleft. When this communication or transmission between cells is completed, the chemicals are taken back up into the transmitting cell in a process called reuptake. Clomipramine and the SSRIs slow the reuptake of serotonin, making more of it available to the receiving cell, and thus prolonging its effects on the brain.

Increasing the amount of available serotonin appears to produce changes in certain structures at the nerve endings called receptors. Think of the receptors as a lock, and serotonin as the chemical key to that lock. To have proper transmission of impulses from one cell to another, there must be a perfect fit between the chemical key and the receptor lock. Further complicating the situation, specific serotonin receptors may be abnormal in people with OCD.

For any given patient, a particular SSRI may not do the trick but another might, so it could be worth trying a different SSRI if the first one isn't effective. A particular SSRI may also affect other brain chemicals important to that "perfect fit" of serotonin and receptor for any given individual. This is why someone may respond to one medication and not to another. You may have to try two or more SSRIs before finding one that works for you.

If none of the SSRIs sufficiently relieves symptoms, other medications may be used in combination with an SSRI to give it a boost. A class of drugs known as atypical antipsychotics, mainly used to treat schizophrenia, are playing an increasing role as adjunctive agents in the treatment of OCD. Your doctor should be knowledgeable about safely combining different medications to best help you with your OCD.

Dosages

High dosages of antidepressants are usually needed to relieve OCD symptoms—higher than the dosages typically used to treat depression. However, some people are very sensitive to side effects at even the lowest dosages. Starting with the lowest dose possible—even breaking pills in half—and gradually increasing the dosage may be effective. Several SSRIs (fluoxetine, citalopram, escitalopram, and paroxetine) also come in liquid form, which makes it possible to start at a very low dose.

Note that a very small number of people who don't experience a reduction of OCD symptoms with large dosages report good results with extremely low doses. The reasons for this aren't well understood, and this result is atypical. First-time users are generally advised to aim for eventually taking the highest dose tolerable.

Medications may take up to twelve weeks to begin working. During the first few weeks, you may experience side effects but no relief of your OCD symptoms. Even physicians may be tempted to give up on the medication too soon, since it usually takes only four to six weeks for people with depression to improve. Even if you aren't experiencing any reduction in symptoms, don't stop taking the medication without consulting your doctor. When these medications are stopped, it's generally important to reduce the level gradually to avoid withdrawal.

Dealing with Side Effects

All medications can cause side effects, and those used to treat OCD are no different. For most people the side effects are mild and tolerable, but for a few they may be quite severe. If side effects are intolerable with one medication, you may tolerate another medication much better. In addition, the side effects often diminish or disappear after you've been on the medication for a while, so give it some time. Many people with OCD needlessly fear and avoid medication because of the possibility of side effects, or they don't keep taking it long enough for their bodies to adjust to it. However, most people who improve and remain on the medication report that the benefits far outweigh problems with side effects.

Be sure to notify your doctor of any uncomfortable side effects or unusual symptoms you have. He or she will let you know if they're dangerous or if your medication needs adjusting. Adjusting the dosage, dividing the dosage over the course of the day, and changing the time of day you take the medication can often relieve side effects. However, these changes must not be made without consulting your doctor. Should you need to stop the medication, you will probably need to discontinue it slowly to avoid withdrawal effects, which may include nausea, vomiting, hyperthermia, headache, sleep problems, and malaise.

Don't allow side effects to deter you from taking medication to treat your OCD. Most side effects are transient and can be dealt with effectively. Tell your doctor about any symptoms you think may be caused by your medications. If they're severe, your doctor may reduce your dosage, supplement what you're taking with another medication or change the medication altogether. Here are the most common side effects and tips for managing them.

Sleep problems. Medications used to treat OCD may cause some people to have difficulty sleeping. If this happens, ask your doctor if you can change the time of day when you take your medication. In general, medications that can activate your system are best taken in the morning, and sedating medications are best taken at bedtime. Be aware that there are individual variations in how people react to medication. A medication that makes some people sleepy may make others feel wide awake.

Restlessness. Some people feel restless or wired on medications that treat OCD, at least initially. Some even experience a temporary increase in their OCD symptoms, lasting a few hours or a few days. If the restlessness and nervousness are severe, your doctor may want to prescribe another medication to be taken temporarily to help you relax.

Weight fluctuations. Be prepared for changes in your appetite. Many people gain weight on SSRIs, while others temporarily lose weight. Adjust your diet and exercise program before you start taking medications that may cause weight gain. If you expect it and take precautions, you are less likely to gain weight—or at least you may not gain as much. Some medications, such as the antiepileptic topiramate (Topamax) and the aminoketone antidepressant bupropion (Wellbutrin), have been known to cause weight loss as a side effect. Your doctor may consider prescribing one of these if you gain weight. Cherry Pedrick gained about thirty pounds the first two years she took SSRIs. Diet and exercise helped her lose the added weight. The weight gain probably wasn't solely due to the medication. It also seemed to be related to depression. When she was very depressed, she lost weight. As she began to feel better, she ate more, and she also ate when she was nervous and anxious. Like many others on SSRIs, she craved carbohydrates, especially sweets. But, for her, this was partly an excuse. She needed to take back control of her diet. When she did, she lost the added weight.

Dry mouth. This common and bothersome side effect of some OCD medications is caused by a reduction of saliva. Sipping on fluids helps relieve the dryness. Sucking on hard candies may help. Try sugar-free candies to avoid tooth decay. Because saliva helps fight plaque and hardens teeth, reduction in amounts of saliva can lead to dental problems. If dry mouth is more than a bit bothersome, your doctor may recommend an artificial saliva to moisten your mouth.

Nausea. Taking your medication with a small amount of food can help control nausea. Rest a bit after taking the medication, but don't lie down, as this can cause heartburn.

Heartburn. If heartburn becomes a problem, don't lie down for two hours after eating or taking medications. You can relieve heartburn at night by adding an extra pillow under your head. If heartburn persists, ask your doctor about medications to relieve it.

Constipation. There are many things you can do to help prevent constipation. Eat a diet high in fiber, fruits, vegetables, and liquids. High-fiber foods include raw vegetables, fruits, and whole grains. Exercise will help too. If these don't relieve your constipation, ask your doctor about taking a fiber supplement or stool softener.

Diarrhea. If you have diarrhea, eat low-fiber foods, such as bananas, and avoid high-fiber foods. Apply petroleum jelly to the anus after bowel movements if you experience soreness, itching, pain, or a burning sensation. Drink plenty of fluids to avoid dehydration. Notify your doctor if you experience weakness, dizziness, or decreased urine output. These can be signs of dehydration. If your diarrhea is persistent, ask your doctor about taking antidiarrheal medications.

Dizziness. Lowered blood pressure, a fast pulse, dehydration due to diarrhea, or nonsymptomatic effects of the medication can lead to dizziness. Notify your doctor to make certain the dizziness is nothing to be overly concerned about. Make sure you're drinking enough fluids. Take precautions to prevent falls or accidents, such as standing up slowly and waiting a few seconds before starting to walk. Don't drive when you're likely to feel dizzy or sleepy.

Sexual dysfunction. Clomipramine and the SSRIs often produce sexual side effects in both men and women. These include lowered sex drive, delayed orgasm, and complete inability to have an erection or orgasm. On the other hand, some people will have increased interest in sexual activity. If you experience these side effects, discuss them with your doctor. Don't be embarrassed; realize that your doctor won't be surprised, as this is common with many medications. Your doctor may be able to prescribe a medication, such as sildenafil (Viagra), to counteract the sexual dysfunction. Some people have been able to reduce sexual side effects and enjoy sexual activity on the weekends by stopping the medication on Fridays and Saturdays. This isn't as effective with fluoxetine because it is longer acting. As always, don't adjust your medication without your doctor's approval and supervision.

Medication Precautions

The medication you take to treat your OCD is an important part of your recovery plan. A few simple precautions will make the medication safer and more effective. When taking any medication, ask your doctor (and pharmacist) to provide you with information about the medication. Here are some questions that we recommend you ask your doctor:

- How does this medication help with OCD symptoms?
- How long does it usually take to see positive effects?
- What is the dosage and how often do I take it?
- How long will I have to remain on the medication, and what is likely to happen if I stop taking it?
- What if the medication doesn't work?
- What are the potential side effects of the medication?
- Which side effects are dangerous? Which should I report immediately?
- What can I do to reduce the severity of side effects?
- Are there any dietary restrictions when taking this medication?

- Will I need any tests before starting this medication or while taking it?

Although doctors are obligated to provide information, you also need to give them information that will aid them in choosing the right medication for you. Notify your doctor of any of the following:

- Any known allergies
- Any other medications you take, even nonprescription medicines
- If you are pregnant, trying to become pregnant, or breastfeeding
- If you have a seizure disorder or heart murmur
- Any other medical or psychiatric problems

The doctor prescribes the medication, but you're the one taking it. Here are some precautions you can take to ensure optimum treatment:

- Make certain the doctor prescribing medication for OCD is a psychiatrist or is very experienced in the treatment of psychiatric disorders.
- Ask your doctor to write out the name of the medication, the dosage, and how often you are to take it. When you get the prescription filled, compare it with what the doctor wrote.
- Provide the doctor with complete medical history, as some medical conditions can seriously affect the doctor's choice of medication for you.
- Report any side effects or new symptoms to your doctor. If you aren't sure a symptom is related to the medication, give your doctor a call.
- Know who you should call if your doctor isn't available.
- Get any tests your doctor recommends before you start the medication and while you are taking it, for example, blood tests and electrocardiograms.
- Tell all of your doctors what medications you're taking.
- Get all of your medications at the same pharmacy. Having one pharmacist who knows all of the medications you take can help you avoid drug interactions.
- Know what your medication looks like. Sometimes you may get the same medication made by a different company. If the tablets or capsules look different than usual, ask your pharmacist about it.
- Don't quit taking any medication or change the dosage without consulting your doctor.
- Ask your doctor before taking any other medication, even over-the-counter medicines.
- Ask your doctor what you should do if you forget to take your medication.

- Let a family member or friend know what medications you're taking. Write them down so you can show the list to doctors or emergency personnel when needed.
- If a medication could make you drowsy or dizzy, adjust your activities. Until you are certain how you will react, don't drive or operate machinery.
- Keep all medications out of the reach of children and pets, even children who visit only occasionally.
- Store medications in a cool, dry place. The moisture in bathrooms may decrease the effectiveness of some medications.
- Make sure you have enough medication before vacations and holidays. Always get refills a few days ahead of time because sometimes the pharmacist must call the doctor for permission to refill the prescription.
- Keep medications in their original bottles, and be sure the label is readable.
- Read the label on the bottle before taking any medication—even those you take every day. It's easy to grab the wrong bottle, especially in the dark.
- Develop a system to help you remember when to take your medications. The weekly pillboxes sold at pharmacies, with a compartment for each day, are a great help. Fill the container at the beginning of the week, and then with just a glance you can tell if you've taken your medication on any given day. It's easy to forget routine activities that you do every day. If you take many medications, you can get a container with multiple compartments for each day.

Caution: Alcohol should be consumed only with great caution when taking medications for OCD, for a variety of reasons. If used in excess, it can interfere with the therapeutic action of the medication. Combining alcohol with medications used to treat OCD may trigger aggressive behavior. Alcohol is also known to worsen depression. In addition, alcohol can have a greater effect on individuals taking medications for OCD—one drink may have the effect of two. If you regularly consume alcohol, be sure to discuss your consumption with your prescribing physician. Consider it another chemical that can interfere with the benefits the medication offers you while you combat OCD.

Parts of the previous section were adapted from "Taking Medications Safely," by Cherry Pedrick, *Mature Years*, Fall 1999.

COGNITIVE BEHAVIORAL THERAPY

Cognitive behavioral therapy is an important part of recovery from OCD. Research by Dr. Lewis Baxter of UCLA demonstrated that behavior therapy results in positive changes in brain activity similar to those brought about by successful drug treatment (Yaryura-Tobias and Neziroglu 1997b). Cognitive behavioral therapy helps those with OCD by providing them with the tools needed to manage their obsessions and compulsions. Continued practice and use of the tools and skills learned in CBT will help keep symptoms manageable. Successful cognitive behavioral treatment requires motivation and daily practice. Initially, it can appear quite challenging, even scary, but obtaining relief from OCD symptoms makes it worthwhile. When used together, medication and cognitive behavioral therapy complement each other. Medication can have beneficial effects on serotonin levels, while cognitive behavioral therapy helps modify behavior by teaching the person with OCD the skills to resist compulsions and obsessions. Medication can reduce anxiety levels, making it easier to implement cognitive behavioral therapy tools and techniques.

Exposure and Response Prevention

Exposure and response prevention is the principal cognitive behavioral technique for treating OCD. The purpose of ERP is to reduce the anxiety and discomfort associated with obsessions through the natural process of sensory *habituation*. Habituation, which is hardwired into the brain, is a natural process whereby the central nervous system gets used to stimuli through repeated, prolonged contact; you might even say the nervous system gets bored with these stimuli. There are endless examples of habituation at work in our daily lives. One example would be the sudden, jolting chill you feel when you dive into a pool of cold water. The sensory neurons in your skin (assigned to detect sensory information about hot and cold) send an initial barrage of temperature-related information to your brain, which interprets this to mean "Boy, this water sure is cold!" However, if you remain in the water, after a few seconds those same sensory neurons on the skin start to fatigue and the transmittal of information about hot and cold virtually stops. The chilling sensations diminish, and gradually the cold water begins to feel almost warm. Obviously, the water doesn't become warmer. Rather, your nervous system numbs out to the chilly sensations as you habituate to the cold water.

There are countless other examples. Here's one you could try right now. Take a mouthful of luscious, flavorful food in your mouth—something you really love—and hold it there for a minute without swallowing. The intense flavors eventually fade away, indicating that habituation to the sensations of flavor have occurred. Likewise, if you've ever worked with the radio blaring in the background or an airplane roaring overhead, you've probably noticed how you can be so absorbed in a task that after a while you may not even hear the continuous background noise. After prolonged, repeated contact with any physical or psychological stimulus, habituation will occur. Habituation also reliably occurs in situations that initially evoke feelings of anxiety and fear. If you stay in persistent contact with those experiences, habituation will occur, providing a natural way to overcome avoidance of anxiety-provoking situations.

EXPOSURE

You can use this process to your advantage by arranging for prolonged exposure to the real-life situations that provoke anxiety and cause you to perform rituals. This is called in vivo, or real-life, exposure. For example, a person with fears related to contamination might be asked to touch or otherwise directly contact some feared object, such as an empty garbage can, without relieving the anxiety by hand washing. Through repeated practice, the person realizes that the feared disastrous consequences don't occur, and the severe anxiety initially associated with that situation decreases.

Exposure is best done in stages, taking baby steps toward the ultimate goal of complete habituation to the feared object or situation. For example, exposure to a "contaminated" garbage can may begin with the person touching a "safe" corner with only a fingernail. Eventually, exposure progresses to touching the garbage can with a finger and waiting as long as it takes for habituation to occur. Then several fingers are used, then the front of the hand, then the back of the hand. With each step, the person confronts the fear, experiences anxiety, then experiences habituation gradually and naturally. (Note: In this book when we use the word "contaminated" in quotation marks, we mean that the person with OCD would consider the object or situation to be dirty, disgusting, dangerous, and to be avoided at all costs, while most people wouldn't consider it dangerous in any way.)

Sometimes it's either impractical or impossible to re-create the feared situation. An example is the fear of becoming sick or losing a loved one. In these cases, *imaginal exposure* is used. This involves prolonged, repeated mental visualization of the feared image or situation, again for as long as it takes for habituation to occur. In combination with in vivo exposure, imaginal exposure is also a useful technique for overcoming the fear of thoughts that so many people with OCD experience. This book offers detailed instructions on how to devise and implement both in vivo and imaginal exposure to help you break free from OCD. With patience and practice, this approach will help decrease the intensity of your obsessions.

RESPONSE PREVENTION

Think of response prevention as the act of voluntarily preventing the rituals (washing, checking, and so on) you typically perform when an obsession triggers anxiety. The purpose of response prevention is to encourage habituation to fear-provoking thoughts and situations, and to ultimately decrease the frequency of rituals. As you face feared stimuli and experience the urge to do rituals, you simultaneously refrain from ritual behaviors such as hand washing or excessive checking. At first you may simply decrease the length and frequency of a ritual as you gradually work toward totally resisting the compulsion. Ultimately, the goal of response prevention is to stop all compulsive rituals. This may sound impossible or even frightening, but with regular effort, practice, and the strong support of a coach, such as a therapist or family member, response prevention is possible—and one of the most powerful keys for breaking free of OCD.

Cognitive Restructuring

The cognitive component of cognitive behavioral therapy involves actively challenging and confronting the distorted thinking and faulty beliefs that drive and maintain obsessions and compulsions. In cognitive therapy, you are encouraged to identify faulty beliefs and replace them with more accurate and realistic appraisals. This approach is traditionally done through interactions between therapist and client in a process sometimes referred to as *cognitive restructuring*, but it's also possible to use this technique in a self-help format, as in the self-directed program in this book. Here are the key cognitive errors of people with OCD, with examples of each.

Overestimating risk, harm, and danger. Examples: "If I take even the slightest chance, something terrible is likely to happen." "The mere possibility of danger equals the probability of danger occurring."

Overcontrol and perfectionism. Example: "Whatever I do, it's intolerable unless I do it perfectly."

Catastrophizing. Examples: "An open sore on my arm means I'll definitely get AIDS if I am around someone I think has AIDS." "If I get angry with my mother, it must definitely mean I'm a violent person."

Black-and-white or all-or-nothing thinking. Examples: "If I'm not perfectly safe, then I'm in great, overwhelming danger." "If I don't do it perfectly, then I've done it horribly."

Magical thinking. Example: "If I think of a bad, horrible thought, it will certainly cause something bad or horrible to happen."

Thought-action fusion (similar to magical thinking). Example: "If I have a bad, horrible thought about harming someone, it feels just as if I've actually done it or as if it makes it more likely to happen in the future."

Overvaluing thoughts. Example: "If I think of a terrible event occurring, the likelihood that it will actually take place is very high."

Overresponsibility. Example: "I must always, at all times, guard against making a mistake that could possibly harm an innocent person, no matter how remote that possibility."

Pessimistic bias. Example: "If something bad is going to happen, it is much more likely to happen to me or to someone I love or care about than to others."

What-if thinking. Examples: "In the future, what if I make a mistake [do it wrong, get AIDS, am responsible for causing harm to someone, and so on]?"

Intolerance of uncertainty. Example: "I can't relax until I'm 100 percent certain of everything and know that everything will be okay. If I'm uncertain about *anything* (my future, my health, the health of loved ones), it is intolerable."

Hypermorality. Example: "I'll go to hell (or be punished severely) for even the slightest mistake, error, or transgression."

The "martyr complex." Example: "How noble and wonderful I am! I'll gladly suffer and sacrifice my life doing endless rituals (washing, counting, checking, and so on) all day long as a small price to pay to protect those I love from danger and harm. And since no one close to me has yet died or suffered great harm, I must be doing something right!"

While changes in OCD-related beliefs are vital to recovery, there is disagreement among clinicians and researchers as to how best to achieve those changes. Some controlled studies show that people improve just as much when they actively challenge their beliefs about the situations that cause them anxiety as when they engage actively in exposure and response prevention to those situations (van Oppen et al. 1995; Cottraux et al. 2001; Emmelkamp and Beens 1991). In other words, some experts that believe that direct exposure to fear provoking situations (like touching a "contaminated" toilet seat) may not be necessary. The approach taken in this book (and that taken by most expert clinicians in the field of OCD treatment), is that ERP is the best way to change OCD-related beliefs and behaviors, but that there is also an important role for actively examining and challenging the faulty beliefs that maintain symptoms (described in chapter 8), especially for people with overvalued ideas or those who find exposure too challenging. For the vast majority of people with OCD, the combination of ERP and cognitive therapy provides the optimum set of tools for fighting and breaking free from OCD.

MEDICATION, CBT, OR BOTH?

Now that several effective treatments for OCD are available, and increasingly so, people with OCD and their family members often ask which intervention to use, especially at the outset of treatment. In general, it's best to think of either medication or CBT as only partial treatment.

Ultimately, most people with OCD will experience the greatest benefits from a combination of medication and CBT, the former delivered by a mental health professional trained in how to use medications (usually a psychiatrist) and the latter delivered by a psychologist or therapist specifically trained in the use of CBT techniques for OCD symptoms. Both forms of treatment offer powerful benefits in the daily management of OCD symptoms. Rather than asking which treatment is better, it's more useful to ask which treatment is the most appropriate for you wherever you find yourself in the treatment process. Each approach offers unique advantages, and also has its drawbacks.

For people with the most severe cases OCD who have never been diagnosed or treated by a qualified professional, it is usually most appropriate to begin with medication. The power of medications to rapidly reduce anxiety, relieve depressive symptoms, and improve mood, focus, and concentration can give the person a big leg up in facing the hard work of CBT. Medication can be likened to water wings, keeping a beginning swimmer afloat as he or she learns the necessary skills (CBT techniques) for swimming with confidence.

However, it often happens that people with OCD take many different medications faithfully, at the proper dose and for the prescribed length of time, yet achieve only modest results. And some people find the side effects of OCD medications so intolerable that they cannot take them at all. For these people, it will probably be important to focus on cognitive behavioral therapy, and specifically exposure and response prevention. Conversely, those who have done the hard work of exposure and response prevention but experienced only limited results are likely to find the addition of medication the key component in gaining control over their OCD symptoms. A well-trained mental health professional who is experienced in the treatment of OCD can provide the best advice as to which treatment component should be your next step in the recovery process.

TRADITIONAL PSYCHOTHERAPY

Obsessive-compulsive disorder appears to be resistant to treatment with traditional psychotherapy, or talk therapy. Decades ago, prior to our present understanding of OCD, the disorder was thought to be solely the result of life experiences, such as an unhappy upbringing, dysfunctional relationships with parents, and distorted attitudes learned in childhood, for example, in regard to cleanliness. In traditional psychotherapy, clients engage in lengthy, in-depth explorations—once or even several times per week, often over the course of many months or even years—talking about their dissatisfactions about their past that contribute to their present frustrations. In this type of psychotherapy, therapists sit patiently and listen attentively to the person, hour after hour, hoping to bring about a "talking cure." While many people with OCD derive some relief from having a trained professional listen to and understand their concerns, few report that this approach actually helps improve their OCD symptoms.

Most competent therapists of all schools of therapy acknowledge a need for a broad, multipronged approach to treating OCD. Talk therapy may be helpful in strengthening coping mechanisms for dealing with the life stresses that can exacerbate OCD symptoms. When psychotherapy focuses on obsessive perfectionism, indecisiveness, doubting, and procrastination, it may be useful in increasing compliance with medication and cognitive behavioral therapy.

NEUROSURGERY

Medication and cognitive behavioral therapy are the treatments of choice for the vast majority of people with OCD, as most will obtain at least some relief from these treatments, either alone or in combination. However, an exceedingly small number of people with extremely severe and disabling symptoms don't get any relief at all from this combined approach. These individuals may qualify for "last resort" treatment with neurosurgery. Worldwide, these delicate surgeries are available only in a few medical centers that possess the equipment and highly skilled staff to perform these procedures successfully.

Neurosurgical procedures for OCD include cingulotomy, anterior capsulotomy, subcaudate tractotomy, and limbic leukotomy. These surgeries are designed to radically disrupt, or "jam," the brain circuits that are overactive in people with OCD. Most of these procedures employ a device called a stereotactic frame to make minute surgical lesions in strategic places where these circuits run. Within the past several years, a device known as a gamma knife has been employed, which uses noninvasive radio waves to create these tiny lesions. This procedure avoids the typical complications of neurosurgeries for OCD, including infections, hemorrhage, seizures, and other complications of wound healing. In addition, it's entirely painless.

Another procedure, deep brain stimulation (DBS), is well established in the treatment of severe Parkinson's disease and shows some promise in reducing symptoms in severely disabled OCD patients who don't respond to medication and CBT. In DBS, the surgeon implants an electrode stimulator in the brain without severing brain tissue or circuitry. The device generates a tiny electrical impulse that reduces OCD symptoms by disrupting the overactive brain circuits.

While neurosurgery for OCD offers relief for some of those most severely affected, it doesn't cure OCD symptoms. Only about 39 to 45 percent of patients who receive this treatment will be considered either much improved or symptom free (Husted and Shapira 2004). However, it can improve the effectiveness of standard treatments that didn't work before surgery. Cognitive behavioral therapy is often an important part of postoperative care, and medication may also be necessary. Improvement of symptoms is likely to be progressive rather than immediate, taking several weeks or months to fully manifest.

Who should have neurosurgery to treat OCD? It is highly unlikely that anyone reading this book will need or qualify for neurosurgery for OCD. Only people suffering with severe, chronic, disabling OCD that never seems to let up—symptoms that severely affect their functioning—would qualify. And all of the medical centers that perform these procedures require that patients exhaust *all* available treatments, delivered by experts in OCD, before undertaking neurosurgery. This includes an intensive course of cognitive behavioral therapy and adequate trials of all of the available medications (at least ten weeks each, at maximally tolerated doses). Most require that patients undergo intensive treatment for a minimum of five years before considering them as candidates for neurosurgery (Jenike 1998).

ALTERNATIVE TREATMENTS

So-called alternative treatments promoted for OCD can include homeopathic methods, acupuncture, biofeedback, and dietary supplements, to name just a few. While these methods may be useful in the treatment of many conditions, their efficacy with OCD has yet to be proven. Why try unproven, so-called alternative treatments for OCD when there are so many studies supporting medication and cognitive behavioral therapies? We can think of a few reasons. People with OCD are sometimes suspicious of traditional medical approaches. For that matter, some people—with or without OCD—have a basic philosophical objection to the use of medications, preferring "natural" treatments. And in spite of the proven effectiveness of cognitive behavioral therapy, many patients avoid it because they think it will be too difficult. It can be scary at first. Others seek out alternatives because, in spite of the availability of proven treatments, in as many as 25 percent of all OCD cases, people simply don't derive much benefit from proven treatments, for a variety of poorly understood reasons. If this is your situation, it may be tempting to turn to the promise of any alternative that offers the hope of symptom relief. Even so, it's important to make certain that any treatment you consider is backed up by legitimate research studies and proof that it works better than a placebo. As we said at the beginning of this chapter, the wrong treatment can be harmful.

MAKE WISE TREATMENT CHOICES

Some people may try unproven methods because they don't have good information about which methods have been proven effective. This leaves them vulnerable to exploitation by mental health professionals who aren't informed or, in a few cases, professionals who are simply unethical. And while the numbers of psychotherapists who are sufficiently trained in cognitive behavioral therapy are increasing, they are still relatively few in number. Cognitive behavioral therapy can be hard work for the therapist, as it often requires leaving the strict confines of the office to work with clients in the real-life environment where their symptoms occur.

It is important to find a therapist who is trained in cognitive behavioral therapy or who is at least willing to study and learn. This book can assist a therapist who doesn't specialize in OCD and help him or her act as your coach or advisor as you work through the self-directed program.

Many people with OCD spend years searching for a magical cure, searching for a cause, and blaming themselves for their illness. If you believe you have OCD, stop blaming yourself or others and take control of your illness and your life. The self-directed program in this book is a powerful first step. In part 2 of this book you will embark on a tremendous journey. While it may be the most difficult journey you've ever taken, it offers you the promise of the greatest reward you can achieve: relief from the burden of OCD symptoms.

HELP FOR FAMILY AND FRIENDS

As a family member, friend, or partner of someone with OCD, your first step is to gather accurate information about the nature of OCD, its causes, and treatment. It's important not to get stuck there, however. The next step is making well-informed treatment choices. Be supportive as your loved one explores the options. Medication decisions are not lightly made, especially for those with OCD. In fact, the very nature of OCD sometimes interferes with the decision-making process. For some people with OCD, their anxious pursuit of the "perfect" treatment decision, combined with fears of making a faulty choice or decision, may needlessly or excessively delay the start of treatment. Patients and family members who routinely go online to research medical treatments commonly become overwhelmed as they wade through the massive amount of sometimes conflicting information about OCD. The actual decision to get help—what kind and from whom—can stop even the most motivated person in his or her tracks. The decision to begin exposure and response prevention can be even more daunting because of the fears that accompany the initial steps toward recovery in this approach.

At this point in your loved one's recovery, patience is definitely a virtue for friends and family members. The process of getting to the starting gate may take much longer than you'd like. The good news is that the upcoming chapters of this book can make the process smoother and easier. Hang in there and be gentle as you help your loved one identify the best treatment option.

PART 2

The Self-Directed Program

CHAPTER 4

Cognitive Behavioral Therapy for OCD: Introduction to the Self-Directed Program

There are risks and costs to a program of action, but they are far less than the long-range risks and costs of comfortable inaction.

—John F. Kennedy

This chapter introduces the self-directed program for breaking free from OCD. The program is grounded in the principles of cognitive behavioral therapy. As mentioned in the previous chapter, CBT differs from traditional talk therapies, which tend to focus on events from the past that may have contributed to current symptoms. In CBT, the focus of treatment is on the present, and specifically on identifying and changing beliefs, thought patterns, and behaviors that currently maintain symptoms. As discussed, a key approach in CBT is exposure and response prevention, which is widely considered to be the gold standard of cognitive behavioral treatment for OCD. Almost thirty years of research, as well as the testimony of thousands of people with OCD, indicate that ERP is a highly effective intervention for reducing OCD symptoms.

ERP consists of two parts: exposure to feared situations with accompanying thoughts, feelings, images and urges; and response prevention, or voluntarily blocking compulsive behaviors. While that may sound simple, it actually involves hard work and a high degree of commitment. It also requires courage, because the images, impulses, and fears associated with OCD seem so real and vivid. The compulsive urges and rituals are so powerful and so persistent that the prospect of change may appear downright terrifying to you. This is to be expected. If you didn't feel this way, you wouldn't have OCD.

WHY ERP WORKS

Exposure and response prevention is based in part on the principle, well-established by scientific research, that we can overcome fear by daring to face the objects or situations that cause anxiety, dread, and avoidance. Exposure relies on two important and related learning processes: habituation and extinction.

Habituation

As mentioned in chapter 3, habituation is the natural tendency of the nervous system to numb out to stimuli through repeated, prolonged contact with a novel stimulus. It has also been referred to as "the remedy of nervous system boredom" (Ciarrocchi 1995, 76). We all experience the process of habituation in our daily lives. In chapter 3 we presented the example of the jolting chill you feel upon diving into a pool of cold water. But after a few minutes, the natural process of habituation enables you to no longer feel the chill of the water.

Exposure and response prevention treatment utilizes this same process of habituation to help you systematically overcome feelings of fear and dread in situations involving people (the homeless, for example), places (such as airplanes), and, in the case of OCD, even fears of your own thoughts. Through frequent and prolonged confrontation with situations you fear and dread, your nervous system will automatically numb out fear responses, bringing them down to more manageable levels.

Here's a simple example of how habituation works to help overcome fear, in this case the irrational fear, or phobia, of water: The fearful individual first approaches the edge of a swimming pool until his or her fear rises to uncomfortable levels, perhaps several feet away, and then waits there. Over the next several minutes, the person's original fear gives way, numbing out as nervous system habituation kicks in. When calm, the person then moves closer to the pool, perhaps a few inches away, until the fear once again rises to uncomfortable levels. Again, the person waits until habituation causes the feelings of dread to diminish to manageable levels. The process is repeated in baby steps. Gradually one toe is placed in the pool, then a foot, then both feet, then the legs up to the ankles, and then the legs up to the knees. Then both legs are entirely immersed, and gradually the whole body is immersed with very little fear. Although this example is simplified, the process of overcoming OCD-related fears takes place in a similar manner. In order for this approach to be effective, it's also necessary to practice response prevention, in other words, to refrain from engaging in compulsive behaviors or responses.

Extinction

Exposure and response prevention is also founded on the basic principle of learning known as extinction. To understand extinction, we need to take a step back and look at how behavior develops. All behavior—that which you can see, such as eating and driving to work, as well as behavior you can't see, such as thinking and feeling—is governed by its consequences. Consequences shape our behavior. They are either positive, such as praise, hugs, paychecks, delicious flavors, enticing aromas, pleasant feelings, or attention from someone important to us, or negative, such as punishment, criticism, embarrassment, parking tickets, fines, or jail. Positive consequences are also known as reinforcers.

Reinforcers work by bringing about feelings of pleasure and satisfaction or by reducing or preventing unpleasant feelings or experiences, such as hunger, pain, or tension. Behaviors such as eating, drinking alcohol, or watching TV as an escape are considered reinforcers when they reduce discomfort or unpleasantness. Reinforcers influence all of our behavior either by increasing feelings of pleasure and comfort or by decreasing discomfort, uncertainty, pain, or tension.

Extinction is what happens when a reinforcer no longer brings about feelings of pleasure or no longer reduces tension or discomfort. Think of the many behaviors you engage in that are reinforced or rewarded: working hard for a paycheck or a bonus, buying flowers for a smile or hug from a loved one, playing your favorite sport for fun or relaxation, and so on. Now, think of what might happen if these same behaviors, for whatever reason, no longer brought the reinforcement you want or seek: your bonus is cut despite your hard work, your loved one no longer smiles or gives you a hug when you bring flowers, or your favorite sport is no longer fun or relaxing. Usually, the result is that these behaviors become *extinguished*—you stop doing them with the same vigor, and eventually you may stop doing them altogether.

Given that behavior is governed by its consequences, it isn't hard to see how compulsive rituals—hand washing, checking, and ordering, for example—strengthen or reinforce obsessive worries and fears. Compulsive rituals reinforce obsessions and worries by reducing, at least temporarily, the tension, worry, and anxiety associated with obsessive thoughts and feelings. In exposure and response prevention, response prevention in the form of refraining from rituals reduces obsessive worries by means of extinction. When you block behaviors that reinforce worries and keep them going, obsessional worries eventually diminish.

EXPOSURE IN VIVO

In vivo means "in life." In terms of exposure, it's used to mean prolonged face-to-face confrontation with anxiety-evoking situations, objects, thoughts, or images in real-life contexts. Here are some examples of in vivo exposures for different types of OCD problems:

- **Washing:** Touching a "contaminated" object, person, or place and not washing afterward.
- **Checking:** Turning off lights, stoves, and appliances only once, or slowly driving a car through an area where small children play and not turning around to check, despite powerful feelings that the car hit a child.

- **Ordering:** Leaving household objects "imperfect" (slightly messy, off-center, or not at right angles), without straightening, balancing, or correcting anything.
- **Primarily obsessional OCD:** Purposely thinking distressing thoughts by writing them down over and over or listening to them on a tape, without avoiding or counteracting these thoughts; simply allowing them to be there.

In order to be effective, in vivo exposure must follow two important rules: It must purposefully and vividly reenact situations that provoke fear, dread, doubt, and avoidance. And it must be prolonged, lasting as long as it takes for the anxious feeling to diminish through habituation. It could take anywhere from a few minutes to several hours before the anxiety reaches tolerable levels.

Exposure changes the way you appraise or interpret danger and harm in specific situations. Recall the analogy presented earlier: diving into a pool of cold water. Your brain and central nervous system naturally adapt (or habituate) to the unpleasant sensations within a few minutes, without you having to do anything about it. The water in the swimming pool doesn't change, your brain's interpretation of the temperature of the water changes. When you do effective exposure, you give your brain the chance to *reinterpret* or *reappraise* OCD's messages. Here are a few examples.

OCD thought		**Reinterpreted thought**
"It is extremely dangerous to do (touch, think) this."	*Becomes*	"Nothing terrible will happen if I do this. I can take a chance."
"I must do this many times."	*Becomes*	"I can do it just once, and that's okay."
"I must be evil to think such a bad thought."	*Becomes*	"It's just one of those silly OCD thoughts."
"I must turn around to make sure no one was hurt."	*Becomes*	"If I turn around, I'm just going to make my OCD worse."

Keep in mind that some fears involve catastrophes that are impractical to simulate in vivo. Feared situations that may occur in the distant future, such as getting seriously ill or dying can't be easily simulated. Other fears are either too complex to confront in vivo or simply too impractical to reenact in vivo alone. These can include fears of causing someone's illness or death or going to jail for doing something illegal or immoral. In these situations, imaginal exposure is useful. In this technique, you imagine or vividly bring to mind the feared situation for a prolonged period of time. Chapter 7 is devoted to the topic of imaginal exposure.

RESPONSE PREVENTION

For exposure to be effective, it is necessary to eliminate, block, or sharply limit all behaviors that neutralize or lessen the feelings of anxiety and discomfort brought about by obsessions. Response prevention refers to the supervised or self-controlled blocking of the compulsive rituals that lessen or prevent anxiety and discomfort. Simply put, response prevention means preventing yourself from performing your usual rituals. Once the ritual is blocked, your brain has the opportunity to provide the natural habituation to the fear-provoking situation. This allows for more realistic and adaptive interpretations of the situations to replace your old, fearful appraisals.

When you block rituals, you are purposefully allowing the anxiety to be present. This allows new adaptations to occur. As with exposure, effective response prevention must be prolonged enough to begin to break down previously acquired associations between anxiety-provoking stimuli and rituals. For example, consider the association between a "contaminated" doorknob and the urge to immediately wash your hands in order to feel safe. Doing response prevention involves the willingness to tolerate initially high levels of discomfort in the face of powerful urges to relieve your tension and fear by engaging in a compulsive ritual, in this case hand washing. Here are some more examples of response prevention:

- Not washing for an entire day (or longer) after touching something "contaminated."
- Not receiving reassurance. For example, you could have your spouse or partner kindly but firmly decline your requests for reassurance about obsessions. Reassurance is often sought for obsessions concerning contamination, safety of others, or having done something immoral or illegal. You will be encouraged to live with your uncertainty and doubt until that gnawing concern subsides on its own.
- Not turning around to check whether you hit someone while driving, despite the sensation of having run over somebody. Instead, you'd allow the fear to rise to uncomfortable levels, then not act upon your urge to check.
- Delaying rechecking that doors are locked or that the stove is turned off (after checking it once) for an agreed upon length of time, say thirty minutes.

Response prevention is one of the key tools you'll learn in the self-directed program. In this approach, you'll make the powerful decision to alter your patterns of rituals in significant ways—by delaying them, shortening them, slowing them down, or eliminating them entirely. This allows you to choose to feel the anxiety, doubt, fear, and dread that you've been avoiding. If doing response prevention doesn't feel at least somewhat uncomfortable, you probably aren't blocking your habitual response enough to make a difference in your OCD. The decision to "feel the discomfort," to just "be with it," or "allow it to be" without acting on it and controlling it will pay off in your progress toward breaking free from the grip of OCD.

Identifying Your Fears About Changing

At the beginning of therapy, a man who had suffered with OCD for forty years vividly described the prospect of confronting his fears and rituals, saying, "It's like being asked to do a swan dive off a five-story building into a bucket of water." Everyone with OCD feels similarly about starting exposure and response prevention, and they often cite similar reasons for fearing making changes. Below, we've listed some of the common fears and concerns we've heard. Check off any that apply to you, and if you have any additional fears and concerns, write them in the space provided. Alternatively, you can write your fears and concerns about changing in your journal:

- ☐ If I don't do my rituals, what will I do instead to feel safe?"
- ☐ If I confront my fear of dirt, germs, AIDS, and the like, how can I be guaranteed that the catastrophe I fear (getting sick, losing a loved one, hurting my children) won't happen?
- ☐ Since there's no cure for OCD, why bother?
- ☐ I know I'll fail. I've failed at everything else.
- ☐ If I fail at this, I'm at the end of the road; there will be nothing left that can help me.
- ☐ If I try this and fail, I'll be considered a loser by everyone who knows me and is pulling for me.
- ☐ I've already done cognitive behavioral therapy, and it didn't work for me.
- ☐ I'd rather just take medication. This is too hard.
- ☐ My rituals are necessary to ward off the dangers I fear.
- ☐ I'm too old to try something different.
- ☐ I'm afraid I'll go crazy (get sick, harm others, and so on) if I'm prevented from doing my rituals.
- ☐ In childhood I was abused (neglected, abandoned, sick, and so on). If it wasn't for my clueless parents (those ignorant teachers, the schoolyard bully, that incompetent doctor, and so on), I wouldn't be in the mess I'm in today!
- ☐ My thoughts are so bad it must mean I have an 'evil seed' inside of me. I don't deserve to get better.
- ☐ If I get better or feel happy, then something bad will surely happen. I don't want to take a chance.
- ☐ Other: ____

- ☐ Other: ______________________________
- ☐ Other: ______________________________
- ☐ Other: ______________________________

As you address your fears about getting started and begin to engage in ERP, you may discover other fears that you didn't note here. Continue adding to the list as you discover other fears. Review your fears and concerns each day until you've dealt with them constructively, or until they no longer bother you significantly. Remember, what's important isn't getting rid of the fear; it's maintaining your freedom and choices in the face of the fear. This is what the self-directed program is designed to do.

DEALING WITH YOUR FEARS ABOUT CHANGING

Now that you've identified the fears and concerns you have about starting the self-directed program, let's look at ways to deal with them.

If I don't do my rituals, what will I do instead to feel safe? Your need to feel perfectly safe is part of your OCD. By taking a chance and not using rituals to deal with your discomfort, you open yourself to other possible ways of handling the discomfort you feel. You are making progress when you take the "risk" of reducing or eliminating rituals.

If I confront my fear of dirt, germs, AIDS, and the like, how can I be guaranteed that the catastrophe I fear won't happen? You can't be guaranteed a life without risk, pain, loss, hurt, error, or injury. The problem is that your brain has made a mistaken connection between your compulsions and feelings of safety and comfort, no matter how temporary those feelings are. ERP can help you break the stranglehold of rituals in your daily life.

Since there's no cure for OCD, why bother? This all-or-nothing way of thinking is typical of people with OCD. Even modest progress can make a significant difference in your quality of life, and your family's quality of life.

I know I'll fail. I've failed at everything else. The only failure would be not trying to succeed by using the self-directed program to improve your life.

If I fail at this, I'm at the end of the road; there will be nothing left that can help me. You are never at the end of the road—ever (until you die). As long as you're breathing, there are always new options to explore, and the search for new and effective treatments is ongoing. You'll never know what the road to recovery is like until you actually travel upon it, putting one foot in front of the other, one step at a time.

If I try this and fail, I'll be considered a loser by everyone who knows me and is pulling for me. Others will judge you by the steadfastness of your commitment to getting better. The specific outcome of your efforts is less important than your dedication to the process.

I've already done cognitive behavioral therapy, and it didn't work for me. Often what people describe as previous experience with cognitive behavioral therapy was actually something other than ERP, such as relaxation training, creative visualization, snapping a rubber band worn around the wrist, hypnosis, or any number of other behavioral techniques, all known to have little or no effectiveness with OCD. And even if you did indeed do expertly conducted ERP treatment in the past without success, a fresh start may yield positive benefits.

I'd rather just take medication. This is too hard. ERP is hard, no doubt about it. And medication definitely plays an important role in the overall treatment of OCD. However, improvement with medication alone is usually limited. In addition, as discussed in chapter 3, some people with OCD simply don't benefit from medications or suffer intolerable side effects. ERP is an important element in optimizing your recovery from OCD. Research evidence indicates that people who have acquired skills such as those offered in the self-directed program suffer fewer problems and are less likely to relapse should they decide, for whatever reason (such as pregnancy or side effects), to discontinue taking OCD medications (O'Sullivan, Noshirvani, and Marks 1991).

My rituals are necessary to ward off the dangers I fear. The degree to which you truly believe, all of the time, that your rituals are necessary—versus knowing at least most of the time that they are dumb, silly, or make no sense—predicts how well you are likely to progress in the self-directed program. If you usually tend to truly believe your rituals are necessary, this is what is known as an overvalued idea. In this case, you may need to address this belief before you start the self-directed program. Turn to chapter 8, Challenging Your Faulty Beliefs, and work through it first, before continuing with this chapter.

I'm too old to try something different. The good news is that treatment for OCD helps no matter when you start. Without treatment, symptoms do tend to get worse with age; however, there is no age group that the self-directed program cannot help.

I'll go crazy (get sick, harm others, and so on) if I don't do my rituals. In over twenty years of working with over a thousand OCD patients, Dr. Hyman has never seen anyone become crazy, sick, or psychotic from ERP. The anxiety experienced during ERP may be uncomfortable, but it is never dangerous. If you find exposure too uncomfortable to do on your own, it's probably best to carry out your ERP with a trained cognitive behavioral therapist who is experienced in the treatment of OCD. The added support and guidance from a trained professional can make all the difference.

In childhood I was abused (neglected, abandoned, sick, and so on). If it wasn't for my clueless parents (those ignorant teachers, the schoolyard bully, that incompetent doctor, and so on), I wouldn't be in the mess I'm in today! Many people with OCD suffered during their childhood. Many people without OCD also suffered in their childhood. The majority of people with OCD have loving, concerned parents who did the best they could, perhaps while dealing with OCD in themselves or other family members. They had the added disadvantage of having access to so much less information about the disorder, and its treatment, than is available today. Blaming your parents or others from your past for your OCD only serves to maintain the problem. It keeps you stuck in the role of victim, leaving you powerless to combat your OCD in the present. The self-directed program offers you the opportunity to powerfully take charge of your OCD problem *now*.

PREPARING FOR CHANGE

Although we've addressed some of the most common fears associated with ERP, you may have some lingering anxiety about the process itself. This is to be expected. Realize that you won't be stopping all of your OCD rituals at once. Chapters 5 through 7 will lead you through the process step-by-step. Yes, you will experience some anxiety while engaging in ERP, but we think you'll find that the anxiety and distress involved in the process of breaking free is much less than what you experience now, in the grips of OCD. Before you turn to chapter 5, it's important to prepare yourself—and your family and friends—for the challenging but rewarding work ahead. The key is to make breaking free from OCD a priority. Here are some tips to help ensure your success:

- Set aside a period of three to six weeks during which you will make the self-directed program the most important priority in your life.
- Be prepared to spend a minimum of two to three hours per day (not necessarily in one single chunk of time)—every day—doing ERP.
- Tell others in your immediate family what you are embarking on, and if you can, get them solidly behind you. Ask family members to read chapter 18, and be sure they read the "Help for Family and Friends" section just below.
- Find a supportive person in your environment who would be willing to coach you in carrying out the self-directed program.
- This can be a close friend, family member, or therapist. It is vital that this person be knowledgeable about OCD, accepting, and nonjudgmental. This person should also have a sincere interest in helping.
- It isn't necessary to delay starting on medication while you do the self-directed program. In fact, in some cases medication may enhance the effectiveness of the program. Likewise, the program is likely to enhance the effectiveness of your medication regimen.
- Alert any mental health professional you're seeing that you're beginning a self-directed program to reduce your OCD symptoms. You can share this book with your care provider to give him or her information about the program.

HELP FOR FAMILY AND FRIENDS

Living with someone who has OCD is frequently painful, baffling, and frustrating. The disorder can challenge the patience and compassion of even the most benevolent family members. Although most loved ones wish only the best for the person with OCD, over the years deep anger and resentment toward the person with OCD may have developed. Negative feelings that aren't acknowledged and managed effectively can be destructive to the recovery process. For a detailed discussion of these issues and how to deal with them, see chapter 18.

Informed and compassionate family involvement is vital to the recovery process. In order to be successful in combating OCD, your loved one will need your support and cooperation. For example, understanding how ERP works—and why—will help you better support your loved one. Reading this book would be helpful. It's also important to understand and confront your own role in perpetuating or enabling the problem by offering reassurance and accommodating the OCD. For example, one way family members perpetuate OCD symptoms is by participating in compulsions in order to keep the peace. The mother who needlessly launders all the family's clothing several times a week to keep her son with OCD comfortably free of "contamination" is, without intending to, contributing to his OCD problem. Such enabling behaviors must eventually be stopped, but it's important to do so gradually and in cooperation with the person with OCD.

You can help your loved one by assisting with the difficult work involved in ERP. Although we aren't proposing that family members function as "junior behavior therapists," you can be helpful in coaching and supporting your loved one's efforts to overcome his or her OCD problem. To be most helpful, you should serve as an encourager, guide, and monitor. To that end, here are some guidelines for providing the most effective support for your loved one:

- Realize that people with OCD cannot control the powerful urges they experience. A chemical imbalance and overheated brain circuitry are ruling their thoughts and behavior. They don't *choose* to have OCD any more than a person chooses to have diabetes or thyroid disease.
- Family members must never force or impose their wishes upon the person with OCD, especially in regard to self-directed treatment. The decision to engage in and follow the self-directed program must be solely the choice of the person with OCD.
- Don't criticize or scold if the person with OCD doesn't fulfill your expectations. Talk about your feelings, but don't blame your disappointment on the person with OCD.
- Do your best to maintain a nonjudgmental attitude. It's especially important that you never judge the person with OCD based on his or her progress (or lack of progress) with the self-directed program.

- Expect relapses and backsliding. Progress is often two steps forward and one step back. Resist any tendency to become discouraged and negative. Stay positive, keep working at it, and the OCD *will* get better!

- Use verbal praise to reward progress, no matter how small and seemingly inconsequential. Even if reducing from fifty to forty checks doesn't seem like a big deal to you, for the person with OCD it may be a major step.

- If the person with OCD is your child or your spouse, stop blaming yourself for the OCD. You didn't cause the OCD. The causes of OCD generally lie in genetic and biological vulnerabilities—factors that are beyond your control. Let go of guilt, as it will only drain you of the energy you need to effectively help your loved one.

- Realize that OCD symptoms typically don't make much sense, and can even be maddeningly inconsistent and unpredictable. Dr. Hyman once had a client who was terrified of germs and lived in constant fear of the possibility of anyone getting saliva on him. But he loved it when, upon arriving home from work, his dog joyously licked his face. That's just the nature of OCD—all too often, it makes no sense.

- Realize that your loved one isn't the OCD. As such, it's best to avoid reading too much into the symptoms. Dr. Hyman recalls a young female patient who considered her father "contaminated" by germs and would therefore avoid any physical contact with him. He read into this pattern that perhaps he was unworthy of his daughter's love despite all the sacrifices he had made to raise her. He took this very hard, and at first he resented his daughter. With counseling from an OCD specialist, he came to understand that the problem was the OCD, not his relationship with his daughter. He realized that the symptoms meant nothing other than "it's just OCD." In time, he was better able to provide emotional support for his daughter in her struggle against the OCD.

- Do your best to help maintain a calm, stable, and consistent environment at home. When OCD symptoms are at high levels, it's especially important to avoid altering daily routines or embarking on major family changes or transitions, even positive ones. Family instability makes OCD worse.

CHAPTER 5

Preparing for the Challenge: Self-Assessment

You gain strength, courage, and confidence by every experience in which you really stop to look fear in the face. You are able to say to yourself, "I lived through this horror, I can take the next thing that comes along." You must do the thing you think you cannot do.

—Eleanor Roosevelt

By now you know what OCD is, and you have a general idea of what is involved in breaking free. You are now ready to actively fight back against OCD using the self-directed program. Before diving into the program, you need to consult a mental health professional—one who is at least somewhat familiar with the diagnosis and treatment of OCD. It's important that a psychiatrist or psychologist confirm that OCD is indeed your primary diagnosis. In addition, you probably shouldn't undertake the self-directed program if any of the following apply to you:

- Severe clinical depression or substance abuse is currently causing more of a problem in your life than OCD is. If these conditions aren't presently under control, they will interfere with your ability to benefit from the self-directed program. Once these conditions are stabilized through proper treatment, you may then benefit from the program. If either of these conditions is currently the primary problem for you, it's especially important to consult with a qualified mental health professional before beginning the self-directed program.

- You're in the midst of a major life stressor, change, or transition, such as the death or severe illness of a loved one, a job change, unemployment, or moving. The stress of these kinds of life changes will probably interfere with your progress in the self-directed program. Once your life stabilizes, you'll be better able to benefit from the program. Of course, there is no such thing as a life without some stress, so don't allow the normal stress of daily life to delay you in starting the self-directed program.
- Your immediate family isn't supportive of your attempts to help yourself. Even the most well-meaning family members can sometimes inadvertently sabotage recovery efforts. If family dynamics seem to be a problem, seek family counseling with a mental health professional familiar with OCD before beginning the program. Enlist the support of as many family members who are willing to help as possible. It is important that the key members of your family be on the same page with you.

An experienced mental health professional can be an excellent source of guidance and support for you as you work through this program. If your therapist doesn't agree with your desire to start the self-directed program at this time, be sure to consider his or her reasons carefully. If you are still unsure of what to do, consult another qualified mental health professional for a second opinion. For help finding someone who specializes in the treatment of OCD, see chapter 19.

ASSESSMENT: THE FIRST STEP ON THE ROAD TO RECOVERY

In this chapter, you'll begin to design your own self-directed program for breaking free from OCD. A thorough assessment of your OCD symptoms and behaviors is the first step. This is vital, since the types of OCD symptoms you have—ordering, washing, or checking, for example—will determine the specific design of your program.

Assessing Your Obsessions and Compulsions

To begin your self-assessment, look back at the OCD symptoms listed in chapter 2. Note the symptoms you checked in chapter 2, then write them down in the appropriate sections in the space provided on the following page. Your particular obsessions or compulsions may vary from those listed in chapter 2. Record the symptoms you experience, and use the examples in chapter 2 to decide where to list them. Use the check boxes beneath "Past" and "Current" to indicate whether each symptom has been a problem in the past or is currently a problem—or both. Then, using the disruption rating below, indicate how much of a problem each symptom is *presently* causing you. To be clear, you only need to provide a disruption rating for current symptoms. (As always, you can do this exercise in your journal if you prefer.)

Disruption rating (for current symptoms only)

1 = a mild symptom, just a slight nuisance or problem

2 = a moderate symptom, causing some anxiety and disruption in daily life

3 = a severe symptom, causing a great deal of anxiety and disruption in daily life

Identifying Your Obsessions

Remember that obsessions refer to unwanted thoughts, ideas, and impulses that come into your mind. An obsession is usually unrealistic, causes a great deal of anxiety, and has a persistent quality—it doesn't let up. Obsessions are usually about trying to prevent something dangerous from happening to you or to others.

Contamination Obsessions (excessive fear or disgust in regard to dirt, germs, or other contaminants, and/or preoccupation with avoiding them)

Symptom	Past	Current	Disruption rating
____________________	☐	☐	__________
____________________	☐	☐	__________
____________________	☐	☐	__________
____________________	☐	☐	__________

Hoarding, Saving, and Collecting Obsessions (excessive acquisition of and failure to discard possessions that appear to be useless or of very limited value)

Symptom	Past	Current	Disruption rating
____________________	☐	☐	__________
____________________	☐	☐	__________
____________________	☐	☐	__________
____________________	☐	☐	__________

Ordering Obsessions (excessive preoccupation with symmetry, exactness, or order)

Symptom	Past	Current	Disruption rating
________________	☐	☐	________
________________	☐	☐	________
________________	☐	☐	________
________________	☐	☐	________

Religious Obsessions and Scrupulosity (excessive fear, worry, and preoccupation with violating moral and religious laws and rules)

Symptom	Past	Current	Disruption rating
________________	☐	☐	________
________________	☐	☐	________
________________	☐	☐	________
________________	☐	☐	________

Body Image Obsessions (excessive fear, worry, and preoccupation with the appearance of specific parts of the body)

Symptom	Past	Current	Disruption rating
________________	☐	☐	________
________________	☐	☐	________
________________	☐	☐	________
________________	☐	☐	________

Health Obsessions (excessive fear, worry, and preoccupation with the possibility of having an illness or incurable disease)

Symptom	Past	Current	Disruption rating
________________	☐	☐	________
________________	☐	☐	________
________________	☐	☐	________
________________	☐	☐	________

Aggressive Obsessions (excessive thoughts, images, or urges related to causing harm to yourself or to others)

Symptom	Past	Current	Disruption rating
______________________	☐	☐	__________
______________________	☐	☐	__________
______________________	☐	☐	__________
______________________	☐	☐	__________

Sexual Obsessions (frequent unwanted, worrisome, and intrusive sexual thoughts, images, or urges)

Symptom	Past	Current	Disruption rating
______________________	☐	☐	__________
______________________	☐	☐	__________
______________________	☐	☐	__________
______________________	☐	☐	__________

Miscellaneous Obsessions (those that don't fit into any of the categories above)

Symptom	Past	Current	Disruption rating
______________________	☐	☐	__________
______________________	☐	☐	__________
______________________	☐	☐	__________
______________________	☐	☐	__________

Identifying Your Compulsions

Think of compulsions as the things you reluctantly do for immediate (but temporary) relief from the anxiety due to an obsession. In OCD, compulsions serve the function of neutralizing the discomfort associated with an obsession. They are usually physical actions, such as hand washing, checking things repeatedly, or seeking reassurance. But they can also be things you do in your thoughts, such as counting, praying, reviewing the past, or thinking the "right" thought. There are three main keys to understanding the compulsions of OCD. First, even though compulsions have the effect of immediately lessening the anxiety of an obsession, the effect is brief and almost always just leads to another obsession.

Second, if you don't carry out the compulsion, you feel extremely anxious, almost out of control. And third, they are extremely frustrating in that you feel you must do them repeatedly, over and over again, in patterns that must be performed just right.

Cleaning and Washing Compulsions

Symptom	Past	Current	Disruption rating
____________________	☐	☐	__________
____________________	☐	☐	__________
____________________	☐	☐	__________
____________________	☐	☐	__________

Checking Compulsions

Symptom	Past	Current	Disruption rating
____________________	☐	☐	__________
____________________	☐	☐	__________
____________________	☐	☐	__________
____________________	☐	☐	__________

Hoarding, Saving, and Collecting Compulsions

Symptom	Past	Current	Disruption rating
____________________	☐	☐	__________
____________________	☐	☐	__________
____________________	☐	☐	__________
____________________	☐	☐	__________

Repeating, Counting, or Ordering Compulsions

Symptom	Past	Current	Disruption rating
____________________	☐	☐	__________
____________________	☐	☐	__________
____________________	☐	☐	__________
____________________	☐	☐	__________

Reassurance Seeking

Symptom	Past	Current	Disruption rating
______________________	☐	☐	__________
______________________	☐	☐	__________
______________________	☐	☐	__________
______________________	☐	☐	__________

Miscellaneous Compulsions

Symptom	Past	Current	Disruption rating
______________________	☐	☐	__________
______________________	☐	☐	__________
______________________	☐	☐	__________
______________________	☐	☐	__________

Assessing Your Avoidance Triggers

Obsessive-compulsive symptoms often lead to the avoidance of numerous situations, people, and places that activate obsessive thoughts and the accompanying anxiety. Situations commonly avoided by people with OCD include using public bathrooms, being in specific places or with people deemed "contaminated," or leaving the house without having someone available to check that the doors are locked. You may also attempt to avoid recurring horrible or disturbing thoughts. To develop an effective self-directed program, you need to identify your avoidance situations. If identifying them is difficult, review the obsessions and compulsions you listed and think about the things you avoid as a result. In the following space or in your journal, list the avoidance situations that are most disruptive to your life and indicate the degree to which you avoid each situation on a scale of 0 to 100:

0 = I never avoid it.

25 = I only occasionally avoid it.

50 = I avoid it about half the time.

75 = I avoid it most of the time.

100 = I completely avoid this situation at all costs.

Avoided situations, people, places, things, or thoughts	Degree to which I avoid (0-100)

Targeting Specific Symptoms

You've probably noticed that you often have several distressing OCD symptoms at the same time. This is common. Still, you may feel helpless and hopeless, and wonder how you'll ever get better, with so many symptoms. It can seem overwhelming to think of making improvements in all of your symptoms at once. The good news is, the self-directed program doesn't involve tackling all of your symptoms at once. This road to recovery is a journey you take one step at a time.

In the following space or in your journal, write down all of the obsessions and compulsions that you assigned a disruption rating of 3. List them in the order of severity, starting with the symptom that disrupts your life the most as number 1. If you need help getting started, we've provided an example.

Target Obsessions (situations, thoughts, images, or impulses that cause discomfort)

1. *What if I'm responsible for loved ones getting sick and dying?*
2. *What if I fail to prevent harm and danger due to germs?*
3. *What if I failed to prevent my house from burning down?*
4. *What if I cause violent harm to my loved ones?*

Target Compulsions (external or internal actions that neutralize discomfort

1. *Washing my hands a hundred times a day*
2. *Taking long, ritualistic showers and avoiding places thought to be contaminated*
3. *Checking the stove, coffeepot, and other appliances twenty times a day*
4. *Repeating, "I love the Lord" six times, in sets of three, in my mind*

Target Obsessions (situations, thoughts, images, or impulses that cause discomfort)

1. ____________________
2. ____________________
3. ____________________
4. ____________________
5. ____________________
6. ____________________
7. ____________________
8. ____________________

Target Compulsions (external or internal actions that neutralize discomfort)

1. ____________________
2. ____________________
3. ____________________
4. ____________________
5. ____________________
6. ____________________
7. ____________________
8. ____________________

Now, go back to the exercise Assessing Your Avoidance Triggers, a bit earlier in the chapter, and choose the five avoidance triggers that cause the most disruption in your life. List them in the space below.

Target Avoidance Triggers

1. ____________________
2. ____________________
3. ____________________
4. ____________________
5. ____________________

ONE STEP AT A TIME

It can be discouraging to attempt to take on the entire problem of OCD all at once. This chapter helped you identify your primary obsessions, compulsions, and avoidance triggers, and then helped you narrow those lists down to the symptoms that are most disruptive in your daily functioning at work, at home, and in your relationships. The self-directed program will be more manageable if you single out one or two of these symptoms and make them the targets of your initial efforts in the program.

As mentioned previously, many people have OCD symptoms in more than one area. For example, you might have contamination fears as well as checking compulsions. You may have an obsession about developing AIDS, intrusive thoughts about harming others, and feel compelled to wash your hands fifty times a day and check door locks, stove, and appliances repeatedly. If this is the case, ask yourself, "Which symptom, if I could be free of it, would make the most difference in the quality of my life?" This is the one to attack first. Once you achieve success with this symptom, you'll probably find it easier to tackle others that are causing difficulty. As with most challenges in life, success breeds success. Breaking free from your worst symptoms will give you confidence that you can break free in other areas, as well. Be patient and continue to work with your symptoms one or two at a time. As you continue to work through this book, we'll help you address your symptoms in a systematic way, starting with the next chapter, where you'll build on the assessments and target symptoms lists you created here to draft a plan for starting to break free from your OCD.

HELP FOR FAMILY AND FRIENDS

In this chapter, your loved one has made a thorough assessment of his or her OCD symptoms and has chosen some of the most problematic symptoms to start working on. In chapter 6, your loved one will draft a plan for confronting and overcoming these symptoms, and it will be important for you to play a supportive role in carrying out that plan. Review the guidelines for being an effective coach, at the end of chapter 4. This would also be a good time for you to do a self-assessment to gauge your own level of support. It's probably too soon to stop participating in your loved one's OCD behaviors or to stop offering reassurance, but it's not too soon to talk about it. As a part of this assessment stage, choose two areas to work on that could make the most difference to your relationship. Here are some examples of actions that would be appropriate at this point:

- Don't scold or criticize a lack of commitment or progress on the part of your loved one. Using an attitude of curiosity and interest, engage your loved one in a discussion about the possible reasons for his or her lack of commitment to the process, and address these as productively as possible.

- Praise your loved one for starting the self-directed program and committing to change.
- Help your loved one complete the exercises in this chapter if you're asked.
- Continue to learn as much as you can about OCD through additional books and reputable websites.
- Talk with your loved one about the ways that you enable his or her OCD, such as assisting with rituals, helping your loved one avoid situations, or offering reassurance.
- Take care of yourself and your family, physically, emotionally, and spiritually. Enter into this process of change as resilient as possible by renewing your strength and staying strong now, at the outset.
- Join a support group for families and friends of those with OCD, either locally or online. For help in finding such a group, see chapter 19 and the resources section.

CHAPTER 6

Your Intervention Strategy: Exposure and Response Prevention

Don't be afraid to take a big step if one is indicated. You can't cross a chasm in two small jumps.

—David Lloyd George

Now that you've done a thorough assessment of your OCD symptoms, you're ready to produce your road map for doing exposure and response prevention work. This road map is called an anxiety/exposure hierarchy. This is simply a list of situations that you fear and avoid, listed in order of the level of fear each provokes. Like a road map, your anxiety/exposure hierarchy shows you where to start, where to finish, and the pathway between.

You'll estimate the level of anxiety aroused in various fear-provoking situations using the Subjective Units of Distress Scale, or SUDS. This is a self-rating system designed to measure the amount of anxiety a person reports feeling. It was first employed in the 1960s by Edward Wolpe, MD, and Arnold Lazarus, Ph.D., both professors of psychiatry at Temple University School of Medicine. This scale will be useful as you design your own anxiety/exposure hierarchy. It's a 100-point scale, with 100 equaling the most anxiety-provoking situation you've ever experienced in your life and 0 equaling no anxiety whatsoever. A SUDS level of 50 indicates a medium level of anxiety—neither very high nor very low.

Think of a few situations you've experienced in your life that caused you the highest levels of anxiety and fear you've ever experienced. Or think of a very scary situation you hope you never have to deal with. If you find yourself not wanting to think much about this, that's okay. This is just a quick mental exercise to give you an idea of the types of situations that would earn a SUDS level of 100.

Next, think of a situation that caused you a moderate level of anxiety—not a lot, but not a little. An example might be seeing your child off for his or her first day of school, or having to take a test for which you are very well prepared, but the outcome is fairly important. Situations like these tend to provoke moderate feelings of anxiety—a SUDS level of around 50.

Now, think of a very neutral or pleasant situation; for example, going to the market, taking a warm bath, or reading a magazine. For most people in most situations, these experiences would have a SUDS level of 0. The word "subjective" in subjective units of distress scale is important. It indicates that every person is different as to the specific situations they give SUDS ratings of low, medium, or high.

TIPS FOR WRITING YOUR ANXIETY/EXPOSURE HIERARCHY

Now that you're familiar with using SUDS levels to gauge your anxiety, you're almost ready to create your anxiety/exposure hierarchy. As you do so, here are some guidelines to keep in mind:

- Your list should include ten to fifteen specific situations that trigger different levels of fear and anxiety: some mild (SUDS levels below 40), some moderate (40 to 70), and some high (70 to 100). For some people, the most useful place to start is with the list of Target Avoidance Triggers you compiled in chapter 5.

- For each situation or trigger, rate the SUDS level based on what you think you would feel if you were faced with the fearful situation and either *could not carry out or were prevented from carrying out* the compulsion you would typically use in that situation. This will help you more accurately assess your true SUDS level for that particular situation or trigger. For example, for the compulsion to check that the stove is turned off, rate your SUDS level based on how it would probably feel if you were unable to check the stove or prevented from checking it more than once. If you have a washing compulsion, rate your SUDS level based on how you'd feel if prevented from, say, washing your hands after touching a doorknob in a public bathroom. This is your true SUDS level for that compulsion.

- The situations, or triggers, on your list should differ from each other by about 5 to 10 SUDS points. You should have at least two or three items in each range (mild, moderate, and high) on your master hierarchy.

- Arrange the items on your list in order according to the amount of discomfort they trigger, with the one that triggers the highest anxiety at the top of the list and the one that triggers the least anxiety at the bottom. You'll work your way through the hierarchy, starting at the bottom items and working your way up to those at the top.

- From your master hierarchy, you can make one or more mini hierarchies that address one single situation, trigger, or avoidance behavior. For example, the items in a mini hierarchy might all relate to the same feared object or situation and differ only in your degree of proximity to that object or situation.

You may find it helpful to see some examples of other people's anxiety/exposure hierarchies before you come up with your own. Below, you'll find examples, including mini hierarchies, from Mary, Melody, Ben, and Jack, whom you met in chapter 1. After you review their hierarchies, we'll help you come up with a hierarchy of your own, targeting your most troublesome symptoms.

Mary's Anxiety/Exposure Hierarchies (Washing)

Let's look at Mary's anxiety/exposure hierarchies. Mary has OCD that began after her oldest son contracted a life-threatening virus five years ago. She has an obsessive fear and avoidance of blood, illness, dirt, and germs, and this has resulted in severely disabling hand washing and showering rituals. She washes her hands about a hundred times a day, her daily showering ritual takes about one hour, and she avoids going near specific places in her town because she considers them contaminated.

Specific triggers for Mary include red-colored spots and objects (because they could conceal bloodstains), homeless people (whom she believes are more likely to have open sores and carry diseases), and hospitals (lots of blood there!). Mary maintains specific "safe and clean" areas in her household that are off-limits to other family members, especially to her husband, who works for a delivery company that makes daily deliveries to local hospitals. She therefore considers him to be contaminated and includes him as an item on her list. Here is Mary's initial anxiety/exposure hierarchy.

Mary's anxiety/exposure hierarchy for fear of contamination by illness	**SUDS level (0-100)**
Anyone entering my bedroom without showering first	*100*
Husband sitting in clean area in the living room without having showered	*80*
Touching red spots on a public elevator	*75*
Touching mail touched by a suspicious looking mailman	*60*
Parking next to a neighbor who was recently ill	*55*
Buying groceries from a sickly looking cashier at the checkout counter	*50*
Touching and using an ATM machine	*40*
Being visited by someone who went to visit someone in the hospital	*35*
Passing or driving close by a homeless person on the street	*30*
Touching a red spot in a book	*20*

Mary's OCD includes avoidance of several "dangerous" situations involving hospitals and homeless people. She therefore constructed separate mini hierarchies addressing those specific situations. The items on each list differ in SUDS levels based on degree of proximity to the feared object or situation: people suspected of having AIDS and the hospitals that treat them, and sickly looking homeless people with "germs." Here's Mary's mini hierarchy for hospital triggers.

Mary's anxiety/exposure mini hierarchy for hospital triggers	**SUDS level (0-100)**
Sitting in a chair at home after returning home from the hospital	100
Touching a chair in a hospital room	95
Sitting in a chair in a hospital room	90
Standing in a patient room in the hospital	80
Touching a chair in the hospital waiting room	70
Sitting in a chair in the hospital waiting room	60
Walking into the hospital and standing in the waiting room	55
Walking into a hospital known to treat AIDS patients, standing for one minute, then leaving	40

Here is Mary's mini hierarchy for her fear of homeless people. Note that the items on her list involve progressively getting closer and closer to her most feared situation (touching the ground in a place where homeless people congregate, then touching the interior of her car, with a SUDS level of 100). Think about how your obsessive fears and avoidance triggers might similarly be broken down into smaller pieces or steps.

Mary's anxiety/exposure mini hierarchy for fear of homeless people	**SUDS level (0-100)**
Touching the ground in an area where homeless people congregate, then touching the interior of the car	*100*
Handing a homeless person a quarter, making sure to touch his skin	*90*
Directly touching the ground in an area where homeless people congregate	*80*
Standing within an area where homeless people congregate	*75*
Walking within 10 feet of an area where homeless people congregate	*70*
Walking within 25 feet of an area where homeless people congregate	*65*
Driving by an area where homeless people congregate, with the windows open	*60*
Driving by an area where homeless people congregate, with the windows cracked one inch	*55*
Driving by an area where homeless people congregate, with the windows closed	*50*

Notice that Mary's second hierarchy and the following examples don't have any items with SUDS levels below 50. That's okay; in fact, it can lead to more rapid progress. But if you find that much exposure too uncomfortable to start with, you'll need to back up and include items with lower SUDS ratings (20 to 50) in your hierarchy. Just be sure that the situation does indeed provoke at least some anxiety. This is necessary in order for ERP to be effective.

Melody's Anxiety/Exposure Hierarchies (Checking)

Now we'll look at some mini hierarchies for Melody, who has extensive checking rituals involving light switches, door locks, and electrical appliances. An important component of her obsession is her fear of being responsible for causing a house fire or a burglary, which intensifies the longer she plans to be away from home.

Melody's anxiety/exposure mini hierarchy for checking appliances	**SUDS level (0-100)**
Leave all small kitchen appliances plugged in overnight	*100*
Check door locks only once prior to going to bed at night	*95*
Leave small kitchen appliances plugged in, leave home, and return home the next day	*85*
Leave small kitchen appliances plugged in, leave home, and return in 6 hours	*80*
Leave small kitchen appliances plugged in, leave home, and return in 3 hours	*75*
Leave small kitchen appliances plugged in, leave home, and return in 1 hour	*70*
Turn off the coffeemaker and leave it plugged in overnight	*65*
Turn the stove off once and walk away without checking	*60*
Shut the refrigerator door once and walk away without checking	*50*

Melody constructed the following mini hierarchy involving her compulsion to check door locks. This list shows how her SUDS level increases the longer she's away from home. This fact will prove useful later on, as she constructs exposure exercises to increase her tolerance for being away from home without having checked the door locks.

Melody's anxiety/exposure mini hierarchy for checking door locks	**SUDS level (0-100)**
Locking the front door once, walk away without checking and stay away overnight	*100*
Locking the front door once, walk away without checking and stay away for 8 hours	*95*
Locking the front door once, walk away without checking and stay away for 4 hours	*85*
Locking the front door once, walk away without checking and stay away for 2 hours	*80*
Locking the front door once, walk away without checking and stay away for 1 hour	*75*
Locking the front door once, check once, then walk away	*70*
Locking the front door once, check twice, then walk away	*65*

Ben's Anxiety/Exposure Hierarchy (Ordering and Symmetry)

Ben, who's had OCD since childhood, requires everything in his home to be arranged precisely. For example, in his pantry, items such as cans of food must be lined up like toy soldiers, in size order, perfectly spaced, and with labels facing forward. His clothing is hung neatly and organized with surgical precision. Rug tassels must lie perfectly straight. Furnishings and display objects must be placed at perfect right angles to the wall. Linen items must be folded and stacked in a precise way. The slightest disarray, disturbance, or misplacement of any object provokes intense anxiety for Ben. Here is his anxiety/exposure hierarchy.

Ben's anxiety/exposure hierarchy for ordering and symmetry	**SUDS level (0-100)**
Move dining room chairs to not perfectly straight position—3 inches off	*100*
Place throw pillows extremely out of place	*95*
Place throw pillows moderately out of place	*90*
Move dining room chairs to not perfectly straight position—2 inches off	*85*
Move dining room chairs to not perfectly straight position—1 inch off	*80*
Move cans of food in the pantry so that they aren't lined up perfectly straight	*75*
Place throw pillows slightly out of place	*70*
Mix clothing so that colored items aren't lined up	*65*

Note that, in general, as objects are placed further from their "perfect" position, Ben's SUDS level increases. As with Mary and Melody, Ben might create mini hierarchies for specific issues; for example, a hierarchy for the dining room, another for out-of-place kitchen items, and so on. As in Melody's case, these hierarchies will be helpful in constructing exposure exercises to overcome his compulsions regarding orderliness and symmetry.

Jack's Anxiety/Exposure Hierarchies (Obsessional Slowness)

Jack has obsessional slowness while dressing and showering. These tasks take him as long as two to three hours because he feels he must perform certain rituals before any piece of clothing feels right. His rituals include repeating (for example, tying shoelaces three times), counting (to a "good" number), and straightening the garment until it feels "just right." Like Mary, Jack takes excessively long, ritualized showers, but for a different reason. Whereas Mary showers excessively because she obsessively fears contamination from germs and HIV, Jack's showers are so lengthy simply because they must be done "just right." For example, body parts must be washed in the "proper" order, and a certain number of "right" times. Contamination is of no concern to him. Here is Jack's anxiety/exposure hierarchy, followed by a mini hierarchy for his lengthy showers.

Jack's anxiety/exposure hierarchy for obsessional slowness	**SUDS level (0-100)**
Leave bedroom without counting to 8 three times	*100*
Leave bedroom with wrong foot first	*95*
Zip up pant zipper only once (rather than a good number of times)	*90*
Place foot in pants touching bare feet to inside of pant leg—the wrong way	*80*
Place shirt in trousers slightly "off," without straightening or tapping	*75*
Tie shoelaces only once, and without performing ritual tapping when finished	*70*
Tie shoelaces only once	*60*
Put on left shoe first (rather than right one first)	*55*
Lay clothing on the bed imperfectly	*50*

Jack's anxiety/exposure mini hierarchy for lengthy showers	**SUDS level (0-100)**
Wash body parts just once, then step out of shower	*100*
Wash body parts wrong number of times, then step out of shower	*95*
While in shower, wash all body parts out of correct order	*85*
While in shower, wash three body parts out of correct order	*75*
While in shower, wash two body parts out of correct order	*65*
While in shower, wash one body part out of correct order	*55*

CREATING YOUR ANXIETY/EXPOSURE HIERARCHY

Using the preceding examples as your guide, construct your own anxiety/exposure hierarchy for one of your target symptoms from the lists you compiled at the end of chapter 5. Make copies of the blank anxiety/exposure hierarchy so that you can repeat this exercise with other target symptoms. Remember, you can break your master hierarchy down into smaller steps and make several mini hierarchies that cover different fears, such as the bathroom hierarchy, the AIDS hierarchy, or the water faucet hierarchy. As always, you may also use your journal to do the exercises in this chapter.

Anxiety/exposure hierarchy	**SUDS level (0-100)**

EXPOSURE AND RESPONSE PREVENTION STEP-BY-STEP

Now that you've constructed an anxiety/exposure hierarchy for your trigger symptoms, you're ready to get into the heart of exposure and response prevention. Exposure consists of confronting situations from your list and thereby creating opportunities to change the way you typically respond to these anxiety-arousing situations. You'll confront these situations in a step-by-step fashion—and in a way that's completely different from your typical way of dealing with them, such as by excessive hand washing, cleaning, or checking. Doing this may seem scary, but remember, you'll be planting the seeds of your recovery from OCD. Below, we'll look at each step in detail, but to give you an idea of the overall process, here's an outline of the steps involved:

1. Choose a hierarchy or mini hierarchy and start with an item that provokes a mild to moderate amount of anxiety.
2. Carry out the exposure for that situation, allowing your discomfort to rise. Stay with it, and do not avoid it!
3. Carry out response prevention while doing exposure.
4. Repeat the exposure task over and over until your SUDS rating goes down to 20 or less. Then move up to the next item on your hierarchy.

Step 1. Start with an Item That Provokes Mild to Moderate Anxiety

It is extremely important that the item you choose for your exposure provokes at least a mild to moderate level of fear. A SUDS level of about 40 to 60 is best, but if this seems too high for you at this time, start with an item lower on your list. If, on the other hand, you don't feel any fear or anxiety when doing an exposure, go to the next situation or trigger on your list. The purpose of exposure is to provide you with firsthand experience of the process of habituation—your nervous system's natural response to prolonged stimuli. With time, your level of fear and arousal will diminish. However, you can only benefit from habituation if you confront a situation that creates an adequate level of discomfort. You've heard it many times before: No pain, no gain! This is key in doing ERP. Because it's highly motivating to see your day-to-day progress, we encourage you to fill out the Daily Exposure Practice Monitoring Form, which you'll find later in this chapter, to keep track of your improvement. Knowing that you're making progress will help you continue with the difficult work of ERP.

In the examples, one of Mary's mini lists focuses on her fear of contamination by a homeless person. Her least anxiety-provoking item is "Driving by an area where homeless people congregate, with the windows closed." Mary carried out this exposure by driving through the "contaminated" area. Her beginning SUDS level was 50. She allowed her feelings of anxiety to emerge.

If you're too uncomfortable with your initial exposure, figure out how to make it a bit easier. For example, if you're afraid of touching a "contaminated" object with your hand, start by touching it with your fingernail or with the tip of a fingernail. If walking away without checking a faucet creates too much anxiety, allow yourself to briefly check it just once to start. If moving an object out of place by six inches is too overwhelming, start by moving it just an inch or two. It's less important where you start than that you start somewhere!

Step 2. Carry Out the Exposure, Allowing Your Discomfort to Rise

As you encounter the triggering situation, feel your SUDS level begin to go up. Stay with the feeling and don't avoid or block it. Even if your SUDS goes up very high, it's okay. The more anxiety you take on now, the better. Too much is better than too little! Try not to fear your discomfort. Although you may feel as if you might die or go crazy, that has never happened as a result of doing exposure. In a while—maybe just a few minutes longer—you'll notice that your SUDS level starts to decrease. This is a sign that habituation is taking place. Your challenge is to stay in continuous contact with the very situations your anxious mind is telling you (or screaming at you!) to run from, escape, or avoid at all costs, until your SUDS level decreases by roughly half, or until you experience a noticeable inner shift in the power and intensity of your urge to escape or avoid the situation. This can take a few minutes or even hours. Hang in there! It's important to stick with it, no matter how long it takes! If you stop the exposure while your anxiety is very high or before an inner shift takes place, you'll miss out on an important opportunity to move forward.

If your SUDS level doesn't go high enough, look for ways you may be blocking your experience of anxiety during the exposure. Here are some typical ways that people block their feelings of anxiety:

Exposure Pitfalls: Typical Ways of Blocking or Avoiding Exposure

- Dulling yourself by purposefully shutting out your experience. It is important to stay alert and connected to the fearful feelings throughout the exposure.

- Relying on a *safety signal*, such as a spouse, therapist, or friend who offers excessive reassurance while you practice an exposure. Although a friend or helper can be a source of motivation, be careful that this person's presence doesn't serve to neutralize your fears. An example would be a friend or helper who, while helping you walk out of the house without checking the door locks and stoves, repeatedly reminds you that you are perfectly safe and nothing bad has happened. Another example would be a friend who shows you passages in medical textbooks about how it's impossible to become HIV positive with just casual contact. Reliance on this sort of reassurance can become yet another compulsion and therefore is self-defeating. If you find yourself relying on others to feel comfortable doing the exposure, eventually try practicing by yourself so that you can obtain the maximum benefit.

- Doing private rituals in the form of counting, praying, and the like in order to neutralize the anxiety or discomfort of the exposure.
- Dissociating from the experience; for example, thinking, "It's not me doing this, but someone else." This is a form of magical thinking that people with OCD may resort to for handling their discomfort during the exposures.
- Being overly perfectionistic about how you carry out the exposures. This can actually interfere with ERP; for example, trying way too hard to find the "perfect" exposure to start with can actually interfere with starting ERP. Likewise, excessively monitoring your anxiety level during exposure to make sure it's high enough can get in the way of habituation. And being extra careful about doing response prevention properly can become, in itself, another obsession. The key is in the idea of "allowing" the exposure experience to happen on its own, along with its attendant discomfort, rather than making it happen. Willingness to immerse yourself in the uncertainty of the exposure situation is much more important to success than devising and executing the perfect exposure.

Spend some time considering the ways you may be tempted to block or avoid anxiety during exposure exercises. List them in the Exposure Pitfalls chart on the next page, then describe what you can do to counteract these problems so that you get the maximum benefit from exposure.

Exposure Pitfalls	
Ways I might block or avoid exposures	**How I can get maximum benefit from exposures**

Step 3. Carry Out Response Prevention While Doing Exposure

As explained in chapter 3, exposure only works when it is conducted hand in hand with response prevention. Response prevention means the voluntary blocking of compulsive rituals, and it is crucial for progress in the self-directed program. Doing response prevention is like resisting the urge to scratch an itchy patch of skin, knowing that if you give in and scratch it, it will only become itchier. If you successfully refrain from scratching, the itch has a chance to go away on its own.

General Rules for Response Prevention

- A relative or friend may be helping you in exposure exercises as a support person. This person also needs to be familiar with the rules, and in the event that you try to violate the rules, your support person should calmly but firmly remind you to follow the rules.
- If you have an urge to perform a ritual or compulsion and are afraid you can't resist, tell your support person before you do the ritual. Ask this person to remain with you until the urge decreases to a manageable level.
- As a general rule, people with OCD shouldn't be physically restrained from doing rituals. There are, however, certain situations where such restraint may be appropriate: if the rituals are causing life-threatening harm to the person with OCD; or if you have agreed, *prior* to starting the self-directed program, to a specific plan for having your support person physically restrain you.

People with OCD are afraid of not doing their rituals for many reasons. Some typical fears include dying, hurting others, failing to prevent harm to someone else, going crazy, causing someone you care about to get sick, being held responsible for something bad happening, going to jail, and losing one's job. The following exercise will help you identify your own fears in regard to response prevention.

In the following chart, list the consequences you fear might happen if you didn't do your rituals. In the middle column, assign a SUDS rating to each fear you listed. Then, in the right-hand column, rate how much you truly believe that the feared consequence will actually occur, using the scale of 0 to 100 percent outlined below. For example, you might list the fear "I or someone I love will get sick and die," assign a SUDS level of 100 to resisting the ritual, and assess your degree of belief at 50 percent.

0% = Not likely at all. I know it is completely senseless and I have no doubt about that.

25% = I don't believe it will really happen, but I don't want to take any chances.

50% = I somewhat believe it will really happen, but I don't want to take any chances.

75% = I strongly believe it will really happen, and I don't want to take any chances.

100% = I'm completely certain this will happen. I have no doubt whatsoever, and I don't want to take any chances.

Feared consequences of not doing rituals	SUDS level (0-100)	Degree of belief (0-100%)

If you assigned a rating of 70 percent or higher to your belief that the feared consequence would occur if you didn't do your ritual, research predicts that exposure and response prevention may not work well for you (Steketee 1993). In this case, we suggest that you skip the remainder of this chapter and chapter 7 for the time being and move on to chapter 8, Challenging Your Faulty Beliefs. Chapter 8 will help you modify the strength of your belief in these feared consequences. If you can decrease the strength of your beliefs, you're much more likely to benefit from the ERP exercises.

Step 4. Repeat the Exposure Task

As discussed in chapter 3, the process of habituation requires extensive and prolonged contact with the situations, places, and objects that provoke anxiety. In general, habituation is evident when your SUDS level goes down by at least half during the exposure session. This is referred to as *within-session habituation*. By repeating the same exposure on successive days, further habituation becomes evident over time. This is referred to as *between-session habituation*. The goal is for your SUDS level to reduce to 20 or less after repeated exposure to the same item on successive days. When this occurs, move up to the next higher item on your anxiety/exposure hierarchy.

Monitor Your Progress

The following Daily Exposure Practice Monitoring Form will help you stick to the program and monitor your progress. Be sure to fill it out every time you practice ERP. You'll want to make copies of the blank form so that you can use it for a variety of different exposure exercises.

Daily Exposure Practice Monitoring Form

Exposure task: ______________________________

Ritual prevention: ______________________________

Initial SUDS (before starting ERP): ______________________________

Goal SUDS level (after ERP): ______________________________

Goal length of time (minutes or hours) per exposure: ______________________________

Frequency of exposures: times per day or week ______________________________

	Length of time		SUDS level (0-100)		
Date	Start	Stop	Beginning	End	Comments

Mary's ERP Program

Mary decided to start her ERP program by working on her mini hierarchy related to fears of contamination by homeless people. She repeated her first exposure (driving by an area where homeless people congregate, with the windows closed) over and over, each time noting the change in her SUDS level. After two days of successive exposure, her SUDS level in the situation had reduced to 20. This situation, which only the day prior had provoked so much fear, had become simply boring.

With her SUDS level at 20 for the first exposure situation, Mary was now ready to move up to the next item on her mini hierarchy (driving by an area where homeless people congregate, with the windows cracked one inch). Initially, this exposure raised her SUDS level to 60 to 70. Despite how illogical it seemed, even to her, Mary's OCD caused her to fear that the "contaminated air" in that area might contaminate the inside of her car. But again, despite her fear, she repeated this exposure over and over in the same day, and on successive days until her SUDS level was below 20 as she entered the situation.

In this way, Mary gradually moved up through the items on her list, repeating steps 2 through 4 with each item. When it was time for her to confront her most feared situation (touching the ground in an area where homeless people congregate, then touching the interior of the car), she became extremely anxious and experienced several fearful thoughts:

- *I'll never be clean again.*
- *If I go from my car into my house, my whole house will become contaminated.*
- *Everything will become contaminated and I can never make it perfectly clean again.*

In spite of her fears, she persisted with the exposure, repeating the task by lightly touching many different places inside her car. When Mary had conquered this task and completed her "homeless" list, she moved on to her "hospital" list. When she found it too frightening to directly touch chairs in the hospital waiting room (which she thought were contaminated with HIV), she lightly dabbed a tiny, quarter-inch corner of a napkin to the backs of the chairs. Then she brought the napkin back to her home and lightly touched many objects there, including the bathroom fixtures, bedroom furniture, and even the kitchen sink, with the "contaminated" napkin.

Mary practiced this exposure for a few hours every day. After a week, she was able to touch nearly all of the items in her home with her napkin and feel very little fear. Her goal was to "avoid avoidances," so any time she had a feeling of wanting to protect an object from "contamination," she countered it by touching the object with the napkin in spite of that feeling. As she gained confidence that nothing terrible would happen to her or her loved ones, her obsessive fears diminished.

ERP FOR SOME COMMON OCD PROBLEMS

Now that you have some familiarity with the basic principles of ERP, we'll give you more details about how to apply these principles to some of the most common OCD symptoms, starting with washing compulsions due to contamination fears. Even if washing isn't an issue for you, read through this section closely, as it provides a good overview of how to approach exposure and response prevention. In subsequent sections, we'll explain how to apply a similar approach to checking, ordering, and "just right" or perfectionistic compulsions that are related to obsessional slowness.

ERP for Washing Compulsions

We'll describe two approaches to ERP for washing compulsions: a "fast-track" method, and a more gradual method. We highly recommend that you use the fast-track method, as it will yield the most rapid results. However, if you find this approach too overwhelming, the gradual method is also effective.

FAST-TRACK METHOD

The fast-track method involves sharply limiting washing and use of water down to normal levels right from the start of your exposure work. Although it may seem frightening at first, if you follow this program rigorously, you can expect more rapid results. For a period of at least three weeks, you should stick faithfully to the washing guidelines below. This will set the stage for an entirely new and healthier washing and cleaning regimen, not dictated by the OCD.

- For the first week, limit showering to one seven-minute shower for men and one ten-minute shower for women every other day. This includes hair washing. If you have long hair, you can add three to five minutes. Use a timer to keep track of the length of your shower. Repetitive or ritualistic washing of specific areas of the body, such as genitals or hair, must be stopped or at least limited as much as possible. If, at the end of your shower, you have the feeling of the wash being "incomplete," you'll know you're on the right track.
- By the start of week two and thereafter, you may take one normal shower per day, as defined above.
- Hand washing should last no longer than twenty seconds (a "normal" hand wash as recommended by the U.S. Centers for Disease Control and Prevention). That's about the length of time it takes to sing "Happy Birthday" to yourself twice. Use only one dime-sized squirt of liquid soap or a quick swipe of a bar of soap to produce a minimum amount of lather. After completing your hand wash, you should experience a feeling of the wash being "incomplete."
- Restrict your hand washing to the following situations:
  - Once before and after meals
  - Once after toileting
  - Once after handling greasy or *visibly* dirty things
  - Once just prior to and after preparing food, especially after touching raw meat, poultry, or seafood

- If you're caring for an infant, wash once after changing a diaper
- Once after emptying a cat litter box, taking out the garbage, or doing the laundry

Your goal over the course of the program is to gradually decrease the number of illegal washes and, after three weeks, to have only "legal" washes. Of course, you need to apply these new washing guidelines while also increasing in your daily contact with the situations that trigger the urge to wash excessively. This is the challenge: to gain, over the course of the program, a greater and greater capacity to withstand those situations without having to resort to compulsive washing to relieve your anxiety.

Additional Washing Guidelines

- Using creams and other toiletry items (bath powder, deodorant, and so on) is okay, except where you use these items to reduce "contamination." Don't use products labeled "antibacterial," including creams, soaps, or other toiletry items.
- If your job requires that you wash your hands more often (for example, if you work with food or in health care), wash as often as required, but following the above guidelines.
- If you live with or care for infants or very young children, adhere to the rules for normal washing, but use common sense and follow your pediatrician's advice as to the most appropriate hygiene procedures. If you use baby wipes with your infant, decide on an appropriate amount to use (for example, one per diaper change), and stick to it.
- Stop any excessive use of hand wipes and instant hand sanitizers, such as Purell. Restrict their use to public situations where there is obvious disease risk, such as in a hospital, day care center, or medical office.
- If you have excessive cleaning rituals, for example, using bleach or unnecessarily strong detergents to clean your body or "contaminated" surfaces, you must remove those items from your home entirely for the duration of time that you're actively engaged in self-directed ERP. Any necessary home cleaning should be done with simple, mild household cleaning products. After you make significant progress with ERP, you may keep on hand a limited quantity of stronger cleansers to use for necessary cleaning tasks.
- The use of latex gloves as a barrier against "contamination" in situations that most people (without OCD) would regard as unnecessary, for example while toileting or grooming, is prohibited.

Keep track of all of your daily washing and showing over the next three weeks using the following form. Make copies and keep your working copy in the bathroom you use most, along with a pen or pencil. All washes that comply with the above guidelines for normal washing are termed "legal" washes; mark them with an *L*. All other instances of washing or cleaning and those that violate the guidelines are termed "illegal"; mark them with an *I*.

Daily Washing Monitoring Form

Date	Hand washes	Showers	Wipes and cleans

For people with contamination fears and washing compulsions, the goal of ERP is to "recalibrate" your relationship to water and the function of cleaning and washing. In cleaning and washing driven by OCD, water, soap, detergents, and cleansers are misused as means to regulate the anxiety that arises due to obsessive worries. In contrast, the goal of normal cleaning and washing is merely to achieve the feeling of being fresh and clean.

GRADUAL METHOD

If the fast-track response prevention method described above seems overwhelming, try this modified procedure, which involves a more gradual reduction in ritualistic washing and cleaning. It is best done in three phases, proceeding at your own pace:

1. During phase 1, for three days use the washing monitoring form above or your journal to monitor your actual number of washes and showers and determine your baseline level of these behaviors. Include the number of wet wipes, plus any other cleaning you do because of your OCD.
2. During phase 2, work toward cutting in half the number and length of hand washes, the length of showers, the number of wet wipes used, and so on. This phase may last from a

few days to more than a week. As soon as you can maintain your reduced washing and cleaning at a consistent level for at least three days, move to phase 3.

3. During phase 3, expose yourself to increasingly anxiety-provoking situations while limiting your washing to the normal levels indicated in the guidelines for the fast-track method above. Follow all of the other guidelines as well, and continue to use the monitoring form to track your progress.

Although you may not progress as rapidly and thoroughly with this gradual method as with the fast-track approach, you may find the gradual approach easier to manage. Both can be extremely effective, and either one can help you toward your goal of breaking free from OCD.

TOOLS FOR ENHANCING ERP FOR WASHING COMPULSIONS

Whichever method you use—fast-track or gradual—there are several techniques you can use to enhance the effectiveness of your exposures for contamination fears. These techniques will speed your progress with either approach.

Full-body exposure. After touching a contaminated object during an exposure session, do a *full-body exposure*. Run your "contaminated" hands up and down your body along your clothing and any exposed skin, toe to head, including touching your hair. Next, hold your "contaminated" hands directly to your face and keep them there for five seconds. As a finale, place a small candy, like a breath mint, in your "contaminated" hand for a few seconds, and then eat it. This is a powerful technique, and if you do it each and every time you do a contamination exposure exercise, it will greatly accelerate your progress.

Total immersion. You can greatly enhance your exposure, and thus your habituation, to a "contaminant" by spreading it throughout your entire living space with your "contaminated" hands. Touch the feared source of contamination, rubbing rub your hands over it if possible, then use your hands to touch a wide array of surfaces throughout your home: in the kitchen, the bathroom, your bedroom, dresser drawers, laundry baskets, washing machine and dryers, closets, and especially the places you are most reluctant to allow to become contaminated. If you spend a good deal of time in your car, "contaminate" it as well. Do this daily for ten days to two weeks, or until you notice a considerable decrease in your urges to clean, wash, and shower.

Using a contamination towel. It's helpful to create a "contamination towel" to use as a tool to enhance response prevention. Lightly touch a washcloth or hand towel to a "contaminated" object to "contaminate" it, making sure that the degree of "contamination" evokes a SUDS level of 60 to 80. Keep this towel on the countertop in your bathroom for easy access. Immediately following all hand washes and showers, touch the contaminated towel with both of your hands, then continue on with your day. If you just showered, do a full-body exposure. This deprives your OCD of the relief from anxiety that it craves and typically obtains through washing and cleaning rituals. Your brain will begin to disconnect the powerful OCD association between anxiety and the use of water to relieve that anxiety. Should you slip up and wash when you weren't supposed to, "recontaminating" your hands with the contamination towel immediately after washing will help you get back on track. Since your brain will eventually habituate to the contamination towel, recontaminate the towel every two to three days to "recharge" it before resuming your exposure practice.

ERP FOR AVOIDANCE DUE TO DISGUST

Some people with washing compulsions don't fear being "dirty" because of potential harm to themselves or loved ones. They simply find contact with certain people (such as the homeless), or objects or surfaces (such as countertops in a retail store) extremely disgusting or unpleasant to a degree that triggers an abnormal level of fear and avoidance. Even though they may acknowledge that there's no great physical danger in touching such people or objects, they avoid contact in a similarly extreme way. ERP works in just the same way here. If you go ahead and do exposure by repeatedly touching or staying in contact with the "unpleasant" object (without washing afterward), the discomfort associated with the object or situation will eventually subside to manageable levels.

ERP for Checking

When doing ERP for compulsive checking, work toward the goal of checking only once in situations where most people would probably check only once. For example, check door locks, faucets, appliances, and so forth only once before leaving the house or going to bed. Check the stove, oven, and other appliances only once after using them. Work to refrain from checking items in situations where they aren't normally checked, for example, repeatedly verifying that you've written the correct amount on a check when paying a bill.

Strict response prevention for checking is very challenging. Try using the following techniques to help strengthen your efforts to deal with the powerful urges to check:

- Instead of checking a door lock over and over, check it once, then plan to check it once every five minutes for an hour. This "overcorrection" makes the checking more cumbersome and therefore may inhibit it.
- Use procrastination as part of your response prevention. In other words, make a deal with yourself to check something later. Often, by the time "later" comes, the urge to check will have passed.
- The urge to ritualize during response prevention is powerful! It's like a strong magnet that tries to pull you back to whatever it was that you didn't check. Coach yourself to resist the pull by taking your mind off the urge. Focus on another activity. Do a chore, make a phone call, or do some sort of vigorous physical activity, such as walking or strenuous exercise.
- Because checking often involves fears and images of catastrophic future events and consequences, use imaginal exposure (explained in chapter 7) along with ERP to face your fears associated with not checking.

- Fight the urge to check by using self-talk techniques, as explained more fully in the section "Correcting Faulty Beliefs," in chapter 8.

Use the Daily Checking Monitoring Form to monitor your progress as you use ERP for checking compulsions, such as checking door locks, the stove, other kitchen appliances, faucets, or the car (lights, radio, air conditioner or heat, and so on). Each time you do an "illegal" check, record it with an *I*. Illegal checking means any checking beyond a single check in any situation. Record legal checks with an *L*. At the end of the day, tally the number of illegal checks you performed that day. You may want to copy this form into a small spiral notepad that you can conveniently put in your pocket or purse. This will make it easier to carry around and keep track of your progress.

Daily Checking Monitoring Form

Date	Checking events	Total illegal checks

When doing ERP for checking compulsions, bear in mind that response prevention itself is the exposure—in this case, exposure to the idea that unless you check excessively, that you are endangering yourself and others. If complying with the "one check rule" seems too difficult to start off with, take two or three days to record how often you typically perform illegal checks; this is your baseline number of checks. Then begin to reduce the number of checks more gradually. For example, if you typically checked the door locks six times before going to bed, reduce that by half for three days, then do one less check for three days. Continue in this way until you check briefly, just once.

The key to all ERP exercises for checking is to purposefully bring on the discomfort by lessening the frequency and duration of your checks. This allows you to habituate to the discomfort.

ERP for Ordering and Symmetry Compulsions

Ordering and symmetry compulsions involve an intolerance for objects not being placed in perfect order and position or being even slightly asymmetrical. For these compulsions, ERP consists of gradually becoming more and more habituated to disorder by purposefully placing objects in "wrong" places or "imperfect" positions. Response prevention involves managing the compulsive urge to restore these objects back to their "perfect" positions.

Use the four-step program outlined earlier in the chapter: To begin, review your anxiety/exposure hierarchy, then start with a situation that elicits moderate discomfort, with a SUDS level in the range of 40 to 60 SUDS. If this feels much too uncomfortable for you, choose a situation even lower on the hierarchy. After purposely moving an object out of its "perfect" position, maintain response prevention by not restraightening. Allow your discomfort to rise, and continue resisting the urge until it lowers to a manageable level. Repeat this exposure until your SUDS level drops to about 20 while the item is "out of place." Then you're ready to move up to the next item on your list,

If you're unable to tolerate even the slightest response prevention, use a gentler, more gradual approach. For example, each day for one week, try "messing up" an item or several items in the house, such as a bedspread or throw pillows. Then try to delay straightening for a predetermined period of time. Experiment and find a length of time that raises your SUDS level to about 50 or 60. That may be fifteen minutes, a half hour, or more.

Repeat this two or three times each day for a few days until you've begun to habituate. You'll know you've habituated because your SUDS levels will be considerably lower and you'll feel more comfortable delaying your straightening rituals. Then increase the length of the delay to two hours. Once you've habituated to two hours, increase the delay time even more, and continue in this way until you can tolerate items being "messed up" and not straighten them for a whole day with minimal discomfort. Don't worry, your family won't mind the house not being "perfect." To the contrary, they'll probably appreciate your efforts to help yourself!

Note that family members sometimes believe they're being helpful by purposefully "messing up" things that are normally kept straight and symmetrical by the person with OCD. Unless this "messing up" is requested by the person with OCD, it is of little help and is likely to antagonize that person and make matters worse.

Many people with ordering and symmetry compulsions fear that being "cured" of their problem will make them disorderly, sloppy, or unorganized. Nothing of the sort is going to happen. Rather, as you break free from this tyrannical form of OCD, you will develop a much healthier and more flexible relationship with the objects in your surroundings.

ERP for Obsessional Slowness

When a person with OCD takes an extremely long time to complete the most basic daily tasks, such as bathing, grooming, shaving, tooth brushing, and dressing, it is often referred to as obsessional slowness. This form of OCD is most often a by-product of an extreme, rigid adherence to perfectionistic standards and intolerance of not doing a task "just right." Often, the activity must be performed in a strict order and is accompanied by counting, repeating, tapping, or various other rituals in order to arrive at the feeling of "just right." The person generally becomes so absorbed in the ritual activity that he or she loses the forest for the trees, as the goal of getting the task done and moving on to something else becomes secondary to getting it "just right."

Slowness is often made worse by trying harder. The more pressure you put on yourself to speed up, the worse the slowness tends to become. When working on obsessional slowness, ERP should focus on habituating to the opposite: "doing it wrong."

REDUCING TIME SPENT ON TASKS

If obsessional slowness is an issue for you, you'll benefit from first monitoring the length of time it takes to do various tasks where slowness is a factor, such as dressing or showering, to establish a baseline. Then decide on a goal for the length of time it should take to complete these activities. Next, set a goal of decreasing the time you take to complete the task by two to five minutes per day. Use a timer or have a friend or family member act as a helper and time how long it takes you to complete the task. We've provided a monitoring form so you can track your progress, preceded by an example filled out by Jack, from chapter 1. (Make copies of the blank form before you fill it out so that you can use it repeatedly for various tasks.)

Jack's Slowness Monitoring Form

Target activity: *Showering*

Goal: *Reduce time to complete shower*

Baseline: *2-hour showers*

Goal time: *15 minutes* **or reduce by:** *25%* **per** ~~**day or**~~ **week**

Date	Start time	End time	Total time	Date	Start time	End time	Total time
3/13/10	8:30am	10:30am	2 hrs.	3/22/10			
3/14/10	8:25am	10:15am	1 hr. 50 min.	3/23/10			
3/15/10	8:30am	10:35am	2 hrs. 5 min.	3/24/10			
3/16/10	8:28am	10:27am	1 hr. 59 min.	3/25/10			
3/17/10	8:32am	10:15am	1 hr. 43 min.	3/26/10			
3/18/10	8:26am	9:56am	1 hr. 30 min.	3/27/10			
3/19/10				3/28/10			
3/20/10				3/29/10			
3/21/10				3/30/10			

Slowness Monitoring Form

Target activity: ______________________________

Goal: ______________________________

Baseline: ______________________________

Goal time: __________ or reduce by: __________ per day or week

Date	Start time	End time	Total time	Date	Start time	End time	Total time

REDUCING REPETITIVE RITUALS THAT CAUSE OBSESSIONAL SLOWNESS

Some instances of slowness are due to repetitive verbal or mental rituals consisting of phrases, numbers, rhymes, or images that must be repeated, either silently or aloud, in order to achieve a "just right" feeling while grooming, shaving, hair brushing, or dressing. If the ritual isn't performed "perfectly," the action must be repeated. In these situations, ERP consists of gradually reducing either the number of repetitions of phrases or the length of the phrases, or otherwise not doing the ritual completely. The procedure is as follows:

1. Make a list of all the activities during which you perform rituals. For each, take a sheet of paper and, at the top, write the activity, such as shaving ritual, hair brushing ritual, dressing ritual, and so on.

2. Make a list of all the rituals you perform while engaging in a given activity. After each ritual you list, designate its SUDS level based on the amount of anxiety or discomfort you'd experience *if you did not do* that ritual. You now have something akin to an anxiety/exposure hierarchy. (An example from Jack appears after this list.) Do this for each activity you listed in step 1.

3. Begin the process of exposure by choosing two or three items on the list with the lowest SUDS ratings, and practice doing those activities while purposefully not performing the ritual that typically accompanies them.

4. Repeat this process for two to three days, until your SUDS levels for those activities go down by at least half.

5. Choose two or three more items with the next higher up SUDS rating and repeat, this time leaving out the rituals for all actions at that SUDS level and below. For each exposure exercise, write down the anticipated SUDS level and the actual SUDS level you experienced.

6. Continue with the process until you can complete the activity while doing only a minimal number of rituals—or none at all.

Jack's shaving rituals	**SUDS level (0-100)**
Pick up the razor and count backward from the number 26.	60
Run the razor under water back and forth twice while reciting the phrase "180 meal ticket."	40
Pick up the shaving cream can and tap the top of the can three times.	80
Press the top and extrude a small dollop of shaving cream, then discard it and repeat saying "all hands on deck" twice, picturing the image of the Pope until his image feels "just right."	90
Spread the shaving cream on my face in symmetric circles on both sides of my face until if feels just right.	50
Begin to shave, starting always on the right side and repeating the strokes; while shaving my moustache, picture the image of the Dalai Lama in lights.	55
Rinse the razor and say "twenty two right" three times in a row.	70
Place the razor on the side of the counter, at a right angle to the mirror, saying "Absence makes the heart grow fonder" six times.	80
Place the top back on the shaving cream can, repeating "thirty-nine steps" six times.	60

REACH BEYOND YOUR FEARS

To break free from all forms of OCD, it is necessary to push your limitations somewhat. You must go to "reasonable extremes" when doing ERP. This means you must be willing to take some reasonable risks and engage in activities that by OCD standards may appear uncomfortable, unsafe, or even quite risky, such as touching an object thought to be contaminated. OCD feeds on these fears and demands perfect certainty, safety, and control in life. Breaking free requires accepting the possible risks and uncertainties—and also opens the door to new and rewarding experiences. Take a chance for a change!

Remember that it's okay and even normal to feel afraid at times when doing ERP; in fact, it's part of the process. Don't be alarmed if your fears and worries increase temporarily. This is actually a good sign and indicates that you're making progress. Your fear and anxiety will diminish with continued ERP work. Get mad at the OCD! Anger can be a great motivator as you continue to face your fears.

Do your best to "avoid avoidance." Realize that any exposure you avoid doing will persist as a fear and eventually erode your progress. Be rigorous with yourself. Make ERP part of your life on a daily basis. As you make progress, you'll find opportunities to practice going beyond your previous limitations.

Keys to Breaking Free Using ERP

- From an early age, many of our learned patterns of behavior—how we walk, talk, eat, dress, and conduct ourselves—are the result of modeling the behaviors, both positive and negative, that we observe in others, You can use this principle of behavioral modeling to gain the courage to do exposures that seem disturbing. Ask yourself, "Would a reasonable person without OCD stringently avoid touching this object merely because it's unpleasant to do so?" If you answer no, then to break free you should consider touching the object. Then ask yourself, "Would a reasonable person without OCD consider touching this object to be dangerous?" (In this context, dangerous means having a high probability of causing immediate harm to yourself or others.) If your answer is no, then you should consider touching the object and doing the exposure.

- If doing exposures to feared or avoided situations seems scary to you, make a distinction in your mind between "possibly harmful or dangerous" and "probably harmful or dangerous." "Possible" means that something could happen—that is, it may or may not happen—whereas "probably" means something is likely to occur. Realize that many more things could go wrong than are likely to go wrong. For example, while walking outside on a rainy day in Florida, you could possibly be hit by lightning, but you probably won't be. Likewise, touching a doorknob and not washing could possibly be harmful, yet in reality it is probably harmless. Walking out of the house and checking the door locks just once could possibly be dangerous, but in reality, it's probably harmless. When OCD is strong, it's hard to distinguish between possibly harmful or dangerous and probably harmful or dangerous. Even unlikely occurrences seem probable. As you confront more and more fear-provoking situations in ERP, it will be helpful to ask yourself, "Even if this situation is possibly harmful or dangerous, is it *probable* that it's harmful or dangerous?"

HELP FOR FAMILY AND FRIENDS

The self-directed program is becoming more challenging now as your loved one is developing anxiety/exposure hierarchies and implementing exposure and response prevention. When people confront situations that provoke fear, it's common for them to become somewhat more anxious and irritable in general for a while. It can be difficult to watch a person with OCD go through the discomfort that's a necessary part of exposure therapy. Your attitude will be instrumental in helping your loved one stick with ERP and get the greatest benefit from it. As far as your supportive role is concerned, less is usually more: the fewer words spoken, the better. Refrain from statements that offer reassurance, such as "Don't worry, it's okay," "You didn't harm anyone," or "Nothing bad is going to happen." Although this may seem supportive, it will interfere with the effectiveness of ERP. However, do offer encouragement and praise for your loved one's courage and willingness to take even small steps forward.

As for your role in reducing your own enabling behaviors, communication is key. Discuss the importance of decreasing your involvement in your loved one's compulsions and rituals. Once you are agreed in principle, start taking small but significant steps toward reducing your involvement. Just as you wouldn't expect someone with OCD to tackle every symptom at once, don't expect to tackle all of your enabling behaviors at once. Start with things you could do that would help reduce the impact of your loved one's OCD on the family without causing too much distress. Ask yourself, "What would really help improve our family functioning the most?"

Relate the changes in your behavior to the challenges your loved one is taking on in the self-directed program. For example, if your husband is working on leaving the house without checking the door and sometimes wants you to check it for him, give ample warning, then stop checking for him. If your daughter is working on limiting hand washing and showering, gradually purchase fewer body care products before starting to purchase only the amount other family members use. If your son has insisted that everyone change clothes as soon as they enter the house, gradually reduce the number of times family members comply over the course of several days, and then strive to stop participating in this ritual altogether.

For all OCD symptoms, reduce reassurance and participation in rituals with the understanding that these enabling behaviors must eventually be stopped. Throughout, stay in close communication with your loved one and other family members. Family members sometimes believe they are helping the person with, say, ordering and symmetry symptoms by purposefully "messing things up." This generally backfires and tends to antagonize the person with OCD and cause further strife in the family.

CHAPTER 7

Imaginal Exposure: Facing Your Fears in Your Imagination

We are healed of a suffering only by experiencing it to the full.

—Marcel Proust

ERP is the core of the self-directed program. You can enhance this approach and make it more powerful by using additional tools and techniques. Imaginal exposure is especially effective for people with OCD, because they are afflicted by recurrent and powerful images of possible dangers. Although the images are often triggered in relatively harmless situations, they tend to be highly charged and frightening. These images about future disastrous events fuel obsessive worry and compulsive rituals.

The object of doing ERP is to free your mind from needless worry about possible dangers and disasters. As explained earlier, in vivo ERP involves confronting the situations you fear in real life, in part so you can learn that what you fear is highly unlikely to happen. However, there are situations that are either impossible or just too impractical to re-create in real life for the purpose of ERP.

This was the case for Mary, whom you've gotten to know in earlier chapters. Her biggest fear involved becoming infected with HIV and then possibly transmitting it to others she cared about. She was well versed in the facts about how HIV is actually spread. Still, she couldn't shake the feeling that harmless events such as using a public restroom, shaking hands, or being in the range of an errant cough or sneeze could expose her to the virus.

Mary washed her hands as many as one hundred times a day and took one-hour showers. Her fear of getting AIDS involved images of increasing inability to take care of her family. The thought of not living up to her responsibilities as a wife and mother was particularly distressing. She also had images of being responsible for others becoming ill, and of shame due to disappointing her immediate and extended family.

Exposure and response prevention for feared situations such as using public bathrooms and shaking hands was very helpful, but Mary also needed to do ERP to break free from her fears of future disaster involving contracting HIV and becoming sick with AIDS. Imaginal exposure allowed her to do this. You can see how this approach would also be helpful with images associated with losing a loved one, "going crazy," being held responsible for a crime, or being rejected by others.

DOING IMAGINAL EXPOSURE

In imaginal exposure, you purposely think uncomfortable, fear-provoking thoughts and hold them in your mind until you become habituated and your distress diminishes. With this approach, you'll eventually be able to experience these thoughts without excessive discomfort. You'll feel less anxious when you have a "bad" thought and learn to accept such thoughts for what they are: just thoughts. In time, your anxiety-provoking thoughts are likely to lessen in intensity. The goal of in vivo exposure is to provide real-life opportunities to become habituated to feared situations, whereas the goal of imaginal exposure is to provide opportunities to become habituated to your own fear-provoking thoughts.

Imaginal exposure is a straightforward process: First you write a detailed narrative describing the feared scenario, then you record it and listen to it repeatedly, as described below. But before you proceed, a word of caution is in order. There are some people who shouldn't try imaginal exposure without the supervision of a qualified therapist. These include people who have borderline personality disorder, a history of psychosis, or severe OCD combined with a strong belief that their obsessive thoughts are real and make sense. Assuming that this doesn't apply to you, you're ready to begin.

Writing and Recording the Narrative

Write a three- to five-minute narrative in the first person present tense ("I am…"), describing what you fear would happen if you didn't check or carry out a compulsive ritual or behavior. Make it as vivid as possible, and include all relevant fear triggers and avoided situations. Write it as if you were describing a scene from a movie, frame by frame. The scene should include all of the following elements (thanks to Dr. Patricia Perrin, via personal communication, for this material). We've included an example from Mary for each element:

1. **The triggering situation:** *While shopping at the grocery store, I accidentally brushed up against a homeless person with a cut on his arm.*

2. **Initial fearful thought:** *What if I was infected with HIV?*

3. **Emotional reactions and physical symptoms:** *I'm feeling sweaty and I'm shaking with fear.*

4. **Additional fearful and doubting thoughts:** *I wonder whether my teenage daughter touched the man with the cut on his arm?*

5. **Urges to ritualize, without following through:** *I wanted to take my teenage daughter into the bathroom at the store so she could wash, but she wouldn't hear of it.*

6. **What this would say about me if the worst happened:** *I'm a bad mom if I don't insist that my daughter take a long shower when we get home.*

7. **Core fear or worst-case scenarios:** *I let it go, and then one month later my daughter gives blood at a local blood bank and discovers that she is HIV positive. Within six months, she dies a slow, painful death, and it's all my fault. I will live in perpetual guilt for the rest of my life.*

As with exposure in vivo, your imaginal exposure should create an initially high SUDS level. The higher the SUDS level you evoke and tolerate with your narrative, the more effective the exposure will be. However, some images, such as the death of a loved one, may seem too scary to include in a narrative, especially in the beginning. In this case, describe a situation that provokes a medium-high level of fear (a SUDS level of about 60 to 75), such as a loved one spraining an ankle or catching the flu. When you've habituated to that situation, do another narrative with more frightening images, with a SUDS level of about 80 to 90. If you're unsure about how to write your narrative, read on. A bit later in the chapter we've provided several examples.

Once you have a vivid, cohesive narrative, record it using a digital recorder or cassette tape. When you use the recording, you'll need to listen to your narrative over and over for about forty-five minutes a day for a full week. If you're using a tape, you may want to record three to five repetitions of the same narrative so you don't have to repeatedly rewind. If you record it electronically, it should be easy to repeat it over and over again.

If you don't like the sound of your recorded voice, you can simply read your narrative aloud over and over again. Similarly, if hearing the recording provokes too much anxiety, you can begin by simply reading your narrative over and over again. Once your SUDS level falls to more manageable levels, record the narrative and proceed as described.

Using Your Recording for Imaginal Exposure

For at least one week, listen to your recording over and over again in an extended session each day. Monitor your SUDS level (0-100) after each repetition of the narrative using the Imaginal Exposure Monitoring Form that follows. (Make copies so you can use it repeatedly; you'll need one form for each session.) Alternatively, you can monitor your SUDS levels in your journal. The goal is to play your narrative over and over until your SUDS level decreases to 20 or less, indicating that habituation has probably occurred. This often takes about forty-five minutes, but everyone is different, and your habituation may take less or more time.

Just as with in vivo ERP, when the images from this narrative no longer evoke excessive discomfort, write another narrative using a more fear-provoking situation and use it for imaginal exposure. Proceed in this way until all of your frightful images have been confronted and your fear of the images reduces.

Imaginal Exposure Monitoring Form

Date: ______________ **Total imaginal exposure time:** ____________________

SUDS	SUDS	SUDS
1. ____________	7. ____________	13. ____________
2. ____________	8. ____________	14. ____________
3. ____________	9. ____________	15. ____________
4. ____________	10. ____________	16. ____________
5. ____________	11. ____________	17. ____________
6. ____________	12. ____________	18. ____________

Average SUDS level for this session (total SUDS divided by number of repetitions): ____________

Mary's Experience with Imaginal Exposure

Because Mary found images of the death of immediate family members too scary to begin with, her first imaginal exposure narrative consisted of frightening images intended to create moderate anxiety (a SUDS level of about 40 to 60). She imagined that she caused someone who was well-known to her to become sick with AIDS and die a long, painful death as a result. She chose a single mother who lived nearby and was a fairly good friend. Her narrative describes a situation (which she knew was extremely unlikely, even preposterous) where her "negligence" resulted in the neighbor becoming contaminated. The scenario involves Mary having to shoulder the sole responsibility for her neighbor's illness and death. Here's the imaginal exposure narrative Mary came up with, using the suggested format:

> *I'm sitting at my kitchen table and the doorbell rings. It's my neighbor, who's come over to borrow some sugar. I hand her a glass bowl of sugar, but as my hands are wet from cooking, the bowl is slippery and it slips out of my hands. It falls to the floor, shattering into a hundred pieces. Some sharp pieces of glass cut my neighbor's skin, puncturing it and causing bleeding. I grab a napkin to wet it with water and wash the cuts, and in that brief moment when I'm looking away, my neighbor walks over to my husband's "contaminated" chair and sits in it so we can tend to the cuts on her leg.*

Upon realizing what's happened, I'm frozen in terror. The open cuts will surely result in her being infected with HIV. I take care of my neighbor's cuts, and she eventually leaves. Six months later, I'm visiting my neighbor at her house, and she tearfully discloses that she has tested positive for HIV and it has already progressed to AIDS, and the cause was what happened six months ago, at my house. I'm totally devastated. My mishap caused this tragedy, and now my neighbor is going to die from AIDS. I'm a careless, irresponsible, and despicable human being!

Over the next few months, I notice the deterioration of my neighbor's health. She's becoming thinner and weaker. I know she has doctor's appointments every week to be treated for her disease. She has four small children who will now be deprived of a mother because of my negligence. Over the next several weeks she becomes sicker and sicker, and eventually she can't take care of herself. I can't bear to look into the eyes of those poor children. My family shuns me for my irresponsible behavior. I can't bear that I must live with this mistake for the rest of my life.

Mary listened to this three-minute narrative for forty-five minutes to an hour daily. For the first week, it evoked powerful feelings of pain and dread, and Mary was resistant to listening to the recording, even terrified. She felt as if merely hearing these thoughts said aloud would somehow magically cause those terrible events to occur. But even so, after hearing the narrative repeated about ten times, she found that she was distracting herself from the horrific images by numbing out or by thinking about innocuous events that just popped into her mind. Each time her mind wandered, she'd make an effort to focus on the images in the narrative. It's important to maintain your focus on the narrative with the intention of eventually becoming bored with the images. In this way, they lose their ability to disturb you.

During the second week, Mary reported that listening to the recording was becoming less disturbing. She also said that she could recite the narrative by heart, like a movie script she'd memorized. And by the end of the second week, her overall SUDS level had dropped to around 30 to 40 and she was starting to become bored with the narrative. The images were having much less impact than in the beginning.

So she devised another narrative, this time involving images of herself becoming infected with HIV due to touching a homeless person. She reluctantly infused the narrative with painful images of being rejected by her family, followed by her death and not being around for her children as they grew up. As before, after listening to the tape over and over again, this more disturbing and fearful imagery began to lose its charge and intensity. It also became less believable that such a thing could just happen. As she continued playing the tape, her "logical brain" was better able to overcome the irrational OCD images. After just one week of daily exposure to these images, she was able to tolerate them with much less discomfort.

Melody's Experience with Imaginal Exposure

Remember Melody, the college student from chapter 1? Her need to check the door, stove, windows, and appliances was taking up more and more of her time, and she was overwhelmed by the fear that she may have harmed someone. She was diagnosed with OCD and her symptoms improved with medication. She graduated from college and passed the bar At age thirty-three, she was single and a successful attorney—and still struggling with OCD.

Melody's symptoms included compulsively checking her car at night. She feared she might have car trouble in the morning because of a flat tire or some sort of mechanical failure. She woke up worried every night and spent one to two hours checking her car for leaks and flat tires. She described feelings of horror at the thought of being late for work, being fired from her job because of it, and her promising career fizzling out as a result. Her ultimate fear was that all of this would make her a disappointment to her parents. Here's the imaginal exposure narrative Melody came up with, using the suggested format:

It's the first day of my new job as an attorney for a prestigious law firm. I'm getting ready to go to work. I leave my apartment, walk downstairs, and look at my car. I'm shocked at what I see. One of the tires is completely flat.

I wonder how in the world I'm going to get to work. I can feel the sweat starting to pour out. I walk around the car and am horrified to see that there's a puddle of oil beneath the engine. I open up the hood of the car and am appalled to see that oil is splashed all over the engine compartment—on the engine, the electrical system, all over the radiator, throughout all the wiring—everything is coated with the thick, slippery substance.

I get into the car to start it, but it won't start. I look at the passenger side and my heart pounds even harder when I see a puddle of oil on the floor of the passenger side. I'm feeling hopeless and helpless. I go upstairs to call a garage for help, but they tell me they're backed up with calls and won't be able to come look at my car for several hours, if at all. I call another garage and they tell me the same story. I call another, and still another... They're all busy and can't help me now.

The sweat is pouring from my body now, and my heart is beating so fast I think I might have a heart attack. I call my new boss to tell him it will be at least several hours before I can get to work today, and that I may not be able to make it at all. He answers me in a cold, harsh, and critical voice: "If this is how you act, then perhaps you don't deserve to work in the law profession! How could someone so irresponsible, someone so careless, be a decent lawyer?" I beg him to take into consideration that something unexpected happened, something beyond my control, but to no avail. My boss replies that as far as he's concerned, I should look for another job, but that it's unlikely that any legal firm in this town would hire someone so irresponsible and careless in her professional responsibilities.

I feel rejected, hopeless, discouraged, and angry. How will I ever find another job in this city? Maybe I'll never get another job... Someone so careless and irresponsible doesn't deserve to work with people in trouble. Word gets out that I'm irresponsible, and after several months and ten different job interviews, nobody will hire me for anything. I can't find any job, anywhere. I start to wonder if I'll always be alone and lonely. No man would want to be with someone so irresponsible. I become a burden to my parents and to society, and eventually I wind up homeless, living on the street.

Melody recorded this imaginal narrative and listened to it over and over for an hour every day, picturing the images in her narrative vividly. During her initial listening, the images provoked intense anxiety, and even tears at the thought of being reprimanded by her boss and losing her job. Her average SUDS level for that first imaginal exposure was 85. After a week of repeated listening, her average SUDS level had only dropped down to about 70.

But by the middle of the second week, she reported that the narrative had become monotonous, even boring. Her average SUDS level decreased to about 25, and with repeated listening, she was better able to access her rational mind and reassure herself that her job performance had been deemed excellent by her boss.

Although thoughts of catastrophic harm to her career still bothered Melody, the idea of actually being fired from her job because of being late became an absurd and remote possibility. An additional benefit of listening to her imaginal exposure tape was that Melody developed an increased awareness of her excessive perfectionism and how it pervaded her life. She started sleeping better, too. The exercise bolstered her ability to resist her nightly rituals of checking her car, and after five weeks of listening to the tape, she stopped getting up at night to check her car and often slept through the night.

Robert's Experience with Imaginal Exposure

Robert, whom you also met in chapter 1, was a thirty-two-year-old salesman with a six-month history of OCD. His symptoms involved obsessive concern and preoccupation with the possibility of harming someone while he was driving. He lived a nightmare of guilt, fear, and dread every time he got behind the wheel. A simple bump in the road, an unexpected noise, a shadow, or flash of light—all triggered a heart-pounding, tire-screeching U-turn back to the scene. To relieve his feelings of panic and dread, Robert had to return to the location where he thought the accident had occurred to make sure it hadn't happened.

As soon as he felt reassured no accident took place, his anxiety was relieved, but only briefly. Feelings of intense doubt and fear would recur, compelling yet another U-turn back to the scene of the "accident." Driving near schools, children, and bicyclists was especially nerve-wracking. Potholes and speed bumps felt like driving over a body, triggering his compulsion to check for signs that he'd injured someone.

In doing imaginal exposure, Robert described his worst nightmare: being held responsible for a driving-related accident that resulted in his incarceration. Here's the narrative Robert came up with, filled with images of guilt, shame, and loss of freedom:

> *I'm out with a couple of buddies. We're blowing off some steam watching a football game at a local watering hole. I have a beer and a snack, and when the game ends, I leave to drive back home. I stop at a gas station a half mile from my house to get some gas.*
>
> *I go in, pay for the gas, and then get back in the car. As I pull out of the parking lot onto the road, I suddenly feel a strong bump, a jolt to the car. I pull over, stop the car, and get out to see what happened.*
>
> *Sure enough, there is the body of a child lying on the ground, bloody and mangled. My heart begins to pound and my stomach turns as I view this horrible, gruesome sight. The girl looks to be about seven years old and is unconscious. Blood is everywhere. I see bloodstains on my fender and know that I hit this poor innocent child. I look up and see a police car approaching, with its flashing lights and siren, then ambulances arrive at the scene. The emotional pain is unbearable. Due to my reckless and careless behavior, this innocent child's life is now hanging by a thread! If I had been more careful, more responsible, this never would have happened.*

The girl is transported to the nearest hospital. Her parents, terribly distraught and in shock, come into the emergency room. They look at me with contempt. They ask me why I did what I did. I'm speechless. I feel like my world is coming to an end. After a few hours, I'm notified that the child is dead. The sickest feeling of all comes over me. I feel like vomiting. The grief and remorse are overwhelming.

After a few days, the sheriff's office notifies me that I'm being charged with vehicular manslaughter and reckless driving. If convicted, I face a prison sentence and years of probation. Rather than fight the charges, I plead guilty as charged. In a brief court appearance I'm sentenced by a judge to ten years in prison. I'm escorted out of the courtroom and taken to a county prison, where I must spend the next ten years of my life with a variety of criminals who have done all kinds of violence to people. The feeling of being confined, of losing my freedom, of my life going down the drain, is too painful to bear.

Robert listened to his narrative for forty-five minutes to an hour daily for ten days. His initial SUDS level was 95. Although he felt extremely uncomfortable at first, his SUDS level lowered to about 50 during the second week of listening. By combining the imaginal exposure with in vivo ERP, Robert was able to get his OCD symptoms under control in a very short time.

Some Tips for Effective Imaginal Exposure

Here are some common problems that may arise while doing imaginal exposure, and some possible solutions:

You can't tolerate the anxiety level your imaginal exposure causes. Intolerance of the anxiety is usually associated with a fear of being anxious. You may hold beliefs that anxiety is somehow dangerous to you or will cause you to lose control. It is important to actively challenge these ideas in gradual steps. First, consider making your narrative shorter and less fear provoking. Aim to have your imaginal exposure create a SUDS level of about 50 to 60, rather than 90 to 100. If you can make the narrative really absurd, even ridiculous, it will take the edge off. When you've habituated to that situation, do another narrative with scarier images, with a SUDS level of about 80 to 90. Remember, as in all ERP, the more discomfort you're willing to experience, the more benefit you'll derive from the exposure.

Your imaginal exposure doesn't arouse much anxiety. Your narrative may be too generalized. Make it more vivid and include specific disturbing images of situations you fear. For example, if you fear being ill in the future, describe a specific image of being in a hospital hooked up to IVs and a breathing machine, or of being alone and unable to call for a nurse for help, and so forth. Also, you may be blocking the full emotional impact of the experience while listening, perhaps by distracting yourself or thinking about other things while listening to the tape. Try to get into the words, feelings, and images as much as possible.

You're relying on safety signals. Another reason why an exposure may not arouse much anxiety is the presence of safety signals. These are environmental or situational cues that provide a feeling of safety and thereby interfere with exposure. For example, having your partner or a friend or family member present during the exposure may be comforting, but it tends to interfere with the activation of your anxiety during the exposure. Another example would be removing all knives from your home while doing imaginal exposure to thoughts of losing control and harming others with a knife. Using safety signals to provide a feeling of protection and security may be a useful strategy when you first begin doing imaginal exposure. However, you must eventually challenge yourself to do the exposures without relying on them. This will give you the best opportunity to benefit from imaginal exposure.

Just imagining the scary scene isn't enough to provoke anxiety. Some people can imagine scenes vividly but don't find that purposely thinking of feared possibilities makes them anxious. If this is your situation, it's best to do in vivo exposure, as described in chapter 6.

MAKE IMAGINATION YOUR ALLY AGAINST OCD

For many people with OCD, the fear and worry involved in attempts to ward off an imagined unlikely feared event can be more emotionally disabling than if some difficult life situation were to actually occur. OCD hijacks your natural powers of imagination to fuel obsessive worries and compulsive rituals. Using imaginal exposure, you can turn the tables and make imagination your ally *against* OCD. Use this powerful technique to face and overcome the OCD fears that can't be re-created in real life. Just as Robert did, you can use imaginal exposure to complement real-life, or in vivo, exposures.

HELP FOR FAMILY AND FRIENDS

Imaginal exposure is a powerful tool for people with obsessive worries about dangers and disasters they fear will happen in the future. The goal is to see the thoughts for what they are: just thoughts. For this approach to be effective, it's vital that the exposure activate the person's fear, dread, and doubt. Offer praise and reinforcement when your loved one appears to be doing imaginal exposures effectively. Do not, however, act like the "exposure police." If you see signs that your loved one is avoiding the imaginal exposure, perhaps through distraction or zoning out, offer gentle reminders of the goals that he or she set in regard to the self-directed program. If necessary, look for a good time to discuss progress. Is your loved one still committed to getting better? If exposure seems to be too difficult for your loved one to do alone, seeking professional help may be a necessary next step.

When people with OCD confront their fears via imaginal exposure, they are also confronting what it means to live with uncertainty and risk. Everyone must learn to live life despite the uncertainties inherent in living. A common way people with OCD avoid accepting uncertainty and thereby perpetuate anxiety is by asking for reassurance from trusted others. In essence, reassurance seeking is a way of avoiding responsibility. It gives the person an "out": "If something bad happens as a result of not doing my ritual, it's not my fault because you told me it would be okay." It's extremely important that family members not feed into the person's craving for certainty. Discuss in advance how you'll handle requests for reassurance during exposure exercises. (See chapter 18 for more guidance on this.) The more often people with OCD face and accept uncertainty without doing their rituals, the more they loosen OCD's grip on their lives.

CHAPTER 8

Challenging Your Faulty Beliefs: Cognitive Restructuring

When I look back on all these worries, I remember the story of the old man who said on his deathbed that he had had a lot of trouble in his life, most of which had never happened.

—Sir Winston Churchill

Although the structure and biological functioning of the brain has been an important focus for scientists studying OCD, there has also been considerable interest in the role patterns of thinking play in people with OCD. Scientists have concluded that faulty beliefs about the risks of danger and harm play an important part in the fear, anxiety, and dread suffered by people with OCD (Salkovskis 1985; Freeston, Rheaume, and Ladouceur 1996). You can also think of these faulty beliefs as inaccurate appraisals or interpretations.

Imagine walking through a densely wooded forest with some friends. It's a beautiful day, and you're enjoying the sights and sounds all around you. You're relaxed and calm as you enjoy the sounds of birds and wildlife. Suddenly, a friend tells you he thinks he just saw a poisonous snake.

An image of the snake slithering through the grass and attacking you triggers your body to prepare for danger. You become edgy, fearful, and anxious. Your heart pounds, your muscles tighten, and your pace speeds up as you think of the fastest way to leave the forest. Slight movements of the bushes and the sounds of rustling tree leaves—phenomena that you ignored or found pleasing just moments ago—now cause you to feel fear. You won't relax until you exit the forest safely.

When you finally leave the forest unharmed, you breathe a sigh of relief. Although you never actually saw a snake, your brain didn't care. Your anxious reaction was solely in response to your appraisal of the situation: your belief about the presence of a snake. Whether there was actually a snake nearby didn't matter. Such is the power of a belief to trigger powerful bodily sensations and reactions.

People with OCD possess strong beliefs about the likelihood of a given situation being dangerous to themselves or others. Often these beliefs can't be supported or justified by the facts, and in fact, there's evidence to contradict the belief. This makes the belief a faulty one. Most faulty beliefs arise from certain categories of cognitive errors. Here are some typical cognitive errors of people with OCD, with examples of the faulty beliefs arising from each.

Overestimating Risk, Harm, and Danger

- I must protect myself (or others or loved ones), even if there is only the remotest chance of something bad happening. I'd rather be safe than sorry. I'll presume the situation is dangerous until it can be proven safe.

Overcontrol and Perfectionism

- I must maintain absolute control over my thoughts, feelings, and actions, as well as all the circumstances in my life.
- Unless I do everything perfectly, it's intolerable to me.
- Extreme harm and danger can come to me, my loved ones, or innocent others if I don't protect them perfectly.
- If it doesn't look or feel just right, it's intolerable.

Catastrophizing

- An open sore on my arm means I'll definitely get AIDS if I'm around someone I think has AIDS.
- If I get into arguments with my mother, it must mean I'm definitely a violent person.

Black-and-White or All-or-Nothing Thinking

- If I'm not perfectly safe, then I'm in great, overwhelming danger. A tiny, one-in-a-million chance of something bad happening is exactly the same as a huge, 99.999 percent chance.
- If I don't do it perfectly, then I've done it horribly.
- If I don't perfectly protect others from harm, I'll be severely punished.
- If I don't perfectly understand everything I read, I feel as if I don't understand anything I've read.

Persistent Doubting

Even though it makes no sense and it's not justified by the facts, maybe I...

- Wasn't careful enough, and something bad will happen as a result
- Harmed (molested, injured, cheated) someone
- Stole (plagiarized, did something awful, improper, immoral, bad)

Magical Thinking

- Thoughts are very powerful. Merely thinking a bad, horrible thought will definitely cause something horrible to happen.

Thought-Action Fusion

- If I have a bad or horrible thought about harming someone, it feels just as if I've actually done it.
- If I think about something bad happening, I'm implicitly responsible should it actually happen.

Overvaluing Thoughts

- If I have a bad thought, it means I'm bad, dangerous, or crazy.
- My thoughts are the true indicator of who I am and what I'm likely to do.
- I'm judged as much for the nature and quality of my thoughts as for what I actually do.

Superstitious Thinking

- By doing my ritual (washing, tapping, repeating, touching, spinning, and so on), I can ward off bad things from happening to me and protect those I love.
- There are bad numbers and good numbers. Bad numbers cause bad things to happen, and good numbers cause good things to happen or can stop bad things from happening.

Intolerance of Uncertainty

- I must be 100 percent certain of everything, and I must be 100 percent sure that everything will be alright. If I'm the slightest bit uncertain about anything (my future, my health, or loved ones' health), it is intolerable and I must do something, anything, to be certain that everything will be alright.

Overresponsibility

- Maybe I caused something bad to happen. My failure to prevent it must mean that I'm definitely a bad person.

- I must always, at all times, guard against making a mistake that can possibly harm an innocent person, no matter how remote the possibility.

Pessimistic Bias

- If something bad is going to happen, it is much more likely to happen to me or someone I love or care about than to others. This occurs for no reason other than because it's me.

What-If Thinking

In the future, what if I...

- Do it wrong?
- Get AIDS?
- Am responsible for injuring someone?

Intolerance of Anxiety

- Anxiety is dangerous to me and I can't tolerate being anxious for even a short period of time. I'll do anything to feel better now.

Emotional Reasoning

- I must be in great danger, otherwise I wouldn't be feeling so anxious.
- It doesn't feel just right, so something must be terribly wrong.

Extraordinary Cause and Effect

- Objects have the ability to defy the forces of nature; for example, stoves can spontaneously turn on, refrigerators can open, locks can unlock—all without human intervention.
- Germs and viruses can leap long distances—even across city streets—and thus contaminate me and others.

THE ABCDS OF FAULTY BELIEFS

The role of faulty beliefs in maintaining OCD symptoms can be understood using the ABCD method. It's based on the original ABC method of cognitive therapy developed by Albert Ellis (1962) and Aaron Beck, Gary Emery, and Ruth Greenberg (1985), in which A stands for *activating event*, B stands for faulty *beliefs* about, or appraisals of, the event, and C stands for the emotional *consequences*—anxiety, doubt, and worry. In this adaptation for people with OCD, D stands for a neutralizing ritual or compulsion. The anxiety, emotional discomfort, and resulting compulsive behaviors of OCD take place in the following sequence:

A = Activating Event and Intrusive Thought, Image, or Urge

An event, such as touching a doorknob or turning off the stove or a light switch, generates an intrusive thought. Here are some examples:

- What if I didn't really lock the door and an intruder destroys my home?
- What if the stove is on and my house burns down and I'm at fault?
- What if this thought about causing danger or harm means that I'm dangerous, crazy, or perverted or that something horrible will happen to me or those I love?

B = Faulty Belief About the Intrusive Thought

The intrusive thought is automatically interpreted literally to mean something very dire is likely to happen unless some action is immediately taken to reduce the anxiety associated with the thought and prevent harm to a loved one or oneself. These intrusive thoughts, rather than being dismissed as "just thoughts," are given great importance and meaning. The list of cognitive errors a bit earlier in the chapter included examples of specific faulty beliefs. Later in the chapter, we'll take a look at some examples of events or situations that typically activate cognitive errors and the unrealistic beliefs that typically result for those who have OCD.

C = Emotional Consequences: Anxiety, Doubt, and Worry

Faulty beliefs or inaccurate appraisals of thoughts trigger high levels of doubt, anxiety, and worry. The feelings of anxiety are, in turn, appraised as intolerable, unacceptable, and dangerous. For a person with OCD, the anxiety spins out of control, resulting in a powerful urge to relieve the anxiety however possible.

D = Neutralizing Ritual or Avoidance

A compulsive action or set of actions such as excessive or ritualistic washing, checking, repeating, or ordering brings the anxiety under control briefly. Persistent avoidance of triggering events and situations can also be considered a compulsion. Either way, it sets the stage for the next activating event, creating an endless cycle. Although the neutralizing ritual may temporarily relieve anxiety, this only serves to reinforce the entire cycle.

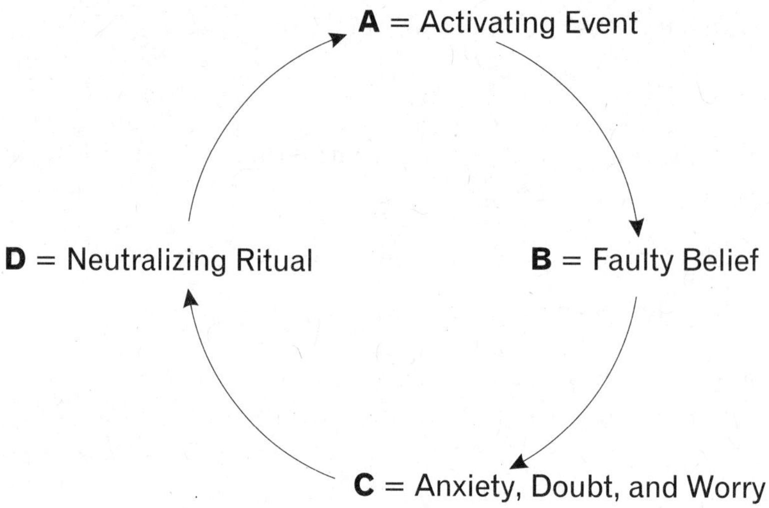

A = Activating event and intrusive thought, image, or urge

B = Faulty belief about the intrusive thought

C = Emotional consequences: anxiety, doubt, and worry

D = Neutralizing ritual or avoidance

CORRECTING FAULTY BELIEFS

Cognitive restructuring is the technical phrase for the process of directly challenging cognitive errors and the resulting faulty beliefs, including those that underlie OCD behaviors. This process doesn't put an end to cognitive errors. Rather, cognitive restructuring helps you in two ways: It helps you see that you have choices as to how you interpret your thoughts and that making different choices can make a difference in the level and intensity of your OCD. And by increasing your awareness of the faulty ways you interpret your thoughts, you can become more objective about them, rather than overreacting to them.

Cognitive Restructuring: How and When to Use It

While cognitive restructuring is useful for correcting the faulty beliefs that maintain OCD behaviors, please consider the following points as you start to work on your faulty beliefs:

- Though some studies have shown cognitive restructuring to be at least as effective as exposure and response prevention (Wilhelm et al. 2005), Dr. Hyman's experience is that cognitive restructuring is best used to enhance and bolster the effects of ERP, not as a substitute for it. According to Dr. Edna Foa, a leading expert on ERP, the best tool for correcting the faulty beliefs of OCD is ERP. It's important to take on the hard work of chapters 4, 5, and 6 first, and then use the cognitive restructuring exercises in this chapter to enhance your progress.

- Use cognitive restructuring to help change faulty beliefs that persist when a course of ERP hasn't been successful at modifying these ideas (for example, that it's likely you'll be contaminated by HIV or burn down the house because of not checking that the stove is off).
- Cognitive restructuring is often helpful for those whose rituals and compulsions are primarily performed mentally.
- In chapter 6, you rated the degree to which you believe in your obsessions and the necessity of your compulsions. If you rated your belief in your feared consequences of not doing rituals at 70 percent or higher, it's best to work on cognitive restructuring first—at least until your degree of belief goes down below 70 percent.
- Remember that, as mentioned in chapter 2, reassuring self-talk or mantras can become compulsions too, if you use them habitually to relieve the anxiety associated with obsessive thoughts. Be careful not to incorporate cognitive restructuring techniques in a manner that provides reassurance or an escape from anxiety. If you find yourself doing this, hold off on cognitive restructuring exercises and focus more on ERP.

Cognitive Restructuring Step-by-Step

By learning to challenge your faulty beliefs, you make the cycle of obsessions and rituals less habitual and automatic. Challenging your faulty beliefs is like throwing a wrench into the gears of the well-oiled engine of your OCD thinking, giving you more freedom and control over the impact that your thoughts have on you and your behavior. Challenging your faulty beliefs is a two-step process:

1. Identify your activating events or situations, plus the accompanying intrusive thoughts, and then identify the faulty beliefs associated with the thoughts.
2. Challenge your faulty beliefs with more realistic self-talk.

STEP 1. IDENTIFY ACTIVATING EVENTS, INTRUSIVE THOUGHTS, AND FAULTY BELIEFS

It's important to know exactly which situations or events activate a specific intrusive thought, feeling, or urge, and what faulty beliefs are involved. The following table provides some examples of common activating events in OCD, the accompanying intrusive thought, along with the faulty belief associated with it. Then, in the right-hand column, we've indicated the categories of cognitive errors those faulty beliefs represent.

Common Activating Events, Intrusive Thoughts, and Faulty Beliefs			
Activating event	**Intrusive thought**	**Faulty belief**	**Cognitive errors**
Locking the front door upon leaving for work	*What if it's not locked?*	*I have to be very careful. If I make a mistake and there's a break-in, it will be my fault and I'll suffer forever.*	• Overvaluing thoughts • Overcontrol and perfectionism • Overestimating risk, harm, and danger • Intolerance of uncertainty • Overresponsibility
Touching the doorknob in a public bathroom without tissue paper	*What if I contract a horrible disease?*	*I'll definitely get sick unless I take measures to prevent it.*	• Overestimating risk, harm, and danger • Intolerance of uncertainty
Seeing the silhouette of a naked child in a shower stall and immediately looking away	*What if I enjoyed what I saw for even a millisecond?*	*Deep down, I'm truly a child molester or pedophile.*	• Thought-action fusion • What-if thinking • Overvaluing thoughts
Looking in a mirror to be sure every hair is perfectly even	*What if people ridicule me?*	*I must keep cutting my hair until it looks perfect, even if it takes hours.*	• Overcontrol and perfectionism • Persistent doubting
Seeing a banana peel on a sidewalk across a busy street	*What if someone slips on it?*	*I'll be guilty of negligence and punished unless I remove it and prevent others from slipping on it and being injured.*	• Overresponsibility • Overcontrol and perfectionism
Switching off a light switch	*Thinking of my daughter dying in a car crash*	*I must turn the switch off five times in a row, perfectly, or something bad will happen to my daughter.*	• Overvaluing thoughts • Overcontrol and perfectionism
Twisting the lids on jars of food closed extremely tightly	*What if they aren't completely sealed?*	*I must make absolutely sure the top of the jar won't open; if the food spoils, someone could get really sick and it will be my fault.*	• Overvaluing thoughts • Overcontrol and perfectionism • What-if thinking • Intolerance of uncertainty

Now that you've seen some examples, it's time to explore your own activating events and associated intrusive thoughts, faulty beliefs, and cognitive errors. Write the activating situation or event in the first column, the related intrusive thought in the second column, and the related faulty belief in the third column. Finally, write the cognitive errors your faulty belief represents in the fourth column, using the lists from earlier in this chapter. (You may also use your journal to do the exercises in this chapter.) Frequently, more than one cognitive error is operating in any given intrusive thought or faulty belief, and some of the errors are overlapping or similar. The important thing isn't to "get it right" or exhaustively list every category that could be involved. Just identify the cognitive errors that seem most fitting to you so that you can come up with coping statements to counter them.

Common Activating Events, Intrusive Thoughts, and Faulty Beliefs			
Activating event	**Intrusive thought**	**Faulty belief**	**Cognitive errors**

STEP 2. CHALLENGE YOUR FAULTY BELIEFS WITH REALISTIC SELF-TALK

Now that you've identified some of your intrusive thoughts, the situations that trigger them, and the associated faulty beliefs and cognitive errors, you can begin to challenge these faulty ideas generated by your "OCD brain." These images and ideas can be very strong and are almost always based on negative feelings concerning future harm and danger, so they feel compelling. To challenge them, you need to note when they occur, and then challenge these unrealistic appraisals of the triggering situations. Note that many people confuse this step with so-called positive thinking. However, the goal is to be an accurate thinker, not necessarily a positive thinker. Accurate thinking means you identify your OCD-based thoughts and label them as such. Even this simple step can give you some much-needed distance from these thoughts. Once you see them for what they are—just thoughts, and OCD thoughts, at that—you'll have more freedom to identify the true facts about the situation and choose to appraise it differently.

To get an idea of how this works, take a look at the following table, which gives some examples of ways to fight specific faulty beliefs and unrealistic appraisals with more realistic self-talk. This strategy can help you cope with difficult situations when obsessive thoughts arise by decreasing their power and thus diminishing the urge to perform compulsive behavior in response to these troublesome thoughts.

Coping Self-Talk

Cognitive error	Faulty Belief	Realistic response
Overestimating risk, harm, and danger	*I must always be protecting myself (or others or loved ones) from danger, even if there's only the remotest chance of something bad happening. I'll presume the situation is dangerous until it can be proven safe.*	• *I must learn to take a chance in order to get better.* • *What would a prudent person (someone who doesn't have OCD) do in this situation?*
Overcontrol and perfectionism	*I must maintain absolute control over my thoughts and actions and over everything bad that can possibly occur in my life.*	• *Maintaining control is so exhausting. I think I'll take a chance on being imperfect for a change, even if it's hard to do.* • *I'm afraid of change, but it's just my OCD brain playing tricks on me.* • *For a change, I'll strive for good enough, rather than perfect.*
Catastrophizing, Black-and-white or all-or-nothing thinking	*Unless I'm sure everything is perfectly safe, I am in terrible danger, or my loved ones are.*	• *What is the evidence of danger here? There's no proof that something bad is inevitably going to happen.*
Persistent doubting	*Maybe I harmed (molested, injured, cheated stole, plagiarized, and so on).*	• *It's my OCD brain playing tricks.* • *I know logically what's what.* • *I'm not buying into these needless fears!*

Magical thinking, Thought-action fusion, Overvaluing thoughts	*Merely thinking a bad thought will cause something bad to happen.*	• *It's only a thought. I am not my thoughts. It's just an OCD thought, and therefore means nothing. Only actions can harm, not thoughts.*
Superstitious thinking	*By doing my ritual I can ward off bad things from happening to me and protect those I love.*	• *These rituals are so tiring. I must take the chance to discover that I can't control the outside world this way. My rituals protect no one, and they torment me and those around me.*
Intolerance of uncertainty	*If I'm even slightly uncertain about anything (my future, my health, and the health of my loved ones), it is intolerable*	• *I can remain calm in the face of uncertainty. Since I can't control everything, why try? By trying to control everything, I only make my OCD worse.* • *If I don't act on my need for absolute certainty, the urge to do a ritual will diminish after a while.*
Overresponsibility	*Maybe I'll cause something bad to happen, and if I fail to prevent it, that will mean I'm a very bad person.*	• *I'm only human. My responsibilities end where others' responsibilities begin.* • *I can be a good citizen without having to be everyone's guardian angel.*
Pessimistic bias	*If something bad is going to happen, it is much more likely to happen to me or to someone I love or care about than to others.*	• *The probability of something bad happening to me or my loved ones is no greater than the probability of bad things happening to anyone else. I'm not so special!*
What-if thinking	*What if I do it wrong (make a mistake, get cancer, get AIDS, cause someone harm)?*	• *The torture I put myself through by worrying about the future is probably worse than anything that could happen. I'll deal with trouble when it happens, not before.* • *Living my life in terms of what-ifs only wastes my time. What are the true odds of getting cancer or AIDS, or causing someone harm? The odds are much smaller than my OCD brain wants to believe.*

Intolerance of anxiety	*I can't stand being anxious for even a short period of time. I'll do anything to feel better now.*	• *I can handle the discomfort. I don't have to do a ritual now. My anxiety level will go down if I just wait it out.*
Emotional reasoning	*This danger feels so real, I cannot not pay attention to it.*	• *My feelings are not the facts. I can treat these feelings as false alarms that I choose not to react to*

Now that you have some idea about how to fight faulty OCD beliefs with coping self-talk in the form of more realistic appraisals, try to come up with some statements to counter the faulty beliefs you identified in the previous exercise. The following worksheet will help you assess how helpful each statement is. Before you start, make copies of the worksheet so that you can use it for a variety of activating events and faulty beliefs. Here are some instructions for using the worksheet:

1. Write down an activating event that regularly triggers your intrusive thoughts and resulting anxiety.
2. Write a description of the intrusive thought that occurs in the situation and the faulty belief that results in anxiety and discomfort.
3. Rate the SUDS level (0-100) of your discomfort associated with that thought.
4. Using a percentage (0-100%), assess the degree to which you believe your appraisal is an accurate depiction of the situation as it really is.
5. Decide which categories of cognitive errors are involved in your faulty belief. There may be more than one cognitive error involved, and if you aren't sure, that's okay too.
6. Write a more realistic response or coping statement that you could use in this situation to talk back to your OCD. When you write your coping statement, you should use the exact words that your logical brain comes up with. If you feel uncertain, use the "Realistic response" column from the preceding table to guide you.
7. Using a percentage, rate the degree (0-100%) to which you truly believe in this more realistic response *right now.*
8. Repeat this exercise for as many different activating events as you can.

Challenging Your Faulty Beliefs

Activating event: ____

____

____

Intrusive thought: ____

____

____

Discomfort (SUDS level 0-100): ______________________________

Faulty belief: ____

____

____

How much do you believe this thought is true? (0-100%): ______________

Which categories of cognitive errors are at work here? (choose from the list above)

____

____

____

Realistic response or coping statement: ______________________________

____

____

____

How much do you believe this realistic response is true? (0-100%): ______________

ADDITIONAL WAYS TO CHALLENGE FAULTY BELIEFS

The previous section helped you challenge your faulty beliefs by changing your self-talk when an OCD thought occurs. This requires consistent practice. Another way to challenge the faulty beliefs of OCD is through the use of a variety of behavioral "experiments." These experiments provide an opportunity for you to dispute your OCD predictions of potential harm and catastrophic danger. By testing out your faulty beliefs in the real world, you will further weaken their grip on your thinking.

Challenging Magical Thinking, Thought-Action Fusion, and Overvalued Ideas

You can use the following exercises to test the faulty belief that thoughts can cause bad events to occur and that thoughts are the same as actions (Freeston, Rheaume, and Ladouceur 1996). While these experiments may at first seem silly, by testing your prediction that your thoughts can cause something to happen against the actual outcome when you purposely think certain thoughts, you can begin to challenge faulty beliefs about the magical power of your thoughts.

Think and win. Purchase a lottery ticket on Monday and think about winning the grand prize for half an hour every day (the typical odds are 27,000,000 to one). In your mind, create as vivid an image of yourself winning as you can. Then, at the time of the drawing for the big prize, note the outcome and ask yourself, "To what extent did my repetitively thinking these thoughts influence the outcome of the lottery? What effect did all of my thinking have on what actually happened?"

Think and break. Choose an old small appliance (like a toaster) that is in good working order. Every day for one week, write on a piece of paper, "The toaster will break." Each day, write it one hundred times and picture the broken appliance in your mind each time. After one week, examine the outcome. Did your thoughts affect the appliance?

Think dying goldfish. Buy a goldfish and a fishbowl from a local pet store. Set it up at home and provide normal, proper care for the fish. For fifteen minutes twice daily, vividly imagine the fish dying. First imagine it gasping. Then imagine it dead and floating on the surface of the water instead of swimming in the bowl. Repeat this every day for a week and observe the effect on the fish. If you believe that thoughts can cause bad events to happen, the goldfish should die.

Challenging Hyperresponsibility

As a person with OCD, you often fail to consider the numerous factors that may contribute to a negative event, such as losing your job or the illness of a loved one. Even when it clearly doesn't make sense, you tend to assume the entire burden for preventing negative events. The pie chart technique can help you attribute responsibility for negative events more accurately and appropriately.

To demonstrate the pie chart technique, let's consider Michael's situation. He has an obsessive concern with the possibility of harming others through his own carelessness. He checks constantly that he hasn't injured others by acting carelessly; for example, by spilling water on the floor and causing someone to slip and fall. He usually keeps his car windows rolled up for fear that something in his car might fly out and cause an accident.

His present obsession is that a piece of paper that flew out of his car window obstructed another driver's view and resulted in an auto accident. He had briefly rolled down the window to get some fresh air. The wind blew a folder on the passenger seat open, and a piece of paper flew out. It wasn't an important piece of paper, but Michael believes it possibly had his name on it, and maybe even his address.

Now he worries constantly about that piece of paper and the accident it may have caused. Sounds silly, doesn't it? Even Michael, an intelligent professional engineer, admits it. Yet despite the complete lack of evidence of any accident occurring as a result, in Michael's OCD-style thinking, he sees his actions as the primary cause of an unfortunate chain of events. This type of thinking ignores all other possible factors that could result in auto accidents, aside from his "carelessness." Using a technique known as the *downward arrow* (Burns 1980), we can take a close look at the sequence of ideas and beliefs that make up Michael's obsession:

A piece of paper blew out of my car.

↓

The paper flew onto the windshield of another driver's car and an accident occurred.

↓

The driver and passengers were seriously injured.

↓

The piece of paper was traced to my car.

↓

I was held responsible for the accident by a judge—found guilty of a crime.

↓

I was fined and sent to jail.

↓

I must live with the perpetual guilt of causing harm to someone through my irresponsible act.

Putting aside that in Michael's case there's no evidence that an accident actually occurred, in every mishap there are a number of possible contributing factors. In Michael's case, some of the factors that might contribute to an auto accident include mechanical problems, the carelessness of other drivers, road conditions, weather, and so on. To begin to more accurately assess the degree to which your actions may have contributed, it's useful to list all of the other potential contributing factors, and then assess the probability that each contributed.

Here's what Michael came up with for this exercise. Note that all of the various factors add up to 100%.

Possible cause of an accident or mishap	Probability that it contributed (0-100%)
1. Defective car	*15%*
2. Driver carelessness	*20%*
3. Paper flying out of my car and onto the road	*5%*
4. Other driver upset over a family member's illness	*5%*
5. Other driver upset by an argument with spouse	*5%*
6. Bad weather conditions	*20%*
7. Poor driving skills	*15%*
8. Other driver's poor vision	*5%*
9. Poor road conditions	*10%*
TOTAL	*100%*

Pictured as a pie chart, all of the competing factors would look like this:

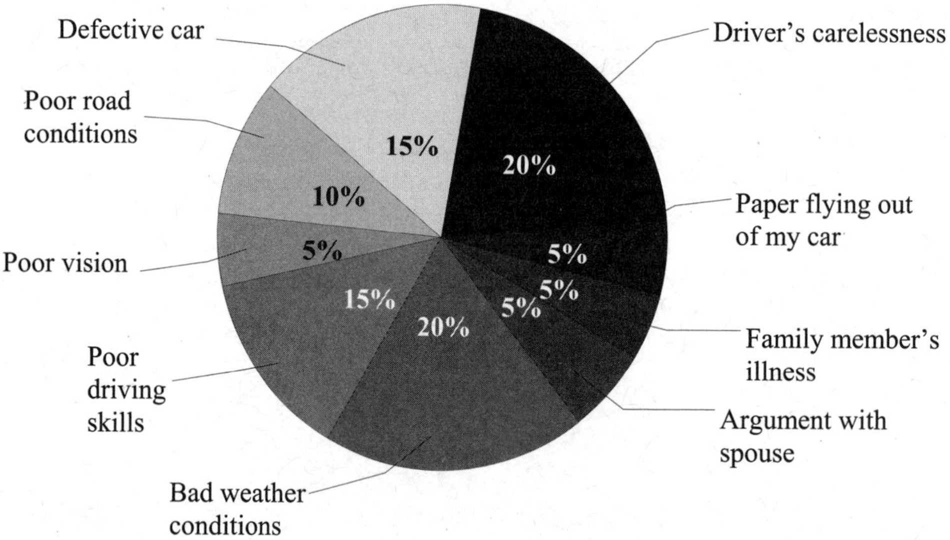

Assigning Responsibility More Realistically

Using Michael's case for guidance, do the following exercise. It will help you brainstorm other possible factors involved in a mishap or potential mishap, and then assess the probability of each and put your own potential responsibility in perspective. This is a very effective way to work on faulty assumptions about your own guilt and responsibility.

Describe in detail your obsessive concern regarding your responsibility for the safety of others and the possibility that others might be harmed. Write a specific scenario where someone could be injured as a result of your negligence:

____

____

____

With this scenario in mind, list all of the possible factors that could result in the consequences you fear. There are no right and wrong responses; just write whatever comes to mind. For each cause, estimate the percentage of its contribution to the scenario. Don't worry if the factors don't add up to exactly 100%; an approximation is fine.

Possible cause of an accident or mishap	**Probability that it contributed** (0-100%)
TOTAL	100%

Now ask yourself the following questions.

Based solely on the possible causes and probabilities you recorded above, if you knew an accident actually had happened and you didn't know anything about the specifics, what is the likely cause of the accident?

____

____

What is the evidence for your decision?

____

____

Is your decision based on your feelings about what might have happened or on the probabilities you assigned above?

____

____

Are you certain about your decision?

____

If you aren't certain, how uncomfortable are you with not knowing for sure?

____

How strongly do you rate your responsibility for the accident or mishap? (0-100%)

____

If you rated your responsibility higher than 50%, is this consistent with the evidence you recorded above, about all of the other factors that could possibly cause it to happen?

____

Based on this exercise, you may now have a clearer idea that, for any accident or mishap, many factors could be responsible, beyond your potential contribution. As you can see, accurately assigning responsibility for something going wrong is complicated. The OCD brain overly simplifies this complex calculation in a way that defies both logic and the facts. In the absence of perfect certainty, people with OCD automatically make assumptions like "It's all my fault, and I'm going to be punished for it."

Challenging the "Evidence" Against You

Many people with OCD have described their experience as feeling like being in a court of law, accused of some act of negligence that resulted in harm to others for which little, if any, real evidence exists. Despite the lack of evidence, you are nevertheless on the witness stand, being vigorously prosecuted by the "OCD attorney." Unlike our present legal system, where a person is innocent until proven guilty, in the courtroom of OCD-related thoughts and ideas you feel guilty until proven innocent. You must somehow prove with absolute certainty that you didn't do something bad, negligent, or harmful. The overbearing, cunning "OCD attorney" in your mind is hurling wild accusations, citing even the most circumstantial, remotely related evidence to cast doubt on your innocence. Each piece of "evidence" brings waves of anxiety and fear, and the more you try to defend yourself or argue with the prosecution, the guiltier you feel—and the guiltier you look to the jury. The following table provides some examples of the type of evidence the "OCD attorney" might cite.

Obsessive thought	**Evidence from "the OCD attorney"**
I must have caused a highway accident while driving because I was distracted.	• *I turned the radio volume up loud, and I was humming to the music.* • *I blinked and my glasses were dirty, so I didn't see the road perfectly.* • *My cell phone rang while I was driving, which distracted me for a second.*
I must have come into contact with HIV while in line at the grocery store. I'll make my child sick unless I wash everything.	• *The cashier had a cut on her arm and could have contaminated my groceries.* • *I had a fresh paper cut on my finger.* • *I placed the contaminated groceries in my car in the place where my child often sits.*
The image of my mother dying popped into my head while turning off the office light. She's now in danger unless I do a ritual to protect her.	• *This thought feels very dangerous.* • *This happens over and over. It must be an omen.*

Facing the "Accuser"

This exercise will help you challenge the accusations of your OCD. First you'll write down your worst fear, such as causing an accident or harm to others or yourself as a result of doing something negligent. Next, you'll record the accuser's "evidence" that the statement is true. It could be some remotely related fact, something irrelevant, or just that "it feels that way." Then you'll rate the degree to which you *truly* believe that the evidence proves that your worst fear actually happened, or that if it did, you would be responsible.

In the second part of the exercise, you'll logically challenge whether the evidence cited *really* proves your obsessive fear. The goal isn't to completely rid yourself of the guilt and discomfort of the intrusive thought, but to reduce it significantly, tolerate it better, and take the air out of OCD's claims that you are guilty or responsible for catastrophes.

The "Evidence" Against You

Obsessive thought:

____

____

____

What is the evidence to support that the feared event took place, or that if it did, you would be responsible? (The "accuser" is pointing the finger at you! Write down as many as you can think of. Most people come up with three to five.)

1. ____
2. ____
3. ____
4. ____
5. ____
6. ____
7. ____
8. ____

Based on this evidence, rate the degree to which you truly believe your worst fear could actually occur, or that if it did, you would be responsible, using a scale of 0 to 100%: ______ %

Challenging the "Evidence"

1. Is the fact that (write evidence #1) ________________________________

   really evidence of danger? Explain why not:

   ____

2. Is the fact that (write evidence #2) ________________________________

   really evidence of danger? Explain why not:

   ____

3. Is the fact that (write evidence #3) ________________________________

   really evidence of danger? Explain why not:

   ____

4. Is the fact that (write evidence #4) ________________________________

   really evidence of danger? Explain why not:

   ____

5. Is the fact that (write evidence #5) ________________________________

   really evidence of danger? Explain why not:

   ____

6. Is the fact that (write evidence #6) ________________________________

   really evidence of danger? Explain why not:

   ____

7. Is the fact that (write evidence #7) ________________________________

   really evidence of danger? Explain why not:

   ____

8. Is the fact that (write evidence #8) ________________________________

   really evidence of danger? Explain why not:

   ____

Once you've argued against each bit of "evidence," answer the following question: Using a scale of 0 to 100%, how would you now rate the probability of your fear actually occurring, or that if it did, you would be responsible? ______ %

At this point, you're probably better able to argue back against the accuser and find some relief from the negative thoughts your OCD presents as "evidence." We have one cautionary note about this approach: Beware of playing into the accuser's game by repeatedly arguing back against the OCD in a compulsive or repetitive manner. This would mean that OCD has hooked you into compulsions again. If this happens, stop immediately. You can make significant progress by merely acknowledging that your accuser's claims are false and just letting them be there without even doing anything to challenge these claims. Eventually, your accuser will get bored and the obsessive thoughts will burn out on their own as a result of your decision to not respond to them.

If you challenge OCD's accusations and find that your belief in the probability of your fear actually occurring hasn't decreased or has decreased only a little, you may be stuck because of overvalued ideas, discussed earlier in this chapter and in chapter 4. If this is the case, medication may help you get your beliefs "unstuck" so you can make progress.

Challenging Overestimation of the Likelihood of Harm

A common theme of the intrusive thoughts discussed throughout this book is an overestimation of the likelihood that some catastrophic event will occur as a result of carelessness. In essence, these thoughts often start with "What if…"; for example, "What if I get AIDS?" or "What if I didn't turn off the stove?" or "What if I ran over someone without knowing it?"

A helpful way to challenge what-if thinking is to use a modification of the downward arrow technique, described earlier, to estimate the perceived probability of the horrific event occurring versus the actual probability. Let's take the example of Michael's fear of a piece of paper flying out of his car window, causing a horrific accident and leading to his incarceration. First, Michael estimates the likelihood, from 0 percent likely to 100 percent certain probability, that such a series of events could occur. He estimates that to be 50 percent, meaning that he believes there's a 50 percent chance that a piece of paper blowing out his car window would result in a horrific accident.

To challenge this belief, Michael constructs a very detailed downward arrow sequence of exactly how he perceives this horrific event occurring:

A small piece of paper accidentally blows out of the window of my car.

↓

The paper is picked up by a gust of wind.

↓

The wind carries the paper into traffic.

↓

The paper flies in front of another car.

↓

The paper lands on the windshield of a moving car.

↓

It lands in the exact spot to block the vision of the driver.

↓

The driver is so startled that he loses control of the car.

↓

The car crashes into another vehicle.

↓

The accident causes one of the passengers, a teenager, to crash into the windshield.

↓

The teenager is killed in the crash.

↓

A forensic investigator at the scene of the accident finds a piece of paper lying at the scene.

↓

The investigator decides that the paper is suspicious.

↓

My name and address are on the paper, connecting me to the accident.

↓

The police arrest me, saying that by throwing paper out of my car, I caused the accident.

↓

I'm tried and convicted of manslaughter.

↓

The judge sentences me to five years in prison and a huge fine.

↓

I go to jail for five years, and I spend the rest of my life living with the perpetual guilt of causing harm to someone through my irresponsible act.

Next, Michael rates the probability (0-100%) of each segment of the causal chain of events. He comes up with the following estimates.

What if a piece of paper blew out of my car?	**Probability** (0-100%)
A small piece of paper accidentally blows out of the window of my car.	20%
The paper is picked up by a gust of wind.	33%
The wind carries the paper into traffic.	5%
The paper flies in front of another car.	5%

The paper lands on the windshield of a moving car.	3%
It lands in the exact spot to block the vision of the driver.	2%
The driver is so startled that he loses control of the car.	10%
The car crashes into another vehicle.	10%
The accident causes one of the passengers, a teenager, to crash into the windshield.	20%
The teenager is killed in the crash.	33%
A forensic investigator at the scene of the accident finds a piece of paper lying at the scene.	5%
The investigator decides that the paper is suspicious.	5%
My name and address are on the paper, connecting me to the accident.	5%
The police arrest me, saying that by throwing paper out of my car, I caused the accident.	3%
I'm tried and convicted of manslaughter.	3%
The judge sentences me to five years in prison and a huge fine.	5%
I go to jail for five years, and I spend the rest of my life living with the perpetual guilt of causing harm to someone through my irresponsible act.	33%

To find the probability of the entire sequence of events occurring, you multiply the probabilities of all of the separate events. For the purposes of multiplication, each percentage should be expressed as a decimal. In Michael's case, he would multiply 0.20 by 0.33 by 0.05 and so on, down the entire sequence. His final answer was an infinitesimal probability: 0.000000000000000012 percent. In fact, even if you calculate the sequence only to the point where the teenager crashes into the windshield, the probability is still an exceedingly small 0.000000002 percent. This exercise helped Michael see that the actual probability of his feared event was nowhere near the 50 percent probability he estimated before the exercise. This allowed him to acknowledge that his intrusive thoughts of causing harm and danger through negligence are greatly exaggerated ideas, not to be given any credence.

Challenging Intrusive Thoughts About Losing Control

A common theme of what-if thinking involves an obsessive preoccupation with the idea of snapping, or losing control and suddenly acting in a way that's alien to how you know yourself to be. People with this obsession often believe that normal emotions, such as fear, doubt, and anger, are dangerous and should be avoided at all costs. For example, Robert, a salesman with OCD, avoided all social situations for fear of getting angry and losing control in a public place. His downward arrow sequence goes as follows:

What if I'm in a restaurant and scream at the waiter, calling him a jerk?

↓

I would become extremely anxious.

↓

Being anxious, I could lose control of myself.

↓

If I lose control, I could go on to call the waiter lots of other names.

↓

I'll be embarrassed in front of all of the other customers.

↓

Everyone will stare at me with contempt or hatred.

↓

I'll go crazy.

↓

They'll take me away in a straitjacket.

↓

I'll be locked up in a psychiatric ward.

↓

I'll go even crazier from being locked up.

↓

I'll never escape the shame of it all.

In Robert's case, what-if thinking combined with the notion that anger is dangerous resulted in extreme isolation due to his avoidance of any public or social situation where anger or anxiety could possibly be triggered.

If you suffer from this sort of what-if thinking, one helpful strategy is to construct an imaginal exposure using the steps outlined in chapter 7. By repeatedly confronting the feared situation in your imagination, the imagery of danger becomes increasingly less potent.

Another strategy is to devise an experiment in getting angry or "losing control." For this approach, you'll need a partner to help you role-play a feared scenario:

1. Make an audio recording of a five-minute role play of a situation that typically or potentially arouses your anger (or whatever emotion you have difficulty with). It can be an ongoing situation from your life or something that typically irks you, such as when it

seems that a salesperson is purposely trying to cheat you. Taking this as an example, allow yourself to argue vigorously with the person playing the role of the salesperson. Allow the dialogue to become more and more heated, and let your language become stronger as your temper rises. You may even start yelling. Punch a pillow if you like. Really let go!

2. Now listen to the recording. If you think you can make it even more dramatic, try recording it again. Once you have the finished product, listen to it and observe your anxiety level as you listen. Does it go up to a SUDS level of at least 60 or 70? If it does, listen again and again until your SUDS level decreases by at least half.

3. If your anxiety level doesn't go up, try practicing your role play in public with a partner. You could do this in a restaurant, a park, a store—anywhere you have a strong fear you'd be embarrassed and lose control. Practice the role play for five minutes and note your SUDS level. Do the role play in different public places that evoke anxiety until you habituate to the worry and are reasonably comfortable experiencing that emotion in public.

WHAT IF YOUR BELIEFS AREN'T CHANGING?

Sometimes the process of changing unrealistic assumptions and faulty beliefs can be quite challenging. Once the powerful cycle of obsessive fears and compulsive rituals is locked into place, it's extremely difficult to change beliefs about what is harmful and dangerous and what isn't. If your beliefs seem extremely resistant to change, here are a few things you can try:

- One key to changing entrenched obsessional fears is to do the opposite of what your OCD beliefs direct you to do. If you can't change the beliefs directly, work extra hard to change what you actually *do* in the face of faulty beliefs. For example, the best way to change the faulty belief that to prevent disease you must avoid sitting on "contaminated" furniture and touching "contaminated" objects is to do the opposite: Take the chance, face your fears, and sit on the feared furniture and touch the feared objects. (This is the heart of ERP, which you learned in chapter 6.) Just do it, even though your OCD brain is sending messages of impending illness and death. If you consistently act in a manner that's opposite to what your OCD beliefs direct you to do, these entrenched beliefs will gradually change.
- Although it may seem scary, work on letting go of being in total control of whatever you worry about. A useful approach to letting go of an obsessional fear or worry is to shout to yourself, *"I'm in charge here, and I'm not going to do this anymore!"* and then walk away without doing your ritual.
- Acknowledge that although the faulty beliefs associated with your OCD may cause you pain, you may be holding on to your faulty beliefs without realizing it. The fact is, you may be reluctant to change them. This makes sense, in an OCD way. For some people with OCD, these beliefs provide a way of feeling safe and in control of a world that often seems scary and unpredictable. Ask yourself if the price you're paying for this feeling of control and safety is worth the impact it's having on your life.

- Consider taking medication for your OCD, or changing medications. The proper medication can help to lessen the grip of intrusive thoughts significantly. When the medication is effective, changing your thoughts, rituals, and beliefs will be easier.

HELP FOR FAMILY AND FRIENDS

As a family member or friend of someone with OCD, could you also be harboring some faulty beliefs about your loved one's recovery? If you're shocked that we would even ask such a question, ask yourself what you think would happen if you didn't reassure your loved one in the midst of an OCD meltdown. What do you think would happen if you didn't participate in rituals or didn't purchase certain items that your loved one demands? Could it be that your loved one is more resilient than you think? Perhaps he or she could further challenge the OCD if you were to withdraw some of your support for OCD behaviors—in an agreed-upon way.

Below, we've outlined some typical faulty beliefs of friends and family members of people with OCD, along with more realistic thoughts. Use these as a guide in challenging your own unrealistic appraisals.

Cognitive error	**Faulty belief**	**Realistic response**
Overestimating risk, harm, and danger	*If I don't reassure my husband, he'll be so uncomfortable that I won't be able to stand it.*	*I can best support my husband's recovery by not throwing him a rescue rope every time he gets anxious. It's the illness that I must stand up to, not my husband.*
	I feel so guilty if my wife is uncomfortable. If something bad happens, I'll never forgive myself.	*By not giving my wife reassurance, I'm taking a stand for her growth and recovery from OCD.*
Overcontrol and perfectionism	*My partner should let me help her more with her exposure practices.*	*It's okay if she'd rather do it herself. The overall goal is to manage OCD on her own.*
Catastrophizing	*My son will never get a decent job or stand on his own two feet.*	*I'm not a fortune teller. No one knows what the future may hold. Plus, negativity and cynicism won't further his progress.*

Cognitive error	Faulty belief	Realistic response
Black-and-white or all-or-nothing thinking	*ERP practice exercises should be done completely and perfectly, or he'll never get better.*	*No exposure practice will go perfectly. What's important is that he's trying and doing the best he can at this point in his recovery.*
	He slipped today and washed illegally. He's such a loser!	*He slipped today. I can help him figure out what might have gone wrong. Then maybe he can correct it and look forward to tomorrow.*
	She should be better by now. Why can't she just get over it?	*She's fighting the battle her of life, and OCD is a horrific foe. I want to hang in there and help her over the long haul.*
Overresponsibility	*If I don't participate in my husband's rituals, he might lose his job.*	*I'll participate in rituals only enough to keep food on the table, and I'll try to support my husband's recovery by cutting back my enabling wherever possible.*
What-if thinking	*What if this program doesn't work? How will my husband cope? How will I survive?*	*I can hang in there as this recovery process proceeds one step at a time. I'll cross those bridges when I come to them.*

CHAPTER 9

Acceptance and Mindfulness Approaches to OCD: Learning to Live Fully—Despite OCD

The reason most goals are not achieved is that we spend our time doing second things first.

—Robert J. McKain

Have you ever noticed that the more that you try to fix certain types of problems, the more things stay the same, or even get worse? This book is largely about techniques designed to help you "get rid of" your OCD, and they can and do help enormously. But sometimes, no matter how diligently people use the tools of cognitive behavioral therapy (CBT), pesky symptoms persist. Indeed, some symptoms may persist because you're unwilling to "try hard" or challenge yourself with difficult exposures even though, ultimately, they can be freeing.

However, even if you're very experienced with CBT and seemingly applying the techniques well, you can become so focused on trying hard and even harder that it has a paradoxical effect of keeping your anxiety high and keeping you stuck in obsessions. We refer to this as being obsessive about obsessing! You can be so consumed with getting rid of your symptoms that you put your life on hold and actually create another obsession. Well stop right there—get off the fixing treadmill, stop trying, and start living *in spite of* your symptoms. A new, so-called third-wave therapy is designed to help you do just that. It's called acceptance and commitment therapy, or ACT (pronounced as one word, not the individual letters), and it just may be the "next big thing" in the cognitive behavioral treatment of anxiety disorders, including OCD. From the viewpoint of ACT, you can control your compulsions, but not necessarily your obsessions and anxiety. When you can think of the goal as controlling your compulsive behaviors rather than controlling your obsessive thoughts and anxiety, you will see your OCD in a whole new way.

ACCEPTANCE AND COMMITMENT THERAPY

Acceptance and commitment therapy (ACT) was developed in the mid-1980s by Dr. Steven Hayes, a psychology professor at the University of Nevada, Reno, who has since been quietly transforming the ways that mental health professionals think about a whole range of disorders, including OCD. While the ACT approach to helping OCD is consistent with the cognitive behavioral principles underlying exposure and response prevention, it differs in several important ways. ACT doesn't focus on getting rid of painful thoughts, feelings, and experiences, and in fact, it views these as inevitable in life. Instead, it's oriented toward learning how to live more in the present, with more of a focus on your goals and values, while making room for difficult internal experiences. ACT teaches people how to engage with painful thoughts and feelings and how to become more comfortable with them through acceptance and mindfulness. Another important goal of ACT is developing self-compassion and flexibility. All of these aspects are aimed at helping people build life-enhancing patterns of behavior. ACT isn't about overcoming pain or fighting thoughts or emotions; it's about embracing life and experiencing everything it has to offer, both the positive, such as joy, and the challenges, including fear, anxiety, and worry. ACT offers a way out of suffering by helping you learn how to live the life you most desire while experiencing whatever you experience along the way. In the following pages we can only provide you with a brief glimpse of what ACT is all about. If you find this approach appealing, there are many books and other resources available to help you learn more about ACT (see the resources section for details on some of these).

ACT has evolved within a solid scientific tradition, and a thriving research community is actively engaged in examining the basic science underlying ACT and the effectiveness of applying ACT techniques to numerous life problems, including OCD, anxiety disorders, depression, and substance abuse, just to name a few. The ACT model is based on six core principles that play an important role in behavioral and psychological flexibility. In this chapter, we'll take a look at how each can be helpful in breaking free from OCD:

- Experiential acceptance (versus avoidance)
- Contact with the present moment, or mindfulness
- Cognitive defusion (versus fusion)
- Self-as-context, or the observing self
- Values
- Committed action

Experiential Avoidance vs. Experiential Acceptance

OCD symptoms are sustained by attempts to avoid internal experiences such as doubt, anxiety, and worry. But thoughts and feelings aren't the problem; from the perspective of ACT, your efforts to control or avoid them are. Avoidance of pain and discomfort works well in the material, physical world. However, avoidance of our private, inner experiences—our thoughts, feelings, impulses, sensations, and urges—doesn't work. The phrase "Whatever you resist persists" is highly relevant here (something we'll discuss in greater detail in chapter 10). Avoidance only gives those uncomfortable inner sensations and feelings more power. Also, consider the costs of your avoidance behaviors. How have you altered your life in attempts to avoid anxiety and obsessions? Our guess is these strategies have made your life smaller, not larger.

Experiential acceptance is the remedy to the quicksand of avoidance. Acceptance can be defined as the act of taking or receiving something that is offered. From an ACT perspective, it means being willing to make room for unpleasant feelings, sensations, and urges, allowing them to come and go without struggling with them, avoiding them, or paying excessive attention to them. Acceptance of uncomfortable inner experiences doesn't mean defeat or giving up. In regard to OCD, the willingness to experience previously avoided thoughts, no matter how repulsive or scary, is a prerequisite to achieving freedom from the terror of those thoughts. However, from an ACT perspective the goal of treatment isn't necessarily to rid yourself of these thoughts; it's learning to not buy into the content of the thoughts and learning to pursue valued directions in life despite their presence. Everyone experiences horrific thoughts from time to time, and the truth is, typically they gently and naturally move to the background of awareness if you don't actively avoid them and instead vigorously pursue a course of life you value.

Contact with the Present Moment

Contact with the present moment, or mindfulness, is the antidote to struggle. Mindfulness is the practice of consciously bringing awareness to your here-and-now experience, including your thoughts, with openness, interest, and receptiveness (Harris 2006). Through practice in mindfulness, you learn how to allow your thoughts and feelings to be what they are, letting them come and go without buying into them or struggling with them. From the viewpoint of ACT, the point of using mindfulness with OCD is to help you find a way to experience obsessions and anxious thoughts that's open and accepting rather than defensive and reactionary.

There are many exercises that can help you develop mindfulness, in ACT as well as in other evidence-based treatments such as dialectical behavior therapy (Linehan 1993), mindfulness-based cognitive therapy (Segal, Williams, and Teasdale 2001) and mindfulness-based stress reduction (Kabat-Zinn 1990). In addition, all of the major religious and philosophical traditions have explored techniques for achieving mindful awareness.

Mindfulness is a skill that is best practiced on a regular basis, both formally and informally. In formal mindfulness practice, called mindfulness-based meditation, you set side a period of time, say thirty minutes every day or fifteen minutes twice a day, to gradually build your mindfulness skills. Informal mindfulness practice means using your mindfulness skills in various situations you find yourself in throughout the day. Both are consistent with the ACT goal of increasing contact with the present moment.

Formal Mindfulness-Based Meditation

Shortly, we'll cover how you can practice mindfulness in regard to your OCD informally, but first, we'll give you instructions for formal mindfulness-based meditation:

1. Create a dedicated, uncluttered space in your environment to practice. (Uncluttered could be a challenge for those with hoarding OCD.) To prevent distractions, turn off your phone, TV, computer, and any music, though with practice, sounds and distractions can become part of your mindfulness practice. Use a timer with a soft ring to keep track of time.

2. Sit in an erect but comfortable position on a cushion on the floor or in a chair. Lower your eyelids slightly and direct your gaze at a spot on the ground a few feet in front of you. If you close your eyes completely, your mind may wander more easily, or you may drift off to sleep.

3. Start your timer. You may want to start with fifteen minutes and gradually increase the time. Take three very deep, slow breaths. After you exhale the third deep breath, breathe normally, without making any special attempt to control or regulate the rate or depth of your breaths. As you inhale, let your breath fall down into your belly. When your belly is full, let the breath continue to rise into your chest. When you exhale, reverse the process.

4. When you're comfortable with the rhythm of your breath, begin to count your breaths. On an inhalation, count "one." Then exhale naturally. On your next inhalation, count "two," and continue in this way until you come to "ten," counting only when you inhale. Don't worry if you lose count or repeat a number. Just pick a place to begin again.

5. After completing a cycle of ten breaths, spend a little while paying attention to any physical sensations you may feel. Notice the mechanics of your breathing, the sensation of the cushion or chair beneath you, the feel of the air against your skin. Listen for any subtle sounds that would otherwise escape you. Pay attention to even the slightest details, such as the feel of your clothing against your skin or the hum of the refrigerator.

6. After a period of awareness of physical sensations, count your breaths for another cycle of ten breaths.

7. Throughout this formal practice, you'll notice thoughts popping into your head, such as "What if I'm doing this wrong?" or "What if this doesn't work?" or "What if I can't control my thoughts?" Thoughts of past and future events naturally occur. When this happens, gently acknowledge them with a phrase such as "Thank you, mind" or "I acknowledge my thought that ______________," and then let them go and gently turn your attention back to your breathing. You can experiment with various ways to acknowledge thoughts when they arise. The key is to gently observe the thoughts without reacting to them, and then let them go. Over time, you'll discover the most useful way for you to respond when thoughts arise.

8. When your timer goes off, take three more deep, slow breaths. Then allow your eyes to open fully and return your awareness to the room. You may want to take a few moments to gently stretch or take a short walk if your legs or back became tight or fatigued from sitting.

Remember that the goal of mindfulness skills is not to reduce the presence of intrusive thoughts. Rather, it is to become more skillful at being an impartial observer of the natural ebb and flow of these thoughts as they come and go in the moment. This is a powerful tool in your arsenal for managing OCD in your life.

Informal Mindfulness Skills for OCD

Applying mindfulness skills to everyday life involves purposefully and nonjudgmentally paying attention to your moment-to-moment experience in the many realms where your daily life occurs. These skills can be applied to OCD thoughts and triggers you encounter throughout the day using the following approach:

1. Notice that you're having the experience of increasing anxiety or fear.

2. Try to take the stance of an impartial observer in relation to it. A statement such as "There's that OCD thought again" can help put some space between you and the thought.

3. Notice the habitual way that you instinctively brace to avoid the discomfort of a thought by immediately turning to a ritual, either mental or physical. Notice how the urge to do a ritual creates changes in your body, such as faster breathing, tightened muscles, tingling in your hands and feet, or numbness in your fingers. Describe what's happening in your body: "I notice feeling ______________ in my hands. I notice feeling ______________ in my feet," and so on.

4. Counter avoidance impulses by focusing on the breath. This will take you into direct contact with your moment-to-moment experience. Then enlarge your awareness to also encompass your fearful thoughts. Breathe in and out slowly, paying attention to the smooth flow of air in and out. Stay present to the moment, taking in all sensations without judgment or labels, such as "good," "bad," or "scary." Make room for all experiences.

5. Continue mindfully breathing until the compulsive urge dissipates on its own. You cannot make the urge go away; you must *allow* it to.

Effectively applying mindfulness skills to OCD triggers takes consistent daily practice. But you will be rewarded—not just by improved mindfulness skills, but by greater freedom to take action in the areas of life most important to you.

Cognitive Fusion vs. Defusion

Cognitive fusion refers to the human tendency to get caught up in our thoughts and assume that thinking has as much power as real events in our lives. But think about it: Is a thought about stabbing someone as bad as actually stabbing someone? No, of course not. One is a thought and the other is an action. In OCD, this dysfunctional tendency is raised to the umpteenth power, especially in the case of primarily obsessional OCD (the topic of chapter 10). The concept of thought-action fusion, discussed elsewhere in this book, is an extreme form of cognitive fusion experienced by people with OCD. Cognitive fusion means that you take your thoughts to be all-important, identify with them, and even fear them.

In contrast, cognitive defusion means being able to step back from one's thoughts and observe them without being caught up in their content. ACT offers numerous cognitive defusion techniques, some of them quite similar to the exposure techniques discussed in earlier chapters. The imaginal exposure exercises described in chapter 7 can be considered a cognitive defusion technique. The goal of defusion is to alter the way you experience your thoughts so that they have less impact on your behavior. Here are a few simple defusion techniques for obsessive or horrific thoughts:

- Write down a disturbing, horrific thought over and over, hundreds of times, until the thought becomes a mere jumble of words. You can also repeat the thought out loud. For example, say the scary phrase "brain cancer" to yourself fifty times. By the fiftieth time, the phrase is stripped of its frightening meaning and sounds more like just a jumble of sounds.

- Make an audio recording of a brief statement of the horrific thought and listen to it over and over until it becomes a mere jumble of sounds. (This differs from imaginal exposure; here, the goal isn't habituation, and you only need to record a very short statement of the thought.)

- Picture your obsessive thoughts appearing like pop-ups on a computer screen—as something you see externally.

- Sing the horrific thought in a happy, sing-song manner.

- Say your thoughts in other voices—for example, a Donald Duck voice.

- Say horrific thoughts over and over, extremely slowly.

- Come up with category labels for your typical obsessive thoughts, then use them in descriptions of private events; for example, "My mind is having one of those 'losing control' thoughts."

Self-as-Context or the Observing Self

Self-as-context refers to the "you" that is always there observing and experiencing, and that is distinct and separate from your thoughts, feelings, sensations, images, and memories. In ACT, this is sometimes referred to as the observing self or the transcendent self. Whatever you call it, it's the enduring, impartial self that cannot be harmed and is always present. For example, experiencing the thought "What if I lose control and stab my child with this kitchen knife?" is divided into two perspectives: the actual thought, and the self who observes the thinking of this thought. The observing self doesn't take sides in the battle for control over anxious thoughts and feelings. In ACT, no thought is dangerous or threatening to the observing self. It's just a thought.

ACT uses a variety of techniques to help people get in touch with this observing self, including metaphors. A useful metaphor for this idea of self-as-context is to think of yourself as a chessboard and your thoughts as the pieces on the chessboard (Hayes, Strosahl, and Wilson 1999), with horrific thoughts on one side and fears of acting upon them on the other. In the game, there is a constant movement of pieces. Sometimes one side is soundly beating the other, sometimes the tables are turned, and sometimes the battle is fairly even. Yet the entire time, the chessboard itself isn't affected, moved, or harmed by the drama being played out by the pieces.

You can develop the perspective of self-as-context by altering typically fused ways of describing your internal experiences. Here are some examples of how to do this with some typical OCD thoughts.

Fused description	**Self-as-context description**
I'm scared.	*I am present to the feeling called "scared."*
I'm thinking about stabbing my child. It's dangerous to think this way!	*In my mind's eye, I see images of stabbing my child that my OCD mind calls "dangerous." It's just a thought.*
What if I lose control and something terrible happens?	*My OCD mind's chatter says "What if something terrible happens?"*
I thought I just brushed against someone with blood on his hand. I'm contaminated and in great danger.	*My mind just made up an episode of ER. It's my choice to buy into it or not.*

Values

In ACT, values are the things that matter most in life. Values aren't dictated by society, family, or other outside influences; they're entirely individual. It's helpful to think of them as directions rather than goals. While goals can move you in the direction of your values, values themselves can never be achieved or possessed (Twohig 2009). Identifying and clarifying values is a unique aspect of ACT that distinguishes it from other cognitive behavioral methods, and perhaps even defines the essential aim of

ACT: helping people live a life of vitality—a life that's meaningful to the individual. In terms of OCD, values can help you redirect your time and energy away from futile and costly goals (trying to control or avoid thoughts, internal images, and sensations), and toward a life that stands for what's important to you. In values work, you're encouraged to actively and specifically define what matters most in your life and the sort of person you want to be.

It's useful to explore how OCD symptoms stand as barriers to moving in chosen life directions. In particular, it can be illuminating and helpful to ask, "What have I given up to the OCD today?" When you're in the downward spiral of OCD and your life is increasingly given over to the impossible task of appeasing or managing obsessions, you move increasingly further away from your true values, whether related to career, relationships with friends and family, or personal and spiritual development. All are put on hold by the struggle with OCD.

What Do You Care About?

Many people with OCD have difficulty defining what's most important to them. This exercise, which involves writing your own epitaph (Hayes, Strosahl, and Wilson 1999), is a powerful way to help you clarify what you care about most.

Imagine many, many years from now, after you are dead and gone, your epitaph is to be engraved on your headstone. On a piece of paper, draw a large semicircle with the open end facing down, depicting a gravestone. Inside the upper portion of the gravestone, write, "Here lies [your name]." Beneath your name, draw four horizontal lines, one beneath the other. This is where your epitaph will go. What inscription would you like to see that would capture your dreams for your life? What do you want to be remembered for? What would you like your life to stand for? Do you really want your headstone to read, "Here lies ______________, who conquered OCD"?

Clarifying Your Values

Here's another exercise that can help you figure out what's important to you. In this exercise, you'll consider various domains of life where people often hold core values, listed in the following chart. Take some time to think about each domain and what's important to you in that area, keeping in mind that values are more like overall life directions than goals.

In the middle column (Importance), rate how important each realm of life is to you on a scale of 0 to 10, where 0 is not at all important and 10 is highly important. For those that you assign a high rating, say 6 or higher, take some time to write in your journal about your values in that domain. What kind of person do you want to be, within the context of that domain? What do you want to truly stand for?

Next, in the right-hand column (Actual), rate how well your actual, current behavior aligns with your values in that area, again using a 0 to 10 scale. In this case, 0 means your values in that realm are not at all manifested in your current life, and 10 means they are completely and fully manifested in your present life. Now, you can compare the numbers in the two columns to see just how well you're doing on living in alignment with your values.

Assessing Valued Living		
Domain	**Importance**	**Actual**
Family		
Intimate relationships		
Parenting		
Friends and social life		
Work or career		
Education and training		
Recreation and fun		
Spirituality		
Citizenship and community life		
Health and physical self-care		

The more deviation between these scores, the more your life is out of alignment with what is most important to you. The point of this exercise isn't to make you feel bad; rather, it's to help you achieve a more fulfilling, satisfying life. One way you can use it to this end is to focus your exposure exercises on domains of life where you hold your most important values. Psychologists George Eifert and John Forsyth and colleagues (2009) call this value-guided action or naturalistic exposure. For example, suppose one of your strongest values lies in the domain of work or career: the desire to make a difference in the lives of children through a teaching career. If you've been buying into the belief that your intrusive OCD thoughts of harming children means you shouldn't have a career involving children, that might seem to make your dream impossible. In this case, you'd focus your exposure and response prevention work on the obsessions that stand in the way of this dream.

Committed Action

If values are like compass bearings, pointing your life in chosen directions, then goals are the road map that gets you where you want to be. Traditional CBT and most other forms of psychotherapy subscribe to the belief that once symptoms are managed effectively, the person's quality of life will improve. ACT differs in placing an emphasis on building improvements in the person's quality of life by working toward goals: committed actions in the service of the person's values. Symptom reduction per se isn't the goal, but it is often a natural side effect of sustained, committed actions toward one's core values.

Having identified your most valued life domains in the previous section, you can now set concrete, short-term goals that will move in you valued directions in each of those domains. As you set your goals, keep the following questions in mind (Eifert and Forsyth 2007):

- Is the goal concrete, practical, and realistic?
- Is it attainable—something you can do and something you actually have control over?
- Does it work with your current life situation?
- Does the goal lead you in a direction that you value?

For example, let's say that some of your most important values are in the domains of parenting. Your value—the direction you want to orient toward—is being a better father to your twelve-year-old son. But your fear of losing control in public has resulted in a pattern of avoiding your son's Little League games. Keeping your value in mind, you can set an achievable, short-term goal of attending your son's games for a brief period of time, say fifteen minutes. During that time, you can work on acceptance and mindfulness and practice a cognitive defusion exercise, such as picturing your fearful thoughts as pop-ups on a computer screen. As your tolerance increases, up your attendance time to, say, thirty minutes, and then longer.

SUMMING UP ACT FOR OCD

In ACT, progress toward treatment goals isn't measured by the degree of symptom reduction you achieve. Rather, your progress is measured by the degree to which you're living your life in alignment with your values, despite the presence of difficult thoughts.

ACT is being evaluated for its effectiveness as a treatment for OCD and other anxiety disorders (Twohig, Hayes, and Masuda 2006; Twohig et al. 2010), and the results are promising. At present, exposure and response prevention is still recommended as the first-line treatment approach for OCD. The self-directed program for OCD presented in chapters 5 through 7 should be your primary strategy. After doing ERP for about six weeks, you may want to utilize some of the ideas in this chapter to supplement your self-directed program. People with particularly strong avoidance tendencies may find ACT to be especially useful.

HELP FOR FAMILY AND FRIENDS

The variety of treatment approaches for OCD can be quite confusing to family and friends. You may wonder what the "right" treatment approach is for your loved one: ACT? ERP? Both? Something else? At this point, we recommend that you view newer evidence-based therapies, such as ACT, with interest and curiosity. If you like the principles of ACT and want to help your loved one find a therapist who specializes in this approach, consult the website of the Association for Contextual Behavioral Science (contextualpsychology.org).

Whether your loved one's therapist uses ACT, CBT, or both, it remains of utmost importance that he or she have ample experience using these techniques with OCD, and that the therapist has worked with many people with OCD. This is the only way to ensure that your loved one is getting the best help available. If an OCD specialist isn't available in your community, you face an additional challenge. More information to assist you is available in chapter 19.

PART 3

Using the Self-Directed Program for Specific Forms of OCD

CHAPTER 10

Primarily Obsessional OCD: Breaking Free from Horrific Thoughts

To want to forget something is to think of it.

—French proverb

The most typical forms of OCD involve obsessive thoughts, feelings, or urges combined with compulsive rituals such as hand washing or checking. However, there is a form of OCD that mainly involves thoughts—intrusive, horrific thoughts and images of causing danger or harm to others or oneself. The thoughts are experienced as originating from one's own mind (rather than as originating from outside one's mind, which is characteristic of psychotic disorders such as schizophrenia), and cause great fear, distress, panic, and, most of all, shame. Perhaps more than with any other form of OCD, people suffering with horrific thoughts feel especially alone and ashamed. As a result, they tend to keep their thoughts secret from anyone and everyone, even those closest to them.

We call this type of OCD *primarily obsessional OCD*. In the past it was called pure obsessional OCD, or "pure o," as behavioral scientists believed that people suffering from this form of OCD didn't perform compulsions or rituals. However, studies of primarily obsessional OCD have revealed that while some people don't perform overt compulsions, many have subtle mental rituals that serve to counteract and neutralize the discomfort of their unwanted, intrusive thoughts (Steketee 1993; Freeston and Ladouceur 1997). For the purposes of this book, we'll consider primarily obsessional OCD to be OCD with horrific thoughts alone, as well as OCD with horrific thoughts and accompanying mental rituals. Let's look at a few examples of primarily obsessional OCD.

Paula, age twenty-five, was playing with her beloved cats while smoking a cigarette. Out of the blue, the thought popped into her mind of burning a cat with the cigarette. The thought horrified her, prompting intense feelings of guilt. She wondered over and over, "How can I think such thoughts? Maybe I don't really love my cats. I must be a horrible person to think of doing that!" From then on, caring for her cats was nerve-wracking because she felt that they were in danger just because of being near her. She avoided touching her animals except when absolutely necessary.

Perhaps you recall Angelita, from chapter 1, who was slicing tomatoes when suddenly a horrific thought popped into her head: "What if I lost control of myself and plunged this knife into my child's neck?" Horrified by the thought, she whisked her two-year-old daughter out of the kitchen. Over the course of several days she placed gates at the entrances to the kitchen to prevent her daughter from coming into the kitchen while she was using knives, and eventually she removed all the knives from her home.

Anthony, a twenty-six-year heterosexual sales associate, had intrusive thoughts of losing control and groping the genitals of good-looking men who stood near him at work. He spent up to two hours each day conjuring up images of having sex with other men in order to reassure himself that he was sufficiently disgusted by the images. Only once he was satisfied about his response could he resume his activities. If he didn't achieve the "right" feeling, he had to keep on imagining the images over and over until he felt sufficiently disgusted. His compulsions started to interfere with his productivity at work, and his job was in jeopardy.

Mario, a forty-eight-year-old teacher who was devoutly religious, had disturbing, intrusive thoughts involving images of Jesus and the Virgin Mary. Often his thoughts involved sexual encounters with them. The images were embarrassing and humiliating. He felt extremely guilty, especially since they tended to increase when he was in church. His thoughts made him feel unworthy, so he quit going to church.

Joshua, a thirty-three-year-old physician, had been married a year when his wife gave birth to their first child. One night while watching his baby girl sleeping peacefully, the intrusive image of touching the child's genitals popped into his mind. Feeling guilty, embarrassed, and ashamed, he started avoiding any physical contact with the child. He didn't dare explain the reason to his wife, and she began to wonder why he refused to change the baby's diapers or even hold her.

These are but a few of the myriad types of horrific thoughts. Here are some other examples:

- What if I assault my teacher with a sharp pencil?
- What if I poke my friend in the eye with a pick?
- What if I lose control and shout a racial epithet?
- What if I lose control and harm myself?
- What if I dump scalding water on my baby?

- What if I think a bad thought about God?
- What if I lose control of myself and go crazy?
- What if I drive my car into oncoming traffic?

THE NATURE OF HORRIFIC THOUGHTS IN PRIMARILY OBSESSIONAL OCD

While horrific thoughts can be extremely disturbing, they aren't actually dangerous. Decades of experience of dozens of clinicians treating thousands of patients with primarily obsessional OCD clearly confirm this. The thoughts all have the same theme: that you will somehow lose control of yourself, your faculties, and your normal, intact sense of judgment about what's right and wrong and act on the horrific thought in a manner that's entirely uncharacteristic of your everyday actions and behavior. Let's take a closer look at what this form of OCD is about.

People with primarily obsessional OCD are extremely unlikely to carry out the horrific acts and urges that pop into their heads. Dr. Hyman, who has worked with over 1,000 patients with primarily obsessional OCD over the last two decades, has been struck by the remarkable consistency of these individuals. Regardless of whether the thought involves violent or sexual images, people with primarily obsessional OCD are not in danger of acting out these unwanted horrific thoughts. People who *do* act on such thoughts—criminals and sexual predators—have what is known as antisocial personality disorder. They lack a conscience and, unlike people with OCD, tend not to worry about their horrific thoughts or the possibility that they might act upon them. On the other hand, people with primarily obsessional OCD almost always tend to display an excess of concern about doing things "right" and according to the rules. Likewise, they tend to rigorously avoid doing things "wrong" and apply overly rigid, unforgiving standards to everything they think, do, and say. Clearly, people with primarily obsessional OCD have a problem with doubt, worry, and fear of their own thoughts, rather than a likelihood of doing bad things or potentially committing crimes.

People with primarily obsessional OCD are not in danger of "snapping." It is common for people with this type of OCD to convince themselves that the presence of persistent unwanted thoughts is evidence that they could or even are likely to suddenly lose all self-control and commit horrific, harmful acts. Despite the incredible degree of discomfort, fear, and frustration these thoughts bring about, no evidence of OCD patients "snapping" exists.

Compulsions make it worse. To control the anxiety and discomfort produced by horrific thoughts, people with primarily obsessional OCD often carry out subtle, covert compulsions that aren't obvious to others. Examples are silently repeating a prayer over and over or compulsively replacing the horrific image with a neutral or positive one in an attempt to neutralize the anxiety associated with the thought. This strategy does two things: It relieves them of the intense guilt associated with having the thoughts in the first place, and it provides a momentary sense of control and reassurance that they won't act out in the manner depicted by the thought. The problem is that the struggle to contain and control these thoughts only intensifies the stranglehold of the very thoughts the person is trying to get rid of.

The thoughts are not the problem; the response to them is. Dr. Hyman's clinical experience with people with primarily obsessional OCD has repeatedly demonstrated that the disturbing ideas depicted in the thoughts are actually in opposition to the person's true character, desires, and intentions. In fact, it appears that these ideas persist *because they are so divergent from* the true desires, intentions, and nature of the person suffering from them. In most cases, attempts to unearth hidden meanings, unconscious motivation, or some root cause of the thoughts are futile and only make the condition worse. The bottom line is that the problem is not the thoughts themselves, as these distressing "hiccups of the mind" appear to be universal. Rather, the problem is the person with OCD's faulty response to these thoughts: a pattern of overcontrol strategies that reinforce a vicious cycle of worry, fear, and dread.

People with horrific thoughts are reacting abnormally to basically normal thought processes. Research studies indicate that, at times, even people without OCD experience unwanted, unpleasant, and even horrific intrusive thoughts (Wilhelm and Steketee 2006; Rachman and de Silva 1978). The difference is that people without OCD can readily dismiss these uncomfortable, distressing thoughts and move on, whereas for people with primarily obsessional OCD, the thoughts get stuck and repeat over and over again. The reasons for this aren't clear, but it seems to be related to the same overactive brain circuits and neurochemical dysfunctions common to all forms of OCD. In OCD, the difficulty arises not so much from the thoughts themselves, but from attempts to alleviate the guilt and discomfort fueled by the thoughts. The resulting efforts to avoid, suppress, or escape these thoughts unwittingly serve to amplify and strengthen them, making them worse and worse. (We'll explain why this is the case later in this chapter.) The person becomes locked into an endless loop of fear, dread, and shame.

Perhaps you'll find it helpful to read some examples of the types of horrific thoughts commonly reported by people who don't have OCD. Here's a small sampling (Wilhelm and Steketee 2006; Rachman and de Silva 1978):

- Thoughts of deliberately crashing the car or driving into oncoming traffic
- Thoughts of stepping in front of oncoming traffic
- Thoughts of poking oneself or someone else in the eye with something sharp
- Images of the death or murder of a loved one
- Wishing someone would be harmed or die
- Impulses or images of attacking, hurting, or killing a loved one
- Thoughts of dropping, kicking, or harming a baby
- Thoughts about running over an animal

THE ANATOMY OF HORRIFIC THOUGHTS

Primarily obsessional OCD begins with an intrusive, distressing thought that the person appraises in a particularly negative way. In the person's mind, the thought is experienced as having the same reality or importance as an action. As a result, the person attempts to avoid or suppress the thought. This leads to various overcontrol strategies to reduce anxiety, including mental rituals. While these strategies may reduce discomfort, the effect is only temporary, and then the cycle begins again. The following figure depicts the overall process, which we'll explain in detail in the following sections.

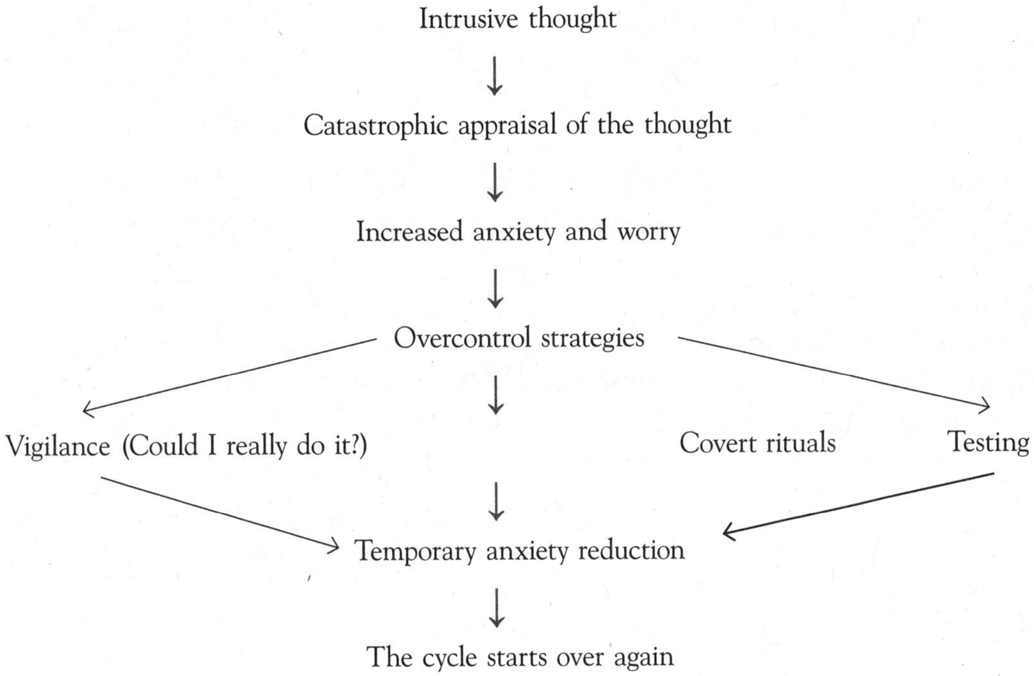

Intrusive Thought → Catastrophic Appraisal

The first step in primarily obsessional OCD is that an intrusive thought, image, or urge pops into the person's mind. These disturbing, embarrassing, or even horrifying thoughts are often of a sexual or aggressive nature and cause guilt and shame. Because doubt is a core feature of OCD, these thoughts can cause your OCD brain to doubt aspects of yourself that lie at the core of what kind of person you believe yourself to be. For example, if you are a responsible parent, it's likely that your OCD may result in the intrusive thought "What if I harm my children?"

The thought may include a strong mental image or an urge to do something embarrassing or humiliating. If you're an especially religious or moral person, your intrusive OCD thoughts may involve blasphemous religious themes with strong sexual or aggressive content. If you tend to be nonviolent, the theme of your obsessive thoughts is likely to be aggressive and hostile. If you pride yourself on being an extremely responsible person, intrusive thoughts and urges are likely to involve committing irresponsible acts, such as setting a house on fire or pushing an innocent pedestrian into oncoming traffic. If you have a strong heterosexual gender identity, OCD may fill your mind with images of homosexual activity. The point is, the intrusive thought always depicts you in your mind as acting in a manner that is the complete *opposite* of how you and others know you to be.

The content of the thoughts often reflects the normal anxieties everyone experiences as they move through life. OCD seems to prey on the self-doubts and fears that people typically have as they move through the phases of the human life cycle. For example, preteens who are becoming more aware of their autonomy and independence are likely to have unwanted, intrusive thoughts regarding doing violent or immoral acts to their parents. Young adults seeking to settle down with a mate may have intrusive thoughts regarding their gender identity. A newlywed overwhelmed at the prospect and responsibilities of parenthood may have intrusive thoughts of harming children.

Catastrophic Appraisal → Increased Anxiety and Worry

As mentioned in chapter 8, many people with OCD suffer from thought-action fusion, a cognitive error in which thoughts are experienced as if they were the same as actions. Likewise, many people with primarily obsessional OCD experience their intrusive thoughts as evidence of the likelihood that they are capable of or will perform the horrific acts that pop into their mind. The OCD logic goes something like this:

I'm having a bad thought. That must mean I'm bad.

↓

I wouldn't be having these thoughts if I wasn't truly bad.

↓

The more bad thoughts I have, the more proof I have that I'm bad.

↓

Because I'm thinking so much about doing bad things,
it must mean that I'm highly likely to do something bad.

↓

If I don't try hard to prevent harm from happening, it's as bad as doing something bad on purpose.

↓

Since it's likely that I'm going to do something bad, I'd better carefully watch out for it.

↓

I must make absolutely certain that others are protected from my bad actions.

Increased Anxiety and Worry → Overcontrol Strategies

Having labeled their thoughts as potentially dangerous, people with primarily obsessional OCD attempt to avoid, suppress, or neutralize their anxiety about their thoughts using a variety of control strategies, including vigilance, covert rituals, and testing. But as mentioned above, these strategies offer only temporary relief at best. When horrific thoughts arise again, as they inevitably will, the cycle starts over and intensifies.

VIGILANCE

After experiencing a number of intrusive thoughts, the mind is constantly on guard. Like a sentry in a watchtower or a cop on the beat, the mind becomes nervously preoccupied with catching "bad" thoughts. Unfortunately, this has the effect of heightening the importance of the occurrence or non-occurrence of the thoughts. With the mind increasingly focused on the next occurrence of the thoughts, more and more energy is tied up in trying to prevent and control them. Attempts to suppress or control the thoughts become more and more elaborate and time-consuming.

The effect of thought suppression is not unlike what would happen if you were to be warned. "Do not, under any circumstances, think about pink elephants!" Try it: Don't think about pink elephants for five minutes and see what happens.

How many times did the thought of pink elephants pop into your head? As you can see, attempts to suppress thoughts only increase their occurrence (Steketee 1993; Wegner 1989). This is because our thoughts are a bundle of associated ideas, concepts, and images that are related automatically one to another. If you doubt this, read the following sentence: "Mary had a little ______________." Even if you try as hard as you can, you'll have a very difficult time *not* thinking "lamb."

Likewise, the idea "I must never, ever think of ______________, and if I do, I'm a horrible, dangerous, and despicable person" inevitably brings up the very thoughts you're trying so hard to suppress. The harder you try to avoid or suppress these thoughts, the more your mind will generate the thoughts. You sink deeper into a vicious cycle. Overcontrol of thoughts simply doesn't work.

COVERT RITUALS

Another control strategy for "undoing" or neutralizing horrific thoughts is covert, or hidden, rituals, such as silent praying ("Forgive me God for having that thought"); "undoing" rhymes or phrases ("I really don't want to do that"); silent, repetitive counting using "good" numbers; and balancing the horrific thought with an opposite "correct" thought or image. Here are some examples of the latter: upon having the horrific thought of your mother dying of cancer, compulsively picturing your mother with a happy smile on her face; or upon having a horrific thought about touching your child's genitals, compulsively picturing yourself lovingly hugging your child.

Despite the designation "primarily obsessional OCD," sometimes overcontrol strategies involve overt behaviors. At times, people with primarily obsessional OCD engage in hand washing or showering in response to the thoughts. They may consider objects physically touched at the very moment when an intrusive thought occurs to be contaminated and therefore to be avoided or immediately cleaned. In this way, they "undo" or neutralize the discomfort of the thought's association with that object. Repeated actions, such as walking back and forth through door thresholds or turning light switches on and off, may be triggered by an intrusive thought that must be neutralized before moving on.

CERTAINTY SEEKING AND TESTING

One of the hallmarks of OCD is intolerance of uncertainty. The persistent search for 100 percent certainty that harm or danger will be avoided often results in dysfunctional testing strategies to reassure the person with OCD that he or she won't act upon the horrific thoughts. Testing behaviors are persistent, repetitive, and sometimes odd. For example, Paula, the woman with the intrusive thought of harming her beloved cats, "tests" herself by holding a lit cigarette near a cat's body for several minutes to reassure herself that she won't lose control and harm the animal. Only when she feels reassured that she wouldn't harm the cat can she put the cigarette down. However, soon the doubts return and the testing behavior is repeated again and again, day after day.

In Anthony's case, his obsessions compel him to purposefully look at pictures of naked men to test whether he's sufficiently disgusted by such pictures. He also compulsively attempts to reassure himself that he isn't gay by picturing images of naked women in his mind and then anxiously noticing whether he feels aroused.

Other examples of certainty seeking by people with primarily obsessional OCD include persistent requests for reassurance from others that the person isn't gay, isn't a child sexual predator, or isn't a psychopathic killer. With the advent of the Internet, people with horrific thoughts may spend untold hours engaged in online research about the nature of being gay or the characteristics of child predators or people with antisocial personality disorder. Although these certainty-seeking behaviors are intended to eliminate doubts, they only serve to increase anxiety, doubt, and fear.

BREAKING FREE FROM HORRIFIC THOUGHTS

You can break free from horrific thoughts. Given the problems with overcontrol strategies, acceptance, rather than control and avoidance, is the key. By "acceptance," we don't mean giving up or resigning yourself to a life of having thoughts you don't want. The solution is to break the cycle of unworkable mental habits and beliefs that keep the thoughts stuck. And what is the reward for this challenging but achievable change? Instead of spending hours each day engaged with your thoughts, you spend a minute or less. A woman recovering from primarily obsessional OCD put it well: "When I let the thoughts be, they let me be." In this chapter, we offer a four-step process to help you do just that. Some of the strategies involved are similar to approaches you learned in part 2 of the book, including using exposure exercises to habituate yourself to these thoughts. Here's an outline of the four steps, which are described in detail below:

1. Write your horrific thoughts down.
2. Try on the belief, despite your doubts, that the thoughts mean nothing about you, your character, or your inherent nature.

3. Accept the presence of intrusive thoughts and resist the urge to control, judge, alter, or modify them in any way. Let go of all avoidance or neutralization strategies.

4. Confront your horrific thoughts directly and do exposure exercises to reduce your anxiety over the thoughts and effectively manage them when they occur.

Step 1. Write It Down

Writing down your horrific thoughts will probably be embarrassing, even nerve-wracking at first, but it's an important first step, so do it! The following exercise will help you examine these thoughts so you can understand how they're triggered and how you're currently responding to them.

List your intrusive thoughts on the Intrusive Thoughts Worksheet that follows. (You may also use your journal to do the exercises in this chapter.) In the second column, assign a SUDS rating (0 to 100) to each thought to indicate how distressing it is. Recall that 100 equals maximum distress, and 0 equals no distress at all. In the third column, note what typically happens just before the thought occurs. This is called a *triggering event*. Examples of triggering events could be holding a child in your arms, noticing a good-looking man at the gym, getting mad at your brother, or entering a church. However, intrusive thoughts sometimes arise without a triggering event. If you aren't sure what to write in this column, you can leave it blank. You might be able to fill it in later, after having another experience of this thought.

Next, think about any neutralizing strategies you may be using to lessen your anxiety about your thoughts, such as testing strategies, covert rituals, or even overt rituals.

Intrusive Thoughts Worksheet

Intrusive thought	SUDS level (0-100)	Triggering event	Neutralizing strategy

Step 2. Try On the Belief That the Thoughts Mean Nothing About You

The combination of doubt, thought-action fusion, and overcontrol strategies in regard to horrific thoughts results in the tendency to wonder, "What if those thoughts represent who I truly am? What if I'm evil at my core, but cover it up well?" The worries and doubt from these thoughts can be overwhelming. Breaking free from this mental hell requires an important shift in thinking: a shift from trying to figure out what the thoughts mean to accepting the thoughts, based on overwhelming evidence from thousands of people with primarily obsessional OCD that the problem isn't you, but your OCD. Rather than thinking that you must be inhabited by some "evil seed," try on the more accurate view that these thoughts are more akin to a neurological "thought tic" or "mental hiccup." And this glitch is maintained by your unworkable responses to these thoughts. When you adopt a more objective and accurate way of seeing these thoughts, they won't seem less disturbing, but you will be able to view them as "just bad thoughts," nothing more and nothing less.

Step 3. Accept the Presence of Intrusive Thoughts

Accepting the presence of these thoughts requires that you allow the thoughts to be there without judgment, opinion, or evaluation. As human beings we feel compelled to create meaning out of our experience, to make judgments. You probably have a long history of judging your intrusive thoughts, so changing this will take attention and effort.

One helpful strategy is to view your thoughts as if you were standing in a train station and watching the thoughts go by like cars of a very long train. The presence of the train or any particular car just is. It is neither good nor bad that it's there. Try to avoid judgments about the thoughts. Simply watch them come and go. Another way to view the thoughts is to imagine yourself at the seashore, standing in water up to your waist. The waves are huge and quite scary as they crash up against the shoreline. When you see a wave coming, you may get scared, but you choose to stay put. So far, so good. You've made a choice not to avoid the thought. But what you do next matters. If you stiffen your body, dig your feet into the sand, and resist the wave, it will smack you and tumble you around in the water. But if you relax your body, float, and go with the wave, it will lift you up and then gently place you back on your feet as it passes by. By taking a more tolerant attitude toward these thoughts, accepting them and allowing them to be there despite the discomfort, you encourage the process of habituation to occur. With time, you'll develop the ability to be a more objective observer of your thoughts, without getting caught up in them.

Step 4. Confront Horrific Thoughts and Do Exposure to Reduce Anxiety

Fear and dread often accompany horrific thoughts. All the classic physiological responses to fear may occur, including a racing heart, sweaty palms, and dry mouth. The process of desensitizing your brain to these thoughts is much like the exposure exercises you learned in part 2 of the book: You deliberately expose yourself to your most dreaded thoughts and horrific ideas until your brain has a chance to habituate. Eventually, this enables you to have the thought without the accompanying fear.

To demonstrate how this works, say your name or the name of someone you have a strong feeling about, attachment to, or reaction to—your child, spouse, parent, or boss, for example. Pay close attention to your emotional reaction to this name. Then repeat the name over and over again, at least fifty times. Observe how your reaction to the name changes. Notice how it no longer has the same emotional impact. It probably sounds like a mere garble of syllables with no particular meaning. This is the process of habituation at work. Because of the constant repetition, your nervous system became "bored" with the name and no longer attaches the same meaning to it. In the same way, when you intentionally repeat a feared, horrific thought over and over again, it loses its power and impact over you.

You may think, "But those are horrible, disgusting thoughts! How could anyone other than an evil, crazy person want to get comfortable with them?" That's an understandable concern. But the point here isn't to get comfortable with horrific thoughts or numb to terrible, even despicable, ideas. The goal is to be able to experience a horrible thought, disgust and all, and to see it for what it is: just a bad thought—nothing more and nothing less. Now let's look at several effective thought exposure exercises.

Written Exposure

Writing your horrific thoughts down on paper, over and over, is a good first step in the process of exposure to horrific thoughts. This will probably feel embarrassing, even nerve-wracking at first, but it's an important start. Notice that as you begin to transfer these thoughts from your head to paper, your feelings of fear and discomfort will increase. This is normal and expected, as what you are now doing feels like letting the cat out of the bag. Acknowledge that those feelings are there, but don't let them get in the way of moving forward with the process. There is a healthy and natural catharsis that goes along with these first difficult steps:

1. Get a pad of lined paper and draw a vertical line down the page so that you have two columns—a wide left column and a very narrow right column. Turn back to the Intrusive Thoughts Worksheet, earlier in this chapter, and choose a thought that causes moderate distress (a SUDS level of 40 to 60). Write this thought in the left column, and then note your SUDS level in the right column.

2. Resist avoiding, distracting, or ritualizing in an attempt to neutralize the anxiety of the thought.

3. On the next line in the left column, write that same thought again, and then write it ten more times. Than, once again rate your SUDS level in the right column.

4. Keep repeating this process, rating your SUDS level every tenth time until your SUDS level diminishes to about half of what it was when you began. You may have to write the thought fifty times or more before this happens.

5. Now choose another horrific thought from the Intrusive Thoughts Worksheet—one that causes even more discomfort, say a SUDS level of 50 to 70. Repeat steps 1 through 4 with this thought. Continue in this way, writing increasingly distressing thoughts from your list for approximately one hour daily until you can tolerate writing your horrific thoughts with minimal distress (a SUDS level of 20 or less).

Intensive Audio Exposure for Extra Sticky Thoughts

Once you feel more comfortable writing down your horrific thoughts, you can make further progress by listening to them over and over, especially any that still cause a fair amount of distress. The goal is to learn to tolerate greater levels of discomfort while holding the thoughts in your mind.

1. Choose two or three horrific thoughts that are still quite distressing. They'll probably start with "What if I…?" For this exercise, write the thought down in the first person present tense to make the exposure more vivid and powerful. Here are some examples of typical horrific thoughts phrased in this way:
   - I'm about to lose control, go crazy, and stab my mother with a knife!
   - I'm a child molester… I delight in touching them in their privates.
   - I'm extremely aroused by gay men (or women).
   - I'm losing control and will burn my cat with a cigarette!
   - I want to pour scalding water on my baby.
   - I'm about to light a match and set this house on fire!
   - I'm losing control and going crazy right now!
   - I'm a murderer and I'm about to drive my car into oncoming traffic!
2. Make an audio recording of the horrific thoughts you've written down, saying each one slowly about twenty times in a row, with a two-second pause after each repetition. Try to add a bit of drama and expressiveness to your voice as you say these phrases. Continue recording repetitions of this thought until your anxiety level has reduced significantly (by at least half).
3. Rewind the tape and listen to all of the repetitions of the thought, and then write down your SUDS level. Be aware that, especially initially, you may try to avoid the discomfort by numbing out or distracting yourself from listening. Resist this tendency.
4. Keep listening to the repeated thought for around thirty minutes to an hour per day, or until your SUDS level goes down to 20 to 30.
5. Repeat steps 1 through 4 until you have done exposure to all of your horrific thoughts.

Total Immersion Audio Exposure

This exercise is a highly effective way to rapidly reduce the intensity and discomfort associated with horrific thoughts. Although it's much the same as the previous exercise, it's more intensive. If you have the time to devote to it (three or more hours per day), it will yield more rapid results. Though many people with horrific thoughts can successfully do this intensive exposure on their own, if it makes you highly uncomfortable, you may wish to do this with the support and coaching of a qualified therapist.

As in the previous exercise, make an audio recording of your horrific thoughts, repeated over and over again, but this time, after repeating the first thought about twenty times, go ahead and record several more thoughts, each repeated about twenty times. Ideally you'd use an endless loop tape or make a digital recording that can be repeated continuously. In this exercise, the goal is to listen to the thoughts for a minimum of *three hours per day*, for a week to ten days.

Play the recording on a portable music player or voice recorder and use a pair of light headphones or earbuds so that you can listen privately as you go about your daily routine, while doing such things as yard work, household activities, watching TV, shopping, or exercising. The only times you may not wish to listen are at school or work, or during other activities that require close attention, like driving or caring for children. While it isn't necessary to give the recorded material your undivided attention (it would be impossible to do so), pay attention to the recorded thoughts as often as you can.

If, while listening, you encounter a situation in which you'd habitually do a ritual (for example, walking through a threshold, turning on a light switch, or flushing the toilet), practice strict response prevention by moving through the situation, horrific thought and all. Doing this day after day will help you achieve a solid level of habituation in those situations.

Combining Situational Exposure with Exposure to Horrific Thoughts

This exposure exercise is very useful for people who overestimate the likelihood that they will do harm to others. It will be highly effective at helping you see that thoughts alone don't have the power to cause harm. Because this exposure can be highly stressful, it's advisable to do it with the support of someone understanding, either a family member or partner, or, better yet, a qualified mental health professional with expertise in the treatment of OCD. A portable audio device with headphones is most useful for this exercise.

1. As in the previous two exercises, make an audio recording of a horrific thought, repeated over and over again. For this exercise, record just one horrific thought—one that involves fear of doing harm to someone specific.

2. Put the headphones on and listen to the recording while looking at photographs of the person whom you fear you might harm or endanger, such as your spouse, child, or parent. Listen to the recording over and over until your SUDS level goes down by at least half. Repeat on subsequent days until your SUDS level is 20 or less for three consecutive days.

3. Listen to the recording (using headphones) in the presence of this person. If it's a child, sit with the child on your lap. Allow your anxiety to rise, and resist avoiding, suppressing, or ritualizing. Stay in the situation for at least forty-five minutes and up to ninety minutes. Your goal is to reduce your

SUDS level to 20 or less through habituation to the frightening thought. Use the Daily Exposure Practice Monitoring Form from chapter 6 to monitor your progress.

4. While listening, you'll probably encounter situations that trigger the urge to do a ritual. Again, practice strict response prevention: Move through the situation, horrific thought and all, noticing your discomfort rise and then eventually fall as you resist your compulsive urge. Practicing these exposures along with response prevention day after day will help you achieve a solid level of habituation in those situations.

Troubleshooting Exposure to Thoughts

There are some typical problems people run up against in exercises designed to help habituate to intrusive horrific thoughts. The first is a fear that if the exercise helps and you no longer have a strong, overwhelming emotional response to the thought, this means that you're indifferent to the horrific content and thus "proves" (by OCD logic) that you may be a murderer, child molester, sexual pervert, or whatever. Don't allow this fear to stop you from doing the exposure exercises. No amount of exposure will brainwash you or make you indifferent to scary, horrific ideas about harm to those you care about. The goal isn't to numb you out to painful thoughts, but to help convince you that you can have these thoughts without fear that you'll act upon them.

Another common fear is rooted in the belief that the absence of anxiety means you're likely to act upon the thoughts. In essence, the anxiety surrounding the horrific thought is perceived as a sort of insurance that you won't act upon it. Again, such thinking is unfounded. In over twenty years of clinical experience, Dr. Hyman has never seen anyone with OCD act on horrific thoughts after becoming habituated to a thought from doing exposure. We always have the choice to act upon our thoughts or not. OCD doesn't alter a person's essential character, judgment, or moral standards.

Some people with OCD report that their anxiety doesn't go up while doing exposure. If this happens to you, it's probably because you're relying on a safety signal in your environment to "protect" you. An example would be the presence of a spouse or partner whom you believe will protect you from acting upon the thoughts. If this is the case, you must do the exposure in gradual steps, with those you rely upon for safety being increasingly unavailable to you for reassurance. Revise your anxiety/exposure hierarchy to include items in which your safety signal is present. For example, "Leaving the house without checking *with* my spouse present" would have a lower SUDS level than "Leaving the house without checking *without* my spouse present." Once you've mastered the exposure in the presence of your safety signal, move on to doing that exposure without the safety signal.

Another reason your anxiety may not go up is because you've already taken precautions to prevent yourself from acting on your horrific thoughts, as Angelita did when she removed all of the sharp knives from her home. In this case, it is vital that you gradually undo whatever "safety" measures you've taken so that exposure to the thought of actually losing control will activate your anxiety. Only then can exposure achieve the desired effect. Remember that habituation to horrific thoughts only occurs when the exposure sufficiently activates your anxiety.

Tools for Managing Thoughts on the Fly

Some people find that they're only anxious if the thoughts are generated spontaneously, on the fly, rather than through a structured exposure exercise. Here are some tools for managing intrusive thoughts on the fly. No single strategy works for everybody, so you'll need to experiment a bit in order to find what works best for you.

Magnification. At the moment the intrusive thought occurs, vividly picture the image of what that would look like if taken to the most extreme degree possible. For example, if your intrusive thoughts involve an aggressive theme, vividly picture the terrifying image of yourself snatching a knife from the counter and charging someone you care about, and hold that image in your mind. If your intrusive thought has to do with potentially sexually assaulting a child, picture yourself becoming inflamed with lust and losing control. Hold that image in your mind for as long as it takes for the thought to lose its potency. This technique may seem scary at first, but the absurd excess of robustly embracing your worst nightmare will actually reduce the force and intensity of the thought.

Watching and waiting. Sometimes doing absolutely nothing in response to a horrific thought can be the most powerful tool you can use to deal with it. Doing nothing deprives your OCD of its tendency to latch onto any behavior that reduces the anxiety and thus create yet another compulsion. Simultaneously, this tactic helps foster an attitude of acceptance in the presence of the thought. Merely watching the thought, without judging it or insisting that it go away, gives it the opportunity to weaken and fade on its own.

Refocusing. In his book *Brain Lock* (1997), Dr. Jeffrey Schwartz describes a refocusing strategy that takes the "watching and waiting" method a step further. At the moment you notice the thought, gently shift to a new behavior that reflects your values and intentions, as if you didn't have the thought at all. The idea here isn't to avoid the discomfort, but to distract yourself from your urge to do something in an attempt to reduce the anxiety. For example, if the thought "What if I stab my child?" occurs as you stand in the kitchen cutting vegetables with a sharp knife, continue what you're doing and refocus on another activity or behavior, such as conversing with your child, reaching for another vegetable to slice, singing a song, noticing your breathing, or thinking of your favorite recipe or the pleasant events of the previous day. It's fine to shift your focus many times as you wait out the storm.

Dealing with Covert Rituals

What about the covert rituals—those you perform in your thoughts? As a reminder, these mental compulsions include repetitious phrases, words, and prayers, as well as counting, recalling the past, and thought balancing, where you balance the presence of a bad thought by compulsively thinking a good thought. Whatever their form, they are compulsive, repetitive thought patterns done as a direct response to an obsessive thought in an attempt to neutralize the discomfort of the thought.

You may be confused about the difference between obsessive thoughts and mental compulsions. You're not alone, as sometimes it's hard to tell. To distinguish between them ask yourself these questions:

- Does the thought cause anxiety, fear, or doubt? If your answer is yes, it's an obsessive thought. In this case, your overarching approach should be to confront, invite, and even encourage the discomfort associated with the thought.
- Does the thought relieve anxiety? If your answer is yes, then it's a mental compulsion, even if it relieves anxiety only briefly. In this case, your overall approach should be to block, reduce, or alter the thought in any way possible. Any strategy that alters the automatic quality of a compulsion is progress in the right direction.

To reduce your covert rituals, in addition to doing the exposure exercises in this chapter, use the principles of response prevention, discussed at length in chapter 6. Deal with these rituals just as you would any overt compulsive behaviors. Here are some especially helpful techniques:

- **Ritual delay.** Put off doing the covert ritual for minutes, or hours, or days—basically, as long as you can.
- **Thought stopping.** Picture a large red stop sign in your mind while screaming, "*Stop!*" (silently, in your mind) *before* you perform the mental ritual. This has the effect of short-circuiting the tendency to automatically use a ritual to relieve the discomfort of the intrusive thought. This isn't intended to stop intrusive, horrific thoughts, which is an exercise in futility. If used for that purpose, thought stopping only increases these thoughts. It is intended only as a tool to help prevent you from doing compulsive mental rituals.

HOPE FOR PRIMARILY OBSESSIONAL OCD

For years, it was widely believed that people with primarily obsessional OCD were much more difficult to help than people with obsessions accompanied by overt compulsions. In our experience, this isn't true. We believe that by using the techniques we've described in this chapter, perhaps in combination with the right medications, you can break free from primarily obsessional OCD. Though the work can be very challenging, even scary, the reward is great: relief from dealing with the constant unpleasant noise in your mind.

The goal of the exercises in this chapter is to help you begin to coexist with your horrific thoughts. Although it's unrealistic to expect your intrusive thoughts to go away magically, you will experience significant relief once you understand that a thought is just a thought, nothing more. Remember the well-worn phrase "Whatever you resist persists." In terms of OCD, this means that the OCD feeds off of persistent attempts to avoid or suppress intrusive thoughts or see meaning in them. When you give up trying so hard to control the activity in your head, the OCD will lessen.

Will your primarily obsessional OCD go away completely and forever? Probably not. Intrusive thoughts tend to flare up when life becomes stressful. But, overall, you can learn to live more comfortably with these difficult thoughts. As they come to be mere occasional background noise, you can enjoy life once again.

HELP FOR FAMILY AND FRIENDS

Cherry Pedrick remembers that years before she had OCD, she didn't want to stand near the edge at scenic overlooks. The thought would cross her mind "If I get too close, I might jump!" That thought was immediately followed by "Where did that thought come from? How silly!" It was disturbing, but she could dismiss the thought easily. While writing this chapter, Cherry could relate to people who have such thoughts and can't dismiss them. During her OCD years, there was a point at which Cherry seldom had a waking moment when she wasn't battling her thoughts—usually worrisome thoughts about having caused harm in the past. For Cherry, it's a joy to be free of those thoughts.

People without OCD have unwanted, intrusive thoughts, often without even realizing it. Chances are, you have such thoughts from time to time. Because they can be so fleeting, you might have to monitor your thoughts for some time before you notice having the types of thoughts that torture the minds of people with primarily obsessional OCD. Imagine if you couldn't easily dismiss those thoughts and felt as if you hardly had a waking moment without an unwanted thought going through your head.

What do these thoughts mean? Will your loved one act on unwanted horrific thoughts? No! If you need reassurance, read the section entitled "The Nature of Horrific Thoughts in Primarily Obsessional OCD." These thoughts are just brain noise. There are no hidden meanings. Your loved one may come to you for reassurance about this, and you may be tempted to offer it. Resist that tendency. Remember, reassurance and debating will only fuel the OCD.

CHAPTER 11

Scrupulosity: When OCD Gets Religious

We can't solve problems by using the same kind of thinking we used when we created them.

—Albert Einstein

Over the past twenty years, scrupulosity has come to be viewed as OCD with a religious theme. It is a condition of "seeing sin where there is none" (Ciarrocchi 1998, 8). Scrupulosity has a very long history. The writings of various major figures in the Roman Catholic and Protestant Churches reveal that these individuals struggled with scruples—ethical or moral considerations that block action, and the historical predecessor of what we now call scrupulosity. For example, John Bunyan, author of *Pilgrim's Progress*, Protestant theologian Martin Luther, and Saint Ignatius Loyola, founder of the Jesuit order, were all tormented by unacceptable thoughts, images, and urges that sound eerily like OCD symptoms as they are described today (Ciarrocchi 1998; Seuss and Halpern 1989).

People with religious obsessions and compulsions are ruled by an overly strict and rigid code of religious, moral, or ethical conduct. Rather than subscribing to religious precepts and laws as guides for living a richer, more peaceful and spiritually fulfilled life, people with scrupulosity become victims of their own beliefs. Their standards and beliefs typically go well beyond those of even the most devout within their religion. They live in a relentless, tortured state of vigilance, always alert to the possibility of committing some immoral or blasphemous act and being punished harshly for it. This robs them of peace of mind. Here are some examples of scrupulosity:

- Repeatedly attending confession to request forgiveness for sins and transgressions for which one has already been forgiven.
- Excessively worrying about having a sexual thought while looking at another person's spouse for fear of violating the commandment "Thou shalt not covet another man's wife."
- Repeatedly reciting the Lord's Prayer over and over until each word is pronounced "perfectly" and without experiencing even the slightest distraction. If any distraction occurs or the words aren't pronounced perfectly, the cycle of prayer must begin again.
- Constantly checking the ground to avoid stepping on an object resembling the sign of the cross and thus desecrating an important symbol.
- Meticulously avoiding swallowing one's own saliva in order to follow the requirement to abstain from eating or drinking during the Jewish celebration of Yom Kippur.

DIFFERENTIATING BETWEEN STRONG RELIGIOUS BELIEFS AND SCRUPULOSITY

Psychiatrist David Greenberg (1984) described five essential principles for distinguishing normal religious beliefs and practices from pathological or overly scrupulous beliefs and practices:

- In scrupulosity, religious practices go far beyond the requirements of religious law and custom, and people may act "more Catholic than the pope." For example, a person who adheres to a kosher diet might try to hold his or her breath when walking by a nonkosher butcher shop for fear of inhaling the "essence" of meat that isn't kosher.
- In scrupulosity, beliefs or practices have an overly narrow, trivial focus. In prayer, excessive attention is devoted to "saying it right" or "perfectly," rather than seeing prayer as a way of developing a relationship with God.
- Healthy religious beliefs don't interfere with the normal practice of the religion, whereas scrupulosity OCD frequently interferes with practicing the religion, such as when a person with blasphemous thoughts avoids going to church altogether.
- The person with scrupulosity spends excessive time and energy on minute, trivial aspects of religious observance, often ignoring more important aspects of spiritual life, such as charity for the less fortunate.
- In scrupulosity, the excessive preoccupation with doing religious rituals until they are "just right," praying repetitively, and confessing unnecessarily resembles the typical symptoms of OCD, such as checking, repeating, and asking for reassurance. Like the typical behaviors of OCD, overly scrupulous behaviors are repetitive, persistent, and unwanted.

Does having strong religious beliefs increase the likelihood of having scrupulosity OCD? Because OCD is seen as a neurobehavioral disorder, a biological predisposition is a necessary factor in developing OCD. Therefore strong religious beliefs cannot be considered to be the cause of OCD. They are only the grist for the OCD mill in a person who is biologically predisposed to it. OCD is sometimes called "the doubting disease," and as such, it attacks, undermines, and wreaks havoc with the very foundation of who you are and who you know yourself to be. For those who don't have strong religious beliefs, OCD will take a different form, such as contamination fears or checking compulsions. Scrupulosity OCD takes well-intended beliefs and precepts and blows them out of proportion. The moral and spiritual aspects of the individual's character become fused with the OCD and become distorted and corrupted.

HYPERMORALITY AND HYPERRESPONSIBILITY

Hypermorality and hyperresponsibility are major behavioral characteristics of people with scrupulosity OCD and can manifest in ways that don't have an overtly religious theme. *Hypermorality* involves an excessive preoccupation with the fear of doing something morally wrong, reprehensible, or condemnable. These individuals set excessive, unrealistically rigid and narrow standards in the areas of their lives touched by the OCD. Here are some examples of hypermorality:

- Checking sales receipts laboriously to make sure an error wasn't made in your favor, for fear that this is the equivalent of stealing
- Reviewing conversations you had with others over and over in your mind to be absolutely sure that you didn't inadvertently tell a lie

People who are *hyperresponsible* have an overly unrealistic sense of accountability. They take on responsibilities that realistically belong to others or take responsibility for things that are beyond anyone's reasonable control. Here are some examples of hyperresponsibility:

- Constantly checking the ground for stray sharp objects that could cause injury if someone were to step on them
- Checking every piece of garbage numerous times to make sure recyclable items are separated, then carrying them by hand to a recycling site to ensure they are not lost, thereby contributing to pollution
- Taking in many stray animals, to the point of endangering your health and your family's

Hyperresponsibility is not to be confused with being highly virtuous or compassionate about the welfare of others. Although people with scrupulosity certainly aren't lacking in compassion for others, they are driven to extremes of worry and anxiety mainly out of fear of possible condemnation. They may be afraid of going to hell, angering God, or living with perpetual feelings of guilt for their failure to protect others from harm or endangerment. Basically, their excessive concern for the well-being of others is an outgrowth of their constant fear for their own fate.

THE SELF-DIRECTED PROGRAM FOR SCRUPULOSITY

To break free from scrupulosity, your self-directed program will be very similar to that outlined in part 2 of the book, with one important difference: It's a good idea to work with a spiritual advisor, as you'll probably feel reluctant to do some of the exposure and response prevention exercises proposed in this chapter out of concern that they are morally, ethically, or spiritually wrong. Or you may fear that changing your behavior will do damage to your spiritual identity and beliefs. So, for scrupulosity OCD, the steps involved in the self-directed program are as follows:

1. Find a spiritual advisor.
2. Keep a daily record of your obsessions and compulsions.
3. Make a target obsessions list.
4. Make a target compulsions list.
5. Devise an exposure and response prevention plan and carry it out.

Step 1. Find a Spiritual Advisor

Choose a trusted, prudent person to serve as your spiritual advisor and guide you through the religious, moral, and ethical challenges you'll experience while doing the self-directed program. This person should have religious beliefs similar to yours and a basic understanding of OCD, and scrupulosity in particular. You may choose your counselor, pastor, rabbi, or other clergyperson. Or it could be your spouse or a parent, relative, or close friend. For the time being, you will need to follow your advisor "as a sheep follows a shepherd."

If you're doing the self-directed program with a therapist, ask if you can bring your advisor to counseling sessions to assist the therapist in your treatment. A trained behavior therapist knowledgeable about OCD will welcome this collaboration. Discuss each exposure task and, for each, ask, "Is this morally acceptable for me to do?" Adjust the tasks until you find those that are morally, ethically, and spiritually acceptable both to you and your advisor.

Whether working with a therapist or on your own, commit to making a sincere attempt to complete the self-directed program you'll develop in the following pages. There will be times when you will doubt your advisor's guidance. However, with time the OCD will weaken and your true moral and spiritual identity will emerge. In the meanwhile, model your behavior after your advisor's example and trust your advisor to guide you as you move ever closer to breaking free from scrupulosity.

To begin, write the names of people you know who might serve as your advisor for these exercises and make a commitment to choose one of these people to act as your advisor as soon as you can.

Step 2. Keep a Daily Record of Your Obsessions and Compulsions

If you have scrupulosity, you probably spend excessive time, effort, and energy warding off thoughts, images, or urges that you consider to be dangerous, unacceptable, offensive, repulsive, or disgusting. These are the obsessions, and they cause intense anxiety and shame. In an effort to neutralize the distress associated with these thoughts, you engage in rituals, either overt or covert; these are the compulsions of scrupulosity.

Before you can develop an effective self-directed program, you need to identify your obsessions and compulsions, the situations that trigger them, and the discomfort associated with those situations. For one week, use the Scrupulosity Monitoring Form to keep a record of your obsessions. Make several copies to last the week, and carry the form with you every day. (You may also use your journal to do the exercises in this chapter.)

Whenever you encounter a situation that triggers obsessive thoughts or worries, record the date in the first column and briefly describe the situation in the second column. Then, in the third column, rate the degree of distress these thoughts cause you by assigning a SUDS rating from 0 to 100, where 0 is no distress and 100 is the greatest distress possible. In the fourth column, write the obsession that arises: thoughts, images, or urges that increase anxiety. In the fifth column write the associated compulsion: excessive thoughts, images, or behaviors intended to neutralize the obsessive concern. We've provided an example to help you see how to use the form.

Scrupulosity Monitoring Form (Example)

Date	Situation that triggers discomfort	SUDS level (0-100)	Obsession	Compulsion
9/21/09	*Thought about an attractive person other than my spouse.*	95	*I'm having an impure thought and God will punish me.*	*Prayed for 75 minutes, until it felt right.*
9/21/09	*Looked at my infant's genitals.*	85	*Maybe I'm enjoying looking and will go to hell for that.*	*Avoided touching the baby or going into the baby's room.*
9/22/09	*Went for a walk.*	90	*I must never step on any living thing. That would violate God's commandments.*	*Kept my eyes on the ground, watching everything I walked on.*

9/23/09	*Sitting in church, looked up at the image of Jesus.*	*75*	*I feel like shouting obscenities at the image of Jesus.*	*Attended confession three times this week to confess my blasphemous thoughts.*

Scrupulosity Monitoring Form				
Date	**Situation that triggers discomfort**	**SUDS level** (0-100)	**Obsession**	**Compulsion**

Step 3. Make a Target Obsessions List

Using the monitoring form you completed in step 2, make a list of your obsessions and rank them in order of the amount of distress they cause you. This is similar to the anxiety/exposure hierarchies from chapter 6. Together with the target compulsions list in step 4, it will help you design an effective program of exposure and response prevention. Here's an example list of target obsessive thoughts, followed by a blank form for you to fill out.

Target Obsessions List (Example)	
Obsessive thought, image, or urge	**SUDS level** (0-100)
Maybe I don't understand this particular passage of scripture and I won't go to heaven after all.	*100*
I'm having an impure thought and God will punish me.	95
Maybe I told a lie without knowing it. That would certainly mean that I'm a bad person.	95
I must never step on any living thing. That would violate God's commandments.	90
Maybe I'm enjoying looking and will go to hell.	85
What if I lose control and shout obscenities at the image of Jesus?	*75*

Target Obsessions List	
Obsessive thought, image, or urge	**SUDS level** (0-100)

Step 4. Make a Target Compulsions List

Now use your monitoring form to make a list of your compulsive behaviors and rank them in order of the amount of distress you would feel if you didn't carry out each compulsion. With avoidance, this can be a little tricky. For example, if the compulsion is something like not going to church, not carrying out that compulsion would mean going to church. In the right-hand column estimate (it doesn't have to be exact!) the amount of time that your compulsions take up in an average day. If the compulsion involves *not* doing something, estimate how many times per day (or week) you avoid that activity. (If you don't practice them daily, estimate your average for an entire week.)

Target Compulsions List (Example)		
Compulsive behavior	**SUDS level if you don't do it** (0-100)	**Time expended or number of times avoided**
Praying for long periods, until it feels right	*100*	*Most of the time*
Repeating "God forgives me" 24 times	*100*	*4 hours per day*
Attending confession frequently to confess blasphemous thoughts	*95*	*90 minutes a day, every day*
Repetitively reading the same scriptures over and over until I understand them perfectly	*95*	*2 hours per day*
Avoiding touching the baby or going into the baby's room	*90*	*About 4 times per week*
Keeping my eyes on the ground, watching everything I walk upon	*85*	*All the time when outside*

Target Compulsions List		
Compulsive behavior	SUDS level if you don't do it (0-100)	Time expended or number of times avoided

Step 5. Devise and Carry Out an ERP Plan

Now it's time to devise a strategy for doing ERP based on your lists of target obsessions and compulsions. To begin with, you'll target the items on your lists that cause a lower level of distress. As you master those, you can gradually move up to dealing with more difficult items.

Here are some key points to keep in mind to ensure that your ERP program is most effective:

- Exposure must be prolonged and repeated—between one and a half and three hours per day, for four to seven days or longer. However, do note that there is no definitive length of time for any given exposure exercise; the key is to remain in the anxiety-provoking situation until your SUDS level diminishes considerably, by at least half. This indicates that you've achieved a significant level of habituation, or what Joseph Ciarrocchi calls the "remedy of nervous system boredom" (1995, 76).

- The exposure must be acceptable to you and not violate your core religious beliefs. This can be tricky. Remember that OCD behaviors are excessive, unwanted, persistent, and not based on the true requirements of a religious or spiritual practice. It's important to separate out OCD behaviors from behaviors that are appropriate expressions of true religious or spiritual belief. Your spiritual advisor or therapist can be invaluable in assisting you in sorting this out, and can also help you find the courage to take the bold steps necessary in confronting your OCD-based scrupulous ideas and behaviors.

- For obsessions regarding feared situations that are difficult to replicate (for example, the fear of going to hell), use imaginal exposure, as outlined in chapter 7. Imaginal exposure will help you hold these uncomfortable or frightening thoughts in your mind with less discomfort.

- As you expose yourself to anxiety-provoking situations, work to reduce your compulsive rituals gradually on a day-by-day, week-by-week basis. Review chapter 6 for how to do response prevention; the following examples will also provide guidance.

- If you feel unsure or unsafe when blocking a ritual, the general rule is do the opposite of whatever scrupulous behavior your OCD mind tells you to do. Over four hundred years ago, Saint Ignatius Loyola, the founder of the Jesuit order, gave the same advice to his scrupulous followers (Ciarrocchi 1995). For example, if your compulsion is to repeat a specific prayer, said "just right," several times a day, refrain from doing so. Or if you feel compelled to repeat going to confession to make absolutely certain that the priest heard your confession correctly, resist this urge with all of your might.

To help you devise a self-directed ERP plan for scrupulosity, we've included a couple of case examples with the details of their ERP plans. A planning worksheet for your own use appears a bit later in the chapter.

Mark's Experience

Remember Mark from chapter 1? A thirty-five-year old businessman, husband, and father of two children, he had a history of OCD that had been well controlled for many years. Because of a job transfer, he and his family moved to a new community and joined a new church. After a few weeks of attending services, Mark started having a disturbing intrusive thought during Sunday services: "What if I lose control and shout obscenities at the image of Jesus in the stained glass window above the pulpit?" The thought made him increasingly uncomfortable because he feared that he'd lose control during services and embarrass himself and his entire family. In response, he repeated the Lord's Prayer over and over to himself to gain a sense of control over his thoughts. After a few weeks, this strategy began to fail him, and his fears increased. Seeking reassurance, he began attending confession for these thoughts, appearing repeatedly at the pastor's door day after day to request a confessional. While confession gave him some relief for a day or two, the thoughts and urges returned, worsening each time he attended church. Eventually he stopped going to church altogether, which upset his wife and drew criticism from his parents and siblings, who knew nothing of his struggle with OCD.

Mark's ERP consisted of exposure to his horrific, blasphemous thoughts, along with response prevention that involved stopping his multiple confessions and avoidance of church services. Mark's plan, which he worked out in conjunction with his spiritual advisor, involved confronting his disturbing thoughts by first writing them repeatedly, and then listening to an audio recording of the thoughts. In Marks's case, it made sense to separate out the exposure and response prevention elements when drafting his plan, as the two were somewhat independent. Here's an example worksheet showing Mark's ERP plan.

Mark's Scrupulosity ERP Planning Worksheet

Target obsessive thoughts, images, or urges: *Intrusive urge to shout obscenities at the image of Jesus.*

Target compulsions: *Attending confession repeatedly, repeating the Lord's Prayer until it sounds right, avoiding attending church services*

ERP strategy: *Expose myself to my horrific thoughts for increasing amounts of time; practice repeating the thoughts while in church. Reduce and eventually stop all reassurance seeking through confession.*

SUDS before starting ERP: *90*

How long (minutes or hours) per exposure, or target SUDS level: *45 to 90 minutes per day, or until my SUDS level is reduced by half in each session*

How often (times per day or week): *Once a day*

Target SUDS level: *0-20*

Avoidances to be stopped: *I must attend church services regularly and tolerate the urge to shout obscenities. I must also refrain from trying to suppress blasphemous thoughts.*

Additional instructions: *Discuss exposures with my spiritual advisor before proceeding! Discuss guidelines for appropriate use of confession and prayer with him.*

Carrying Out Mark's Exposure Plan

Week 1, days 1-3: *Write down my blasphemous thoughts on paper repeatedly, one at time, 20 times each, focusing hard on the content of the thought and evaluating my SUDS level after every 20 repetitions. Continue with the first thought until my SUDS level reduces by half, then move on to the next thought and do the same thing.*

Week 1, days 4-7: *On day 4, make an audio recording of my blasphemous thoughts, repeating each one 20 times. Continue until my SUDS reduces by one-half. Then, move on to the next thought. Listen to this recording on days 5 through 7.*

Week 2, days 1-4: *While holding a picture of Jesus in my hand, listen to the audio recording of my blasphemous thoughts. Repeat each thought until my SUDS level reduces by half.*

Week 2, days 4-7: *Listen to the recording of my blasphemous thoughts while sitting in an empty church. While listening, look at the image of Jesus until my SUDS level reduces by half.*

Week 3, days 1-4: *Listen to the recording of my blasphemous thoughts while sitting in church during actual services. While listening, look at the image of Jesus until my SUDS level reduces by half.*

Carrying Out the Response Prevention Plan

Week 1: *Reduce confessions to two per week; reduce Lord's Prayer to twice per day.*

Week 2: *Reduce confessions to one per week; reduce Lord's Prayer to once per day (a normal prayer schedule).*

Week 3 and beyond: *Stop all compulsive confessing, praying, and avoidance of church services.*

Lydia's Experience

Lydia provides another example of doing ERP with scrupulosity OCD. Lydia's obsession involved an excessive and literal adherence to the religious and moral principle "Thou shalt not kill." Specifically, she thought she might accidentally, without realizing it, step on bugs or small animals while walking on city streets. The thought that she might have violated this sacred principle caused her enormous guilt and anxiety. She struggled to neutralize her worry by always keeping her eyes focused on the pavement immediately in front of where she walked. If it occurred to her that she might have been distracted for a moment, she turned around, retraced her steps, and checked the pavement for signs of a crushed bug to reassure herself that nothing horrible had happened. As a result, a simple walk down the street took a great deal of time, so she was consistently late for social and work-related appointments. As her checking became more extensive, her anxiety escalated and she began to incorporate more and more compulsions, such as carrying a crucifix in her hand and praying once she arrived at her destination. After a while, she couldn't walk anywhere without assistance from a trusted friend or family member who could reassure her that nothing terrible happened.

Lydia's ERP strategy involved exposure to the doubts that she had possibly stepped on small bugs in her path, combined with response prevention in the form of resisting her urges to look down when walking, retrace her steps, use safety signals, and pray in response to her worries. Because Lydia's compulsions were closely interwoven with her obsessions, her plan was simpler than Mark's; exposure and response prevention occurred at the same time. Here's an example worksheet showing what she and her therapist came up with.

Lydia's Scrupulosity ERP Planning Worksheet

Target obsessive thoughts, images, or urges: *If I cause the death of any living thing, even without knowing it, I'm a murderer and I'll be punished.*

Target compulsions: *Looking down while walking outside, retracing my steps, checking for signs of dead bugs or animals, touching the crucifix in my pocket, praying to myself*

ERP strategy: *Accept the uncertainty that I may accidentally cause the death of a living thing while walking outside. Walk for increasing lengths of time without retracing my steps and checking the ground for dead bugs or animals.*

SUDS before starting ERP: *95*

How long (minutes or hours) per exposure, or target SUDS level: *30 minutes per day, or until my SUDS goes down by at least half in each session*

How often (times per day or week): *Two sessions per day for 3 to 4 weeks*

Target SUDS level: *20*

Avoidances to be stopped: *I won't avoid walking outside.*

Additional instructions: *Discuss exposure with my spiritual advisor before proceeding. Avoid saying prayers repeatedly while doing the exposure or holding any safety objects my OCD relies upon, such as my grandmother's crucifix.*

Carrying Out Lydia's Plan

Day 1: *Walk for 5 minutes without looking down or retracing my steps.*

Day 2: *Walk for 10 minutes without looking down or retracing my steps.*

Day 3: *Walk for 20 minutes without looking down or retracing my steps.*

Day 4: *Walk for 40 minutes without looking down or retracing my steps.*

Day 5: *Walk for 80 minutes without looking down or retracing my steps.*

Days 6-9: *Walk for 80 minutes without looking down, retracing my steps, or holding the crucifix.*

Days 9-12: *Walk for 80 minutes without looking down, retracing my steps, holding the crucifix, or saying prayers silently to myself.*

Developing Your ERP Plan for Scrupulosity

As you saw in the sample worksheets, sometimes exposure and response prevention can be combined in a single plan. Other times it's clearer to draft one plan for exposure and another for response prevention. We've designed the worksheet with separate spaces for those two elements to make it flexible, but it's fine for you to create a simpler plan, as Lydia did. Make copies of the blank form so you can use it repeatedly.

Scrupulosity ERP Planning Worksheet

Target obsessive thoughts, images, or urges: ____________________

____

Target compulsions: ____________________

____

ERP strategy: ____________________

____

____

SUDS before starting ERP: ____________________

How long (minutes or hours) per exposure, or target SUDS level: ____________________

How often (times per day or week): ____________________

Target SUDS level: ____________________

Avoidances to be stopped: ____________________

____

Additional instructions: ____________________

____

Carrying Out the Exposure Plan

Day or week 1: ______________________________

____

Day or week 2: ______________________________

____

Day or week 3: ______________________________

____

Day or week 4: ______________________________

____

The Response Prevention Plan

Day or week 1: ______________________________

____

Day or week 2: ______________________________

____

Day or week 3: ______________________________

____

Day or week 4: ______________________________

____

Using Imaginal Exposure with Scrupulosity

As you saw in Mark's example, it may be difficult to use real-life scenarios to confront feared situations in scrupulosity OCD. Mark used techniques from chapter 10, on horrific thoughts, to confront his intrusive thoughts. You can also use more in-depth imaginal exposure, as described in chapter 7, to help you habituate to intrusive, blasphemous thoughts. This approach is particularly useful if the obsessive fears involve some sort of suffering or condemnation far in the future. Lydia decided to use this approach to enhance her real-life ERP. Here's what she came up with. (Refer back to chapter 7 for full instructions.)

1. **The triggering situation:** *While walking down the street downtown and talking to my husband, I suddenly feel something underfoot. Not thinking anything about it, I keep walking for fifteen minutes.*

2. **Initial fearful thought:** *Then the thought occurs to me: What if I stepped on a small animal or insect and killed it?*

3. **Emotional reactions and physical symptoms:** *Suddenly, my body breaks out in a sweat, my heart starts pounding, and I start shaking with fear.*

4. **Additional fearful and doubting thoughts:** *I'll never know for sure what happened.*

5. **Urges to ritualize, without following through:** *I want to go back and retrace my steps, but I know it's impossible to do that now.*

6. **What this would say about me if the worst happened:** *I'm a hypocrite and an evil person for being so casual, so uncaring about possibly killing a living thing.*

7. **Core fear or worst-case scenarios:** *I must live forever with the guilt of knowing that I killed a living thing. I will be condemned by God for my transgressions and be denied his eternal grace.*

Using Lydia's example as your guide, write your own imaginal exposure script, including plenty of details to give it an added sense of drama and emotion. Then follow the instructions in chapter 7 for using your narrative to conduct imaginal exposure.

You can double up, doing both imaginal exposure and ERP during the same period of time. Or if you're too anxious to do ERP initially, you can start with imaginal exposure for a few weeks as a way to ease you into ERP. Either way, remember that the goal isn't to get rid of your obsessive thoughts; rather, it's to learn to not buy into their irrational content. With time and practice, you'll be able to disengage from your obsessive thoughts more easily, leaving more time to live the life you value, including practicing your faith in a healthier and more wholesome manner.

Troubleshooting ERP for Scrupulosity OCD

To gain the most from exposure, be sure to avoid engaging in any safety behaviors or using safety signals when doing exposure. As in other forms of OCD discussed in this book, having your partner or spouse nearby may make your exposure feel safer. Other forms of safety seeking that commonly occur with scrupulosity include saying prayers silently over and over or relying on religious objects such as pendants, a rosary, or prayer beads. Despite their symbolic or sentimental value, using these objects in a compulsive way to relieve anxiety prevents you from attaining maximal benefit from the exposure experience. You must eventually relinquish reliance on any these safety signals and challenge yourself to do the exposures without them.

CAN YOU DO ERP FOR SCRUPULOSITY AND STILL BE SPIRITUAL?

Psychiatrist and author Dr. Ian Osborn researched how leaders from many branches of Christianity have dealt with their obsessive-compulsive disorder over the centuries. Martin Luther, John Bunyan, Saint Thérèse of Lisieux, Saint Ignatius of Loyola, Saint Jane Frances de Chantal, and Saint Alphonsus Liguori came to similar conclusions, all without cognitive behavioral therapists, and most without adequate spiritual counsel.

In his book *Can Christianity Cure Obsessive-Compulsive Disorder?* Dr. Osborn states, "After successfully treating his own obsessive-compulsive disorder, Ignatius counseled others on how to overcome similar problems… It boils down to two principles. First, it is necessary to identify the source of a scruple (or obsession), that is, what exactly is causing the anxiety and disquiet. Secondly, one must oppose the scruple by acting in a manner contrary to it, such as stopping excessive confessions. Perhaps this great Catholic saint deserves to be called the first OCD behavioral therapist" (2008, 139).

The advice is the same for people of any faith. In fact, Cherry had been giving similar spiritual advice to people who emailed her with problems with scrupulosity for years before Dr. Osborn's book was published. The obsessions and compulsions were always similar: "Have I lost my salvation?" "Did I commit an unforgivable sin?" "Am I saved?" "If I don't pray, read my Bible, or recite verses, won't something terrible happen?" These people were almost always surprised by Cherry's advice: Stop praying the moment you feel you must continue praying. Stop reading the Bible verses you feel compelled to read. Stop doing whatever spiritual activity you feel you just have to do for fear of something terrible happening. While on the surface this may look like abandoning spiritual practices, in these situations the practices are no longer spiritual activities; they're rituals—symptoms of obsessive-compulsive disorder.

The point isn't to abandon all spiritual activities. It's important to develop new spiritual activities that are *different* from those affected by your OCD rituals and compulsions. For example, set aside some quiet time each day for reading spiritual texts and praying. If reading and praying aren't for you or are affected by your OCD, spend this time meditating. You could also get involved in a local church, synagogue, or other type of faith community as a means of expressing your spirituality. In the following space (or in your journal), brainstorm a list of some fulfilling spiritual activities that could serve as alternatives to those affected by your OCD:

____

____

____

You may ask, "Isn't that avoidance?" It isn't. The goal is to maintain and broaden your spirituality while doing the challenging work of ERP around those worship activities that are most affected by your OCD. Initially, you may experience an increase in anxiety and worry as you make fundamental changes in your spiritual practice. This is normal, and a sign that positive changes are taking place. Stick with it! It will get easier with time. Write your worrisome thoughts down in your journal and come back to them during your quiet time to challenge or dispute them.

A THERAPY OF TRUST

Dr. Osborn discusses responsibility modification therapy, an approach in which accountability is transferred to someone else (2008). This approach isn't often used in traditional cognitive behavioral treatment for OCD because of the obvious shortcomings: A person willing to assume responsibility isn't always available, and therapists typically want clients with OCD to become more independent of external sources of accountability in their lives, not less so.

As mentioned, Martin Luther, John Bunyan, and Saint Thérèse of Lisieux all had what we now know as OCD. Although they lived in different centuries and had great influence on different Christian denominations, each included a type of responsibility modification strategy in his or her theology because this is the way all of them broke free from their OCD. Responsibility modification involves giving the responsibility for all obsessional fears completely and absolutely to God. Dr. Osborn describes a three-step process for doing this that can also be used by people of other faiths:

1. Recognize obsessions when they strike. (For example, "What if I'm not going to heaven?" or "What if something really will happen to my mother if I don't repeat these verses?")

2. Transfer responsibility to God. (For example, "I'll turn it over to God to decide whether I'm going to heaven.") Leave the matter there.

3. Affirm your faith and trust by resisting all behavior that aims to seek certainty, such as repetitive praying that must be done "just right." (For example, "Because I trust God, I'll resist rereading and repeating a scriptural passage.") If this feels difficult, remember that compulsions undermine genuine faith and strengthen the grip of OCD symptoms.

According to Dr. Osborn, believers have another incentive for resisting compulsions: "In doing so they demonstrate or prove, both to God and themselves, how much they trust him and love him" (2008, 145). In a personal communication, Dr. Osborn expanded on that, saying, "The trust is not that the obsessional fear won't come true, although there is a sense of hope for that. The trust is that whatever God arranges to happen will be for the person's best—even if for reasons not understood, the worst fears come true." In the process of eliminating rituals entirely, Dr. Osborn recommends trying to win small, daily victories over OCD by, for example, shortening the time spent on rituals or postponing them.

Keys to Breaking Free from Scrupulosity

- In ERP for scrupulosity, you aren't planning to act on your fearful thoughts, only to think about them. Discuss the relationship between thoughts and actions with your spiritual advisor. You will progress further once you can accept that thoughts do not equal actions.
- If you have difficulty resisting a ritual, try postponing, delaying, or changing it. If you usually do a ritual quickly, do it very slowly. If you recite a phrase or prayer to yourself (for example, "I love you Lord. Please let me bring about good and not harm. Don't let anything bad happen because of what I do"), sing it to yourself or change it in some other way, for example, leaving out a word so it sounds "imperfect."
- Tell your spiritual advisor, friends, and family members to reassure you only once when you request reassurance. And keep in mind that rephrasing the question or asking a second person to get another reassuring answer is self-defeating and won't help you get better. Think about your questions before you ask them and resist the urge to ask to relieve your anxiety. The discomfort will be short-lived compared to the persistent suffering that comes with giving in to your compulsive need for certainty.
- When you want to avoid a situation or activity, remember that you pay a price for avoidance. If you feel an urge to do something to alleviate your anxiety, fight that urge with everything you have. The anxiety always goes down eventually if you resist. If you aren't sure what you should do, consult your spiritual advisor or ask yourself, "What would a reasonable, prudent person do in this situation?"
- If you find an exposure too threatening, break it down into smaller steps that are easier to manage and master.

CHALLENGE OCD DAILY

To overcome scrupulosity, it's important to make ERP a central part of your life. Daily, find the courage to place yourself in situations that will trigger symptoms. Avoid avoidance! When doing ERP, expect and even invite and welcome discomfort. Don't expect to feel good while you're doing ERP—you won't. You will, however, begin to feel good, even great, as you experience small, gradual successes in letting go of obsessions, eliminating rituals, and reclaiming your true spiritual self. When you aren't doing ERP tasks, occupy yourself with the present moment and day-to-day activities. Notice your surroundings and pay attention to conversations around you. Observe details. Allow uncomfortable thoughts to pass through your mind like distant clouds crossing the sky. Accepting obsessive thoughts for what they are—just thoughts—and not reacting to them will weaken them, whereas fighting against them strengthens them, causing them to grow and multiply.

Practice the art of letting go, in this case letting go of your need for certainty. Religious belief requires faith. If you had total certainty in your life, you wouldn't have a need for faith. Let go of your extreme and compulsive religious rituals and develop a more personal faith. Find ways to replace your religious rituals with sincere spiritual practices. For example, you might spend more quality time with your children, do volunteer work, spend time with a lonely person, or help a neighbor.

HELP FOR FAMILY AND FRIENDS

The biggest question you have is probably *why*: Why does your loved one have this type of OCD? Your loved one's religion is one of the most important parts of his or her life, so why would the OCD attack there? That is precisely why it attacks there. OCD often attacks the part of a person's life that matters the most. Don't think of this as a sign of weak faith; view your loved one's scrupulosity as another collection of OCD symptoms to be tackled.

As part of your loved one's recovery from scrupulosity, he or she may need, at least for a while, to do things that seem foreign to your notion of religious practice: praying less, reading scripture less, or attending worship services or confession less often or even not at all until the OCD symptoms let up. Don't misinterpret this as a loss of faith. Instead, read this chapter carefully and then discuss it with your loved one. When religious practices are excessive, they represent OCD symptoms, not religious observances. During this time, it's important that your loved one consult with a spiritual advisor. This advisor should be your loved one's primary source of advice in these matters.

CHAPTER 12

Hit-and-Run OCD: Hyperresponsibility Behind the Wheel

I believe that anyone can conquer fear by doing the things he fears to do, provided he keeps doing them until he gets a record of successful experiences behind him.

—Eleanor Roosevelt

Hyperresponsibility is a common theme among people with OCD. It involves repetitive thoughts about the possibility of causing harm to others as a result of one's negligence or carelessness. One of the more crippling types of OCD problems related to hyperresponsibility involves a preoccupation with the possibility of accidentally hitting, injuring, or killing someone while driving a car. "Hit-and-run" OCD was aptly named by a long-suffering patient with the disorder. People with this form of OCD live a nightmare of worry, fear, and dread every time they get behind the wheel.

Remember Robert, from chapter 1? For him, a simple bump in the road or an unexpected noise, shadow, or flash of light triggered a heart-pounding, tire-screeching return to the site where he thought he might have hit someone or caused an accident. Once at the site, he felt reassured that no accident had occurred. This relieved his anxiety—but only briefly. Feelings of intense doubt and fear would recur, compelling Robert to do yet another U-turn back to the scene of the "crime." He would repeat this many times, until at last he felt "right" could drive on. Yet even then, he experienced lingering feelings of doubt and anxiety that persisted for hours or even days.

For people with hit-and-run OCD, driving near schools, children, and bicyclists can be especially nerve-wracking. Potholes and speed bumps may feel like hitting a body, triggering the compulsion to go back and check the site. Checking behaviors may go to such extremes as routinely reading accident reports in newspapers or online, watching TV news programs specifically for information on local accidents, and chasing ambulances to accident scenes. Some people with hit-and-run OCD repeatedly check the surfaces of their vehicles for dents or bloodstains.

Some people with this problem may actually endanger themselves by getting out of their cars in traffic to check underneath the car for signs of injured pedestrians. The number of people who suffer from hit-and-run OCD isn't known, but from Dr. Hyman's anecdotal experience it appears as a symptom at some time in as many as 30 percent of his patients. It seems to occur equally in males and females.

People with hit-and-run OCD suffer a particular sense of shame and humiliation about their problem. Like most people with OCD, they are aware that their behavior is irrational and makes no sense, but they can't control it. Many resort to driving only with a suitable "witness" in the car, and some avoid driving altogether.

SELF-DIRECTED PROGRAM FOR HIT-AND-RUN OCD

The self-directed program for hit-and-run OCD follows the same general guidelines for exposure and response prevention as outlined in part 2 of the book. The basic steps are as follows:

1. Assess your hit-and-run problem by keeping a record of your obsessions and compulsions.
2. Make an anxiety/exposure hierarchy.
3. Devise an ERP plan and carry it out.
4. Use imaginal exposure concurrently with ERP to assist in habituation to thoughts.

Step 1. Assess Your Hit-and-Run Problem

Before you can devise an effective plan, you need a good understanding of your problem with hit-and-run OCD. We'll start with some questions that will help you describe the problem in detail, and then you'll record what you actually experience for one week before developing an ERP program. (You may also use your journal to do the exercises in this chapter.)

How often do you feel anxious while driving? (For example, all the time, some of the time, rarely, only when anxious about other things, or when driving alone.) ______________________________

____

What places and driving situations cause you the most anxiety and fear? ______________________

____

____

What are your specific triggers for anxiety? (For example, bumps in the road, pedestrians passing by, children walking by, emergency sirens, or cyclists.) ______________________________

____

Overall, how anxious do you feel when driving? (Indicate your average anxiety by assigning a SUDS rating from 0 to 100, where 0 is no distress and 100 is the greatest distress possible.)

____

What other factors affect how anxious you are? (For example, fatigue, alcohol, or a "witness.")

____

____

How much do you avoid driving? (All the time, some of the time, rarely, or not at all?) __________

____

Are there any special circumstances in which you avoid driving, or places or situations you avoid? ___

____

____

What do you do to relieve the anxiety when it occurs? (For example, returning to the scene, asking for reassurance, checking the car for signs of blood or dents, checking accident reports, or calling the police department.) ____

____

____

Next, use the following Hit-and-Run Monitoring Form to record what you experience in actual driving situations for one week. Make several copies to last the week and carry the form with you whenever you drive, but don't try to fill it out while driving; just do so as soon afterward as possible. (If you currently avoid driving, you might still make a few entries by thinking about past driving experiences.) Note specific anxiety-provoking situations and the date they occurred, the SUDS level associated with each situation, associated intrusive thoughts and images that trigger anxiety and worry, and the compulsive rituals or behaviors you use to neutralize the anxiety. We've provided an example to help you see how to use the form.

Hit-and-Run Monitoring Form (Example)				
Date	**Situation that triggers discomfort**	**SUDS level (0-100)**	**Intrusive thought**	**Compulsion**
2/3/09	*Driving by a bicyclist*	95	*Maybe I hit him.*	*Checked in the rearview mirror and returned to the area to check to see if an accident occurred.*
2/3/09	*Switching lanes*	75	*Maybe I forced someone off the road, causing an accident.*	*Returned to check whether an accident occurred. Asked my passenger for reassurance that I didn't hit anyone.*
2/4/09	*Driving over a bump in road*	90	*Maybe I ran over someone.*	*Turned around and returned to place where it occurred. Checked for signs of an accident, harm, or injury.*
2/4/09	*Pulling out of a parking space*	85	*Maybe I ran over a child behind the car.*	*Got out of the car and checked to make sure no one was behind or under the car.*
2/4/09	*Hearing police sirens, then seeing a police car racing to an accident scene*	100	*Maybe I caused that accident.*	*Checked police reports of accidents occurring in the area where I'd driven.*
2/5/09	*Turning my head while driving*	75	*Maybe I didn't see what was in front of me and I hit someone.*	*Checked in the rearview mirror to make sure I hadn't caused an accident.*
2/6/09	*Parking and getting out of the car*	80	*Maybe I injured someone. I'd better make sure.*	*Checked around car for signs of dents or blood.*
2/7/09	*Driving by a school where children are walking on the sidewalk*	95	*I've run over a child and will be punished for it.*	*I must avoid driving near schools in the future.*

Hit-and-Run Monitoring Form				
Date	Situation that triggers discomfort	SUDS level (0-100)	Intrusive thought	Compulsion

Step 2. Make an Anxiety/Exposure Hierarchy

After you've compiled a record of the situations that cause you distress while driving, use the following form to list them in order, from least distressing at the bottom of the list to most distressing at the top. Again, we've provided an example.

Robert's anxiety/exposure hierarchy for driving	**SUDS level (0-100)**
Hearing a police siren, then seeing a police car racing to an accident scene without following the police car to the accident scene	*100*
Driving by a school where children are walking on the sidewalk without checking	*98*
Driving by a bicyclist on a residential street without turning around to check	*95*
Driving by a bicyclist on a main street without turning around to check	*90*
Driving over a bump in the road without turning around to check	*85*
Driving by an elementary school during recess without turning around	*80*
Backing out of a parking space without getting out of car to check for harm	*75*
Parking and getting out of the car without checking under the car for body parts	*70*
Turning my head for half a second while driving on a residential side street after school	*65*
Turning my head for half a second while driving on a four-lane highway	*60*
Switching lanes while driving on a four-lane highway	*55*
Blinking my eyes while driving with the radio on, on a residential side street after school is out	*50*
Blinking my eyes while driving, on a four-lane highway with the radio on	*45*
Blinking my eyes while driving on a residential side street	*40*

Anxiety/exposure hierarchy for driving	SUDS level (0-100)

Step 3. Devise and Carry Out an ERP Plan

The key to overcoming anxiety associated with driving lies in an effective ERP program: exposure to fear-provoking driving situations, combined with blocking the behaviors you typically use to neutralize anxiety, such as returning to the scene, checking the exterior of the car, and checking accident reports. When planning your exposure strategy, it's important to *not* repeat the same exposure activity in the same location on the same day, as that would allow you to check and reassure yourself that no accident occurred. Instead, do several different exposures in different locations during one session, starting with those at the bottom of your hierarchy. For fastest results, incorporate as many different triggers as possible into each session. The more discomfort you experience while also resisting the urge to check, the faster your progress will be.

Once your SUDS levels for the first set of triggers has reduced by half for three days in a row, move to items higher on your hierarchy, and proceed in this way until you've confronted all of your triggers and your overall SUDS level while driving is 20 or less.

Here's Robert's ERP plan for his hit-and-run OCD, followed by a blank form for your use. Make copies of the blank form so you can fine-tune your plan later or make a new plan, if need be.

Robert's Hit-and-Run ERP Planning Worksheet

Target intrusive thought: *What if I ran over someone or caused an accident without knowing it?*

Target compulsion: *Turning around and returning to the scene of the possible accident to check that nothing happened*

ERP strategy: *For the first week, practice daily exposures to items at the bottom of my hierarchy, with a SUDS level of 40 to 60, without turning around or checking in mirrors for reassurance. When my SUDS level for those items reduces by half, hopefully within a week, move to items higher up on the hierarchy—with SUDS levels of 60 to 80. Continue with this strategy until I've conquered all items on my list.*

How often (times per day or week): *Practice daily for three to four weeks—or as long as it takes.*

How long (minutes or hours) per exposure: *About one hour per session, fitting in as many different triggers as I can manage in one driving session.*

Target SUDS level: *20 or less whenever driving*

Avoidances to be stopped: *Stop avoiding driving near schools or near bicyclists, or in heavy traffic.*

Additional instructions: *Adjust all mirrors out of position for exposure sessions. Don't turn around or otherwise return to any location during an exposure session.*

Carrying Out Robert's Plan

Week 1, days 1-3: *Drive on residential side streets for 20 minutes, purposely blinking every minute or so. Turn on the radio and drive on a four-lane highway for 20 minutes, again blinking every minute or so. With the radio still on, drive through a different neighborhood for 20 minutes, still blinking every minute or so.*

Week 1, days 4-7: *In the afternoon, about the time school lets out, drive on a four-lane highway for 20 minutes, changing lanes every few minutes. While still driving on the highway for another 20 minutes, turn my head for a half second every couple of minutes. Then drive through a residential neighborhood for 20 minutes, continuing to turn my head every couple of minutes.*

Week 2, days 1-3: *Drive to an area with a lot of stores. For an hour, drive to different stores, get out of the car, and go into a store for a few minutes. Return to the car, back out, and drive away, to another store, without ever checking the car for signs that I hit someone.*

Week 2, days 4-7: *Drive by a couple of local schools during recess, just once, without turning around to check. Find some nearby roads with potholes or other damage and drive down those once without turning around to check. Find an apartment complex or neighborhood where I can drive over speed bumps.*

Week 3, days 1-3: *In the afternoon once kids are home from school, take half an hour to drive on streets near the university or near the bike path in the park. Spend the other half hour driving through a neighborhood with lots of kids who might be out riding their bikes.*

Week 3, days 4-7: *At about the time school lets out, drive around the local schools. Once I've driven by both schools, I could work on the bicycle exposures a bit more. I'll look for an opportunity to resist my urge to not follow police cars.*

Hit-and-Run ERP Planning Worksheet

Target intrusive thought: ______________________________

____

____

Target compulsion: ______________________________

____

____

ERP strategy: ______________________________

____

____

____

____

How often (times per day or week): ______________________________

____

How long (minutes or hours) per exposure: ______________________________

____

Target SUDS level: ______________________________

Avoidances to be stopped: ______________________________

____

Additional instructions: ______________________________

____

____

Carrying Out the Plan

Week 1, days 1-3: ______________________________

____

____

Week 1, days 4-7: ______________________________

____

____

Week 2, days 1-3: ______________________________

____

____

Week 2, days 4-7: ______________________________

____

____

Week 3, days 1-3: ______________________________

____

____

Week 3, days 4-7: ______________________________

____

____

Step 4. Use Imaginal Exposure to Assist in Habituation

Because hit-and-run OCD involves hyperresponsibility and obsessional ideas about being responsible for causing awful things to happen in the future, it's a good idea to use imaginal exposure to enhance your real-life ERP practice. We highly recommend that you employ this approach. Turn back to chapter 7 for full details on imaginal exposure. In that chapter, you'll find an example of Robert's imaginal exposure for hit-and-run OCD, which may help you in devising your own narrative. Once you have a vivid, cohesive narrative, follow the instructions in chapter 7 for using your narrative to conduct imaginal exposure.

REALISTIC SELF-TALK FOR HIT-AND-RUN OCD

In breaking free from hit-and-run OCD, you may find it helpful to use realistic self-talk to challenge your unrealistic anxiety-provoking thoughts. (If you need a refresher on this approach, see chapter 8.) Here are some examples of typical OCD thoughts related to driving, with more accurate appraisals for each.

Self-Talk Strategies to Deal with Intrusive Thoughts and Urges to Check

Intrusive thought	**Realistic self-talk**
I can't stand it if I don't check.	*I can resist the magnetic pull of the urge to check.* *If I just wait, the urge will reduce to manageable levels.*
Maybe I hit or ran over someone. I'll surely go to jail.	*It's just my OCD brain giving me false messages.* *It's just ghosts and goblins—they look real, but they aren't.*
I'll have to give in and check later.	*If I check, it will only make my OCD worse.* *Instead of checking, I can do something different now.*

Keys to Breaking Free from Hit-and-Run OCD

- When doing ERP for hit-and-run OCD, expect your compulsions to be very strong at the beginning. The urge to check or turn around will probably be powerful, and you're likely to feel worse for a while before you start feeling better. With repeated ERP practice, the urges will lessen over time. Persistence and resistance are the keys.
- It's helpful to use props to simulate the actual sensation of hitting or driving over a large object. You can use twenty-five-pound sacks of concrete mix, sand, or mulch or a two-by-four to simulate driving over bumps in the road. To simulate hitting a body, use a padded department store mannequin or a rolled-up piece of heavy carpet. Have a friend or helper toss the mannequin or carpet at the car while it's moving to simulate the feeling of the car hitting a heavy object.
- If the urge to check or perform another compulsion is too strong during your exposures, move to items that are lower on your hierarchy and work to master those first, before trying the more challenging exposures.
- Beware of overly relying on safety signals such as rearview mirrors, which enable you to easily see behind you to check that no harm was done. As you work your way up your hierarchy, place your mirrors purposefully out of position to activate more discomfort. Other safety behaviors include driving way under the speed limit or having a "witness" in the car—a person you rely on for reassurance that no accident happened.

THE ROLE OF HYPERRESPONSIBILITY

Hit-and-run OCD is similar to other types of OCD problems that involve hyperresponsibility, such as scrupulosity and checking compulsions intended to prevent harm and danger to others. At the heart of hyperresponsibility is the feeling of a dark cloud always hanging overhead, as though if you aren't constantly on guard, disaster could strike at any moment, you'll be held responsible, and life will turn into a horror show of perpetual guilt and suffering.

Because driving is an activity that places you in a machine well-known to potentially inflict pain and death, it's a perfect breeding ground for hyperresponsibility. Progress with hit-and-run OCD, and all types of OCD that involve hyperresponsibility, requires accepting the risks inherent in living life fully. Fear and an excessive need to control events can prevent you from being fully in charge of your life. Only by letting go of the need for control do we truly gain the freedom to choose how to live our lives.

HELP FOR FAMILY AND FRIENDS

Hit-and-run OCD can affect the entire family. Because people with this form of OCD typically resist driving, you may have gradually taken on more family responsibilities. Are you taking your children to school and picking them up when your spouse once did? Or perhaps you have a friend with OCD who asks you to take him or her to the grocery store, or who asks you to go along as a passenger and then frequently seeks reassurance about possible driving mishaps. While it may seem helpful, agreeing to help by doing any of these only reinforces the person's avoidance of driving and maintains the OCD. Repeatedly answering such questions as "Did I hit something?" or "Should I go back and check?" to reduce your loved one's worries will only deepen the problem and delay recovery. Discuss a timetable for decreasing and eventually eliminating enabling behaviors. As always, let your loved one "take the driver's seat" in the recovery process by dictating the pace at which reassurance will be withdrawn.

CHAPTER 13

Health Anxiety: Hypochondriasis

Life is either a daring adventure or nothing. Security is mostly a superstition. It does not exist in nature.

—Helen Keller

Health anxiety, or hypochondriasis, is defined as an obsessive preoccupation with fears of having a serious disease—a preoccupation that persists despite repeated reassurance from medical professionals that the person is physically healthy. Here are some examples of hypochondriasis:

- Juan repeatedly checks his lymph nodes for signs of swelling. He has read that swollen lymph nodes in patients with advanced cancer can indicate a life-threatening metastasis of the cancer. As a result of his repeated checking, the lymph nodes in his neck are swollen, and Juan considers this to be evidence that he may have cancer.
- Every morning, Monique, a university professor, takes over an hour to check her body for unusual moles and lesions. She's convinced that she must check to ensure that she has no symptoms of skin cancer. At times, she demands that her partner check her skin as she doesn't trust that she will detect a suspicious mole.
- A close friend of Bob's was recently diagnosed with multiple sclerosis. Now Bob goes for a full physical and neurological examination every three months in order to reassure

himself that he doesn't have multiple sclerosis. His doctors have repeatedly told him that the exams are unnecessary and that he is perfectly healthy.

The "bible of psychiatry," the *Diagnostic and Statistical Manual of Mental Disorders* (American Psychiatric Association 2000), classifies hypochondriasis as a somatoform disorder, meaning a psychological disorder characterized by physical complaints for which there appears to be no physiological cause. However, many people with hypochondriasis display symptoms that have a great deal in common with OCD. They experience obsessions (intrusive, unwanted thoughts that provoke feelings of anxiety and dread), in this case related to fears of having an illness. Here are some typical obsessions in hypochondriasis:

- What if I'm sick from an undiagnosed fatal illness, or will get sick from some dreaded disease in the future?
- What if the doctor missed some key sign of a disease that can be fatal?

People with hypochondriasis also engage in compulsions (repetitive, unnecessary actions that are taken to relieve the anxiety or dread). These compulsions are triggered by the obsessive health concerns and are meant to relieve the anxiety or dread associated with those thoughts. Here are some typical compulsions in hypochondriasis:

- Repeatedly checking the body for signs of disease
- Repeatedly asking doctors or loved ones for reassurance that no disease exists
- Going for repeated medical consultations and tests to confirm that no disease exists
- Repeatedly checking additional sources of medical information on Internet websites (cyberchondriasis) such as www.webmd.com, www.healthline.com, or www.easydiagnosis.com

UNDERSTANDING HYPOCHONDRIASIS: A COGNITIVE BEHAVIORAL PERSPECTIVE

Let's take a look at hypochondriasis using the cognitive behavioral model of OCD discussed earlier in this book. This model can help you better understand how the symptoms are sustained and what you can do to get them under control:

A = Activating event (in this case, usually a bodily sensation)

↓

B = Faulty belief about the dangerousness of the activating event

↓

C = Emotional consequences: anxiety, doubt, and worry in response to the faulty belief

↓

D = A neutralizing ritual: an action taken to relieve the fear, distress, or worry (checking one's body, asking others for reassurance, going for unnecessary medical tests, and so on)

In hypochondriasis, this process repeats over and over again because the net effect of these actions increases the likelihood that another activating bodily sensation or thought will soon occur. The sequence becomes a vicious cycle that locks the person in a pattern of worry and distress that can seriously interfere with normal life. Let's now look more closely at the model.

A = Activating Event

The model starts with the idea that that the human body is "noisy"—that even healthy people experience, on a daily or weekly basis, bodily sensations that are mild, transient, and not associated with any serious disease but could be interpreted as symptoms. Here are some examples of benign or harmless bodily sensations:

- Dizziness, faintness, or a rapid heartbeat from not eating for a long time
- A rapid heartbeat from eating a meal rich in carbohydrates
- Arm and joint discomfort from sitting or standing in one position for a long time
- Stomach pain from overeating or indigestion
- A headache from being out in the sun too long
- Muscle pain after a lengthy workout

Clearly, our "noisy" bodies generate a variety of bodily sensations and experiences. For those who don't have hypochondriasis, these typically cause little psychological distress or worry and can be dismissed relatively easily.

In the following space (or in your journal), list the bodily sensations or symptoms that activate your fear and worry. Indicate which ones contribute most to your fear with notations such as +, ++ (more), and +++ (even more):

____

____

____

____

____

B = Faulty Belief

Problems arise if you begin to interpret those harmless bodily sensations to mean that something is seriously wrong with you. Here are some of the categories of faulty beliefs commonly involved in hypochondriasis, with examples of each:

Black-and-White or All-or-Nothing-Thinking

- Bodily complaints are always a sign of disease.
- I'm only sure I'm healthy if I don't have any uncomfortable bodily sensations.
- Unless I'm absolutely sure that there is nothing wrong, I must assume the very worst.

Persistent Doubting

- Doctors can't be trusted because they often make mistakes.
- Just because my doctor says I'm healthy doesn't mean I am. My doctor could be missing something.

Catastrophizing

- I have a headache. I must have a brain tumor.
- My back aches. I must have bone cancer.

Intolerance of Uncertainty

- I must have 100 percent proof that I'm not ill, otherwise I'm probably sick.
- I must frequently check my body and watch my health carefully in order to catch the first signs of serious illness.
- If I stop thinking about my health, even for a short time, it's dangerous.

Superstitious Thinking

- If I tell myself I'm healthy, I'm tempting fate.
- The coincidence of seeing a TV show about herpes at the very same time that I'm worrying about it is an omen that I probably have it.
- Worrying about my health will keep me safe.

Emotional Reasoning

- There must be something terribly wrong with me; otherwise I wouldn't be feeling so anxious.

Think about your own beliefs about illness. In the following space (or in your journal), list some the faulty beliefs and cognitive errors that may be contributing to your fear, doubt, and worry in regard to illness. Indicate which ones contribute most to your fear with notations such as +, ++ (more), and +++ (even more):

____

____

____

____

____

C = Emotional Consequences: Anxiety, Doubt, and Worry

The combination of A (an activating event) and B (a faulty belief) triggers a strong emotional response of fear, dread, doubt, and worry, and with it a laserlike focus on those bodily symptoms or sensations. These fears demand a great deal of attention on a daily basis.

In the following chart, list the "symptoms" that you tend to focus on, then, in the right-hand column assign a SUDS rating (0 to 100) to your degree of distress.

Feared "symptom"	**SUDS level (0-100)**

D = Neutralizing Ritual or Avoidance

In all likelihood, you probably engage in neutralizing rituals in response to the fear, distress, and worry that arise as a consequence of your faulty beliefs about physical sensations, illness, and health. Here are some common forms of these maladaptive behaviors and compulsions:

Medical Reassurance Seeking

- Repeatedly asking others, especially doctors, for reassurance that you aren't seriously ill
- Searching the Internet for disease-related information to rule out the possibility that you have a fatal illness (cyberchondriasis)

Excessive Body Checking

- Examining one's body for "suspicious" signs; for example, looking for moles, palpating the body for an enlarged liver or lymph glands, or repeated swallowing to check for throat cancer
- Insisting on unnecessary medical tests and procedures

Using Safety Signals (unnecessary items used to alleviate disease-related anxiety)

- Wearing an unnecessary medical alert bracelet
- Always keeping an EpiPen nearby to dispel fears of anaphylaxis
- Programming your cell phone to speed dial doctor's offices or 911
- Purchasing portable medical equipment such as a defibrillator

Avoiding Disease-Related Situations

- Avoiding hospitals and people who "look sick"
- Avoiding homeless people on the street
- Not giving blood
- Not undergoing standard or necessary medical tests and exams

All of these strategies are designed to relieve fear, doubt, and worry. However, studies of people with health-related anxiety have concluded that rather than allaying fears, these behaviors have the unintended effect of reinforcing faulty appraisals and perpetuating health anxiety (Salkovskis and Warwick 1986; Slavney 1987). They do so by intensifying your focus on illness and exposing you to further alarming medical information.

In the following space (or in your journal), list neutralizing or compulsive behaviors you engage in to seek reassurance, check for symptoms or signs of illness, utilize safety signals, or avoid disease-related situations. Indicate the ones you use most often with a notation such as +++.

Medical reassurance seeking: ______________________________

____

____

Excessive checking for signs of illness: ______________________________

____

____

Use of safety signals: ______________________________

____

____

Avoidance of disease-related situations: ______________________________

____

____

CHALLENGING YOUR FAULTY BELIEFS

Now that you've analyzed the components of your health-related anxiety, you can start working on getting your fears under control. According to the model outlined at the beginning of this chapter, hypochondriasis is perpetuated, in part, by the inability to generate believable, alternative explanations for health-related fears. The person jumps to catastrophic conclusions, either ignoring or discounting plausible alternative explanations.

The following worksheet will help you actively dispute your beliefs. First you'll cite the evidence both for and against a belief. Then you'll come up with some coping self-talk to help you counter the faulty belief. Make several copies of this exercise so that you can challenge a variety of health-related concerns. (You can also do this exercise in your journal.) If you need help getting started, we've provided an example. You can also refer back to chapter 8 for more information on thought challenging and coping self-talk.

Challenging Your Faulty Health-Related Beliefs (Example)

Activating event: *I have a bad headache.*

Faulty belief (automatic irrational thought): *I must have a brain tumor.*

Discomfort (SUDS level: 0-100): *95*

How much do you believe this appraisal is true? (0-100%): *90*

Which categories of cognitive errors are at work here? (choose from the list above): *Catastrophizing, intolerance of uncertainty*

Evidence in support of the faulty belief: *I read on the Internet that a headache is the first sign of brain tumor. My aunt's niece, who complained of headaches, died of a brain tumor. People die every day because of ignoring their body's pain signals.*

Evidence against the faulty belief: *I'm healthy overall. Based on numerous tests, doctors have assured me that I don't have a tumor. When I'm busy taking care of my baby, I don't get caught up in this idea. The people who care most for me don't seem concerned.*

Realistic appraisal or coping self-talk: *My pain is most likely just a tension headache. I've had a lot on my plate lately, and I have a history of headaches when I'm under stress.*

How much do you now believe this appraisal is true? (0-100%): *70*

Challenging Your Faulty Health-Related Beliefs

Activating event: ____

____

Faulty belief (automatic irrational thought): ________________________

____

Discomfort (SUDS level: 0-100): ______________________________

How much do you believe this appraisal is true? (0-100%): __________

Which categories of cognitive errors are at work here? (choose from the list above)

____

____

____

Evidence in support of the faulty belief: ________________________

____

____

Evidence against the faulty belief: ____________________________

____

____

Realistic appraisal or coping self-talk: __________________________

____

____

How much do you now believe this appraisal is true? (0-100%): _________

EXPOSURE AND RESPONSE PREVENTION FOR HEALTH-RELATED ANXIETY

Exposure and response prevention can be very helpful in health-related anxiety that has strong avoidance and ritualistic elements (Visser and Bouman 2001). As you'll recall from chapter 6, the key to ERP is to intentionally confront situations that arouse anxiety, allowing you to habituate to these situations and find new ways of responding. Here are some examples of typical health-related avoidance behaviors. These are the types of behaviors you'll want to target in your ERP plan:

Cancer-Related Avoidance

- Avoiding movies with actors who have died of cancer
- Avoiding writing or reading words with the letters "C-A-N" in sequence
- Avoiding hospitals that have cancer wards
- Avoiding books, TV programs, or movies about cancer

HIV/AIDS-Related Avoidance

- Avoiding walking around in the "gay" part of town
- Avoiding contact with homeless people
- Avoiding TV programs and magazine articles related to HIV and AIDS
- Avoiding writing or reading words with the letters "H-I-V" or "A-I-D-S" in sequence

Herpes-Related Avoidance

- Avoiding using public toilets
- Excessive hand washing when using public restrooms
- Worrying excessively about coming too close to people's mouths when they speak

Avoidance Related to Fear of Death

- Discarding the section of the newspaper that has the obituaries
- Avoiding driving by cemeteries
- Avoiding going to funerals or discussions of making out a will

Creating an Anxiety/Exposure Hierarchy

The procedures for conducting ERP described in chapter 6 will be equally effective here. As a reminder, self-directed exposure treatment is best conducted in steps. First, draw up a list of everyday situations that cause you health-related anxiety and doubt. Include a variety of situations that cause anxiety levels ranging from moderate to extreme. Assign SUDS ratings to these items based on the amount of anxiety the situation would provoke *if you were to not carry out any compulsions or employ any of your safety signals*. Arrange the items by SUDS level, from lowest to highest. Here's a sample anxiety/exposure hierarchy for anxiety related to multiple sclerosis, followed by a blank form for you to fill out.

Health-related anxiety/exposure hierarchy (example)	**SUDS level (0-100)**
Shaking hands with an MS patient without wearing gloves	100
Shaking hands with an MS patient while wearing gloves	95
Sitting on an empty hospital bed in a ward that treats neurological disorders, without barriers	90
Touching a sign on an MS clinic door without wearing gloves	85
Touching a sign on an MS clinic door while wearing gloves	75
Sitting in a hospital waiting room where patients with MS sit, without wearing gloves	70
Sitting in a hospital waiting room where patients with MS sit, wearing protective latex gloves	65
Touching photos of patients with MS in a magazine article	60
Reading a magazine article about deaths due to MS	50

Health-related anxiety/exposure hierarchy	SUDS level (0-100)

Now that you've developed your hierarchy, the next step is to carry out exposure exercises either alone or with a support person. See chapter 6 for more detailed instructions on how to carry out your own ERP plan. Remember, for exposure exercises to be optimally effective, it's important to do the exposure fully, without distracting yourself or blocking the experience. A sense of risk and uncertainty is necessary to help raise your anxiety levels as high as you can handle during any given exposure. As mentioned earlier, most people can handle much more discomfort than they think they can, so really go for it!

Response Prevention

Exposure is important, but it isn't enough. Remember, ERP stands for exposure and *response prevention*, so you'll also need to make a conscious effort to *not* engage in behaviors you typically use to reduce your uncertainty or worry. Examples include seeking reassurance from doctors, searching the Internet for proof that you don't have a dreaded disease, excessive washing or disinfecting, excessively checking your body for signs of illness, and excessive use of barriers such as latex gloves and masks. If incorporating response prevention into exposure practice seems too difficult, take it in stages, as in the example above, where eliminating the safety signal of wearing latex gloves was always a second step. However, responses such as seeking medical reassurance should be done in one fell swoop, if possible. If this prospect is too threatening, you can take a more gradual approach, as long as you completely eliminate the behavior as soon as possible.

Keep in mind that the goal of ERP is not to achieve total relief from anxiety in the situations that typically provoke your fear; rather, the goal is to change your beliefs about the dangerousness of the situation from something like "I can't tolerate this, and the only way to be perfectly safe is to avoid anything that feels unsafe" to something more like "I can handle the uncertainty of not knowing for sure. I'm not afraid to be anxious." Achieving this takes patience and persistence. We suggest that you do at least one exposure per day, lasting fifteen minutes to an hour, for two to three weeks. You can use the Daily Exposure Practice Monitoring Form in chapter 6 to keep track of your exposure practices. You can also keep track of this information in your journal.

THE EFFECT OF ATTENTION

People with health anxiety tend to be highly vigilant for changes in their bodily sensations and symptoms. Studies of people with health-related anxiety have shown that the more attention a person directs toward the body, the more intense the sensations they perceive will be (Mechanic 1983; Pennebaker 1980). In addition, a persistent focus on physical sensations may increase the likelihood of detecting these sensations. We've all had the experience of itching, yawning, or coughing when someone nearby itches, yawns, or coughs. In such cases, our attention is drawn to a sensation that we previously ignored. Conversely, the more externally focused we are, the less likely we are to notice our "noisy" bodily sensations. A classic example is football players who are so focused on the game that injuries sustained on the field go unnoticed until later. Here are some quick experiments you can do that will demonstrate how attentional focus can increase your experience of bodily sensations:

- Focus intently on the sensations on your fingertips. Keep focusing until you notice feelings and sensations there. It's likely that you'll notice sensations that you weren't aware of just a moment ago.
- Focus completely upon sensations in your throat, noticing any itchiness or dryness. As you continue to focus, you may feel the need to cough or clear your throat.
- Focus your attention on an area of your body that's distant from an area that concerns you, and stay focused on that area for a few minutes. Notice how your focus on the new area might have changed the sensations in the area you're concerned about.

INCREASING ATTENTIONAL FLEXIBILITY

People with health anxiety are often advised to just stop paying attention to the bodily sensations they worry about. This is good advice. However, as everyone who has health anxiety knows, it's very difficult to shift attention away from the fear-provoking thoughts and bodily sensations. Making this attentional shift requires flexibility. The following exercise can be extremely helpful in developing this flexibility.

Attention Training

Attention training, developed by British psychologist Adrian Wells (1997), can help reduce health anxiety by redirecting your attention. The following script is designed to help you increase your ability to redirect your attention. Make an audio recording of the script in your own voice, or ask a family member, a friend, or your therapist to record it for you. The narrator should speak in a soft, calm voice with a measured pace. The narrator will need to tap a table or other surface where indicated in the script. You'll need to practice in a room with a ticking clock. If that isn't possible, have the narrator substitute another environmental sound, in the third paragraph. Depending on where you practice, the narrator may need to substitute other sounds toward the end of the script.

> *I am now going to ask you to focus your gaze on a dot marked on the wall for a few seconds (wait about 10 seconds). That's good. I would like to begin by asking you to focus upon the sound of my voice. Pay close attention to that sound, as if no other sound matters. Try to give your entire attention to the sound of my voice. Ignore all of the other sounds around you. Focus only on the sound of my voice. No other sound matters... Just focus only on the sound of my voice.*
>
> *Now, while still gazing at the dot on the wall, focus your ears on the sound of me tapping on the table. Focus only on the tapping sound, as no other sound matters* (pause). *Closely monitor the tapping sound* (pause). *If your attention begins to stray or is captured by any other sounds, refocus all of your attention on this one sound* (pause). *Give all of your attention to this sound* (pause). *Focus on the tapping sound and monitor this sound closely, filtering out all of the competing sounds, for they are not important now* (pause). *Continue to monitor the tapping sound* (pause) *and keep all of your focus and attention on that sound. If you find yourself distracted, that's okay... Bring yourself gently back to paying attention to that sound* (pause).
>
> *Now, while still gazing at the dot, focus on the sound of the clock ticking in the room. Focus all of your attention on that sound* (pause) *as no other sounds matters. Focus on that sound, paying close attention to it and not allowing yourself to be distracted* (pause). *This is the most important sound and no other sounds matter* (pause). *Give all of your attention to that sound. If your attention strays, refocus on the sound of the ticking clock* (pause). *Focus only on this sound, giving it all of your attention* (pause). *Continue to monitor that sound closely, paying full attention to it* (pause). *If you find yourself distracted, again, gently bring yourself back to paying attention to that sound.*
>
> (The above instructions should be repeated for at least three more sounds in the near distance; for example, sounds of people in the hall, the sound of traffic outside, the sounds of the ventilation system, birds chirping, and so on.)

Now that you have identified and focused upon different sounds, I would like you to rapidly shift your attention between the different sounds as I call them out (pause). *First focus on the tapping sound, as if no other sound matters. Give all of your attention to that sound* (pause). *Now focus on the sound of the ventilation system, paying attention only to that sound* (pause). *Now switch your attention and focus to the sound of traffic outside. Focus only on that sound as if no other sound matters... Now* (picking up the pace) *switch your attention to the sound of my voice* (pause). *Now refocus on the sound of the traffic outside* (pause); *and now back to the tapping sound* (pause). *Now the sound of the ventilation system; now focus back on the tapping sound... Now the sound of the traffic* (pause), *now the sound of the ventilation system...now the sound of my voice...* (and so on, continuing for about three minutes).

Finally, expand your attention, making it as broad and deep as possible and try to absorb all of the sounds both within and outside the room all at the same time (pause). *Count the number of sounds that you can hear at the same time* (pause). *Try to hear all of the sounds simultaneously. Count the number of sounds that you hear at the same time.*

This concludes the exercise. How many sounds were you aware of at the same time?

The goal of this exercise is *not* to rid you of your anxiety. Rather it is intended to help you increase your control over what you pay attention to and thereby enable you to develop more accurate beliefs about your physical symptoms. Try practicing this for 15 minutes per day, twice each day, for several days. At the end of each session, note the date and time that you did the exercise in your journal or in the space below. In addition, rate the degree to which you were able to achieve a state of external focus on a scale ranging from –3 to +3, where –3 means entirely internally focused and +3 means entirely externally focused.

To further expand upon the training, you can creatively incorporate other sense modalities as the focus of your shifting attention. For example, you can use various fragrances and scents as the focus of your attention. Or try tasting small samples of different foods or experiencing various tactile sensations using fabrics of various degrees of smoothness and coarseness. The goal here is to find ways to "get external." With practice, you'll greatly enhance your capacity to break free from the stranglehold of body-focused worry and fear.

HELP FOR FAMILY AND FRIENDS

If your loved one suffers with anxiety-related bodily sensations, it's important for you to recognize that the discomfort he or she is feeling is real. Don't dismiss complaints by saying things like, "It's all in your head" or "Your stomach can't be hurting because the tests all came back negative." To some degree, all pain is "in your head," as different people perceive similar pain differently. We all have our own unique nervous system pathways and mental filters through which we perceive the sensations we call "pain." So it's important not to discount your loved one's discomfort just because no medical cause has been found.

While you shouldn't dismiss complaints, it isn't a good idea to give them undue attention, either. There may be times when your loved one will ask you to help with body checking (checking for signs of skin cancer, for example) or seeking medical care. Have a discussion with your loved one to decide together on an appropriate response. Here are some examples of how you might respond to future requests:

- You asked me not to check spots anymore, so it's best that I not do it.
- You'll have to decide whether to go to the doctor or not. I'm no good for you if I keep feeding your fears.
- I know your stomach hurts. How about helping me with the dishes, and later on we can do something (e.g., go to the gym, take a walk, play a card game, call Grandma).

You may be helping your loved one with the attention training exercise by narrating the script on page 230. As you join your loved on in becoming more skilled in "getting external," you can be creative by suggesting more varied, unusual sounds, tastes of food, smells, and textures. Make a game out of seeing how many different and varied sensory experiences you can focus upon and pay attention to in the course of a day! You will find that this simple, even fun exercise in purposeful attention shifting can do a lot to lessen the overall focus upon bodily symptoms and their accompanying fears and worries.

CHAPTER 14

Hoarding OCD: When You Have Too Much Stuff

By perseverance, the snail reached the ark.

—Charles Haddon Spurgeon

Compulsive hoarding is a widely recognized symptom of OCD. It is defined as acquiring and failing to discard possessions that appear to be useless or of limited value (Frost and Gross 1993). While everyone is familiar with someone whom they consider a pack rat or chronic saver, people with hoarding OCD are distinguished by the sheer quantity of objects collected, and by their strong emotional attachment to items most would clearly consider useless. The objects hoarded can be almost anything, but often include such things as newspapers, clothing, foodstuffs, books, papers, junk mail, and old appliances. One person with hoarding OCD aptly described her apartment as "something between a wastebasket and a suitcase" (Greist and Jefferson 1995, 3).

People with hoarding OCD seem to overvalue these objects and therefore develop an excessive attachment to them that prevents them from discarding the objects. Often, the rationale is "What if

I need it in the future? I'd better not throw it out." Meanwhile, piles of clutter rise to the ceiling and only a little space is left for walkways. Navigating through the cluttered home of a person with hoarding OCD can be challenging.

Estimates of hoarding behaviors range from 18 to 31 percent of all people with OCD (Damecour and Charron 1998; Frost and Steketee 1998), with the onset occurring most often when people are in their early twenties (Greenberg 1987). It appears to affect both genders equally. Although many theories exist about the cause of hoarding, for years psychologists have theorized that compulsive hoarding develops from a perfectionist effort to control the environment (Salzman 1973).

People with hoarding OCD are often extremely resistant to changing this behavior. They tend to ignore the impact it has on themselves and others and see their hoarding as necessary to feel in control of their lives. When the clutter becomes intolerable or health hazards develop, family members may make an effort to remove some of the clutter. The person with hoarding OCD may react to this with intense anger and threats of violence, prompting an emergency situation. Should a move from the property become inevitable, it is likely that the hoarding will only continue in the new environment.

Five features generally characterize people with hoarding OCD: indecisiveness, categorization problems, faulty beliefs about memory, excessive emotional attachment to possessions, and excessive need to feel in control of their possessions (Frost and Steketee 1998). Let's look at how these traits tend to manifest.

Indecisiveness. The simplest decisions of everyday life, such as what to wear in the morning, what to eat for dinner, and where to take a vacation, are troublesome for compulsive hoarders. This indecisiveness appears to be related to a perfectionist fear of making mistakes. Hoarding useless objects may therefore be a means of avoiding making bad decisions or decisions that may be regretted later. By hoarding even seemingly useless objects, the person avoids any potential regrets or pain over not having these objects (Frost and Steketee 1998).

Categorization problems. People with hoarding OCD have difficulty sorting objects into categories that would determine if they're useful or not. Each object seems as important and vital as any other. A gum wrapper may have as much importance as a recent tax return. Decisions about keeping or discarding objects become exceedingly complicated by the person's inability to differentiate between what is truly valuable and what is not.

Faulty beliefs about memory. People with hoarding OCD typically display obsessional concerns about the reliability of their memory, even though there's little objective evidence of this. They fear that their "faulty" memory will prevent them from having access to all of their possessions. This lack of confidence in their memory renders compulsive hoarders reluctant to put items away and out of sight for fear they will be forgotten. Therefore, useless objects are everywhere within sight in the person's home, contributing to the extreme clutter.

Excessive emotional attachment to possessions. People with hoarding OCD regard their stuff as part of themselves. They attach much more sentiment to objects than nonhoarders do, and they find an extreme degree of emotional comfort in their possessions (Frost and Gross 1993). Taking great delight in things also results in a marked tendency toward excessive purchasing, or shopaholic behavior.

Excessive need to feel in control of ownership. People with hoarding OCD have an exaggerated need to feel in control of their possessions to protect the items from harm or irresponsible use. Hence, they feel extreme discomfort or even feel personally violated if the objects are touched or moved by anyone else.

SELF-DIRECTED PROGRAM FOR HOARDING OCD

For some people, hoarding is the major symptom of OCD, and it can be so severe that it greatly interferes with maintaining healthy living standards. More commonly, hoarding is just one more type of OCD symptom. Either way, the self-directed program for hoarding OCD can help you break free from hoarding. Because the solution is partly logistical, there are more steps than in many of the other self-directed programs in this book, but all of the steps are straightforward:

1. Set a realistic goal that you're willing to achieve.
2. Assess your hoarding problem.
3. Put a moratorium on all accumulating.
4. Develop an organization plan for your home.
5. Decide where to start.
6. Establish a few simple rules for placing, storing, and discarding, and *stick to them.*
7. Pace yourself.
8. When an area is cleared, decide how the cleared space is to be used.

Step 1. Set a Realistic Goal That You're Willing to Achieve

Most often, people with hoarding OCD feel overwhelmed at the idea of getting rid of their collected stuff and therefore resist doing so. If you feel this way, instead of thinking that you must get rid of most of your possessions, start small and set more realistic goals. A good place to start is to commit to becoming less indecisive and making your living space better organized and less cluttered.

Step 2. Assess Your Hoarding Problem

The following questions (adapted from Frost and Steketee 1998) will help you gain a better understanding of your hoarding problem. You can also write your answers in your journal if you like.

How much of the house is cluttered? Which rooms?

____

How much discomfort does the problem cause you?

____

How much discomfort does it cause your family members?

____

How severe would you say the clutter problem is (very bad, somewhat bad, not too bad)?

____

What types of items do you save?

____

For each type of item, what are your reasons for saving it?

____

____

____

____

Do you have any form of organization for the stuff in your home? How do you decide what item goes where?

____

How does the problem affect your relationships with family members?

____

____

____

____

Step 3. Put a Moratorium on All Accumulating

For the duration of time you are working on the self-directed program for hoarding, temporarily suspend accumulating all but the most essential items for your household. This will help you see progress more quickly and enhance your success in gaining control over your hoarding problem.

According to psychologist April Benson (2008), most instances of compulsive shopping arise out of a need or impulse to replace uncomfortable, unwanted internal experiences such as anger, anxiety, depression, or boredom, or in response to stress, loss, or trauma. Shopping can provide a soothing sense of being in control when circumstances in life are out of control. While compulsive shopping is a complex problem with numerous factors contributing to it, the following steps can help you overcome the problem:

1. Identify the key triggers that contribute to your vulnerability to compulsive shopping. These may be situations, thoughts, or emotions.

2. Challenge the faulty beliefs that underlie your compulsive shopping.

3. Learn alternative, healthier means of handling your triggers.

4. Repeatedly practice behaviors other than shopping in response to your triggers.

5. Develop "mindful" shopping skills as an alternative to impulsive shopping.

Step 4. Develop an Organization Plan for Your Home

Using the following worksheet, make a plan for how you intend to use the space in all of the areas of your home. Use the blank rows to add any areas not listed in the worksheet. For each space, write down exactly how it is presently being used. Then estimate approximately what percent of the usable space is presently cluttered. In the fourth column, indicate how you'd like to use each space (for example, to entertain guests, watch TV, or eat meals). In the fifth column, indicate your goal for the amount of clutter allowed in that room. Be sure to include ample areas for storage in your plan.

Organizational Plan

Area of home	How is it presently used?	How cluttered? (% of usable space)	Goal for use	
			Function	% Clutter
Living room				
Kitchen				
Dining room				
Family room				
Master bedroom				
Second bedroom				
Third bedroom				
Hallway				
Closet, master bedroom				
Closet, second bedroom				
Closet, third bedroom				
Closet, hallway				
Bathroom				
Garage				

Step 5. Decide Where to Start

The decision about where to start can be hard. One of the best places to start is in an area where uncluttering will provide a high degree of satisfaction, such as the kitchen table or your entryway. This will make your initial efforts more rewarding. Another way to start is to pick a type of item that you have many of in one small area, such as books, clothing, or types of papers, and work only on that type of item first. Since it's easier to sort and store large groups of similar objects, the job will go faster and provide satisfaction more quickly.

Step 6. Establish Rules for Placing, Storing, and Discarding

Place three empty large boxes in the area you'll work on. Label one box "Store," the next box "Sell" or "Donate," and the third box "Discard." ("Store" items refers to things that you currently use.) One helpful rule for uncluttering is to only handle an item once (Frost and Steketee 1998). This means that once you've touched an item or picked it up, you can't return it to the clutter pile. It *must* be placed in one of the three boxes.

Because discarding causes the most anxiety, you may find it helpful to have a rule for what to discard. We recommend that if you don't have a specific use for the object now (including displaying it) and you don't foresee a specific use for the object in the next six months, discard it. Keep only items that you know for a fact have a distinct function within your home.

To help with the anxiety associated with getting rid of possessions, start by discarding items that provoke the least anxiety. Assign a SUDS rating (0 to 100) to your level of discomfort when you discard items in a specific area. First discard the items that provoke the lowest SUDS scores, say less than 40. Then move to more anxiety-provoking items, with SUDS levels ranging from 40 up to 80. Finally, discard items with a SUDS level higher than 80. If discarding an item is too distressing, place it in the "Store" box. But be sure to find a place to store the "Store" box!

Perhaps you feel paralyzed by the fear of making a mistake. You may feel that you will mistakenly discard something you could use later. Ask yourself, "What's the worst that could happen if I never saw this object again?" Chances are, after some initial discomfort you'll forget you discarded it. It's helpful to make a distinction between what you feel you'd use and what you know for a fact will be used for a distinct purpose within the next six months. Basing your decision on what you feel you may use someday will only perpetuate your hoarding problem; in most cases, "someday" never comes. A helpful change would be to base your decision on the facts only, and to keep this saying in mind: When in doubt, throw it out!

Remember, your goal is to create usable living space, not a museum of past memories. If you have a particular attachment to an item that takes up too much space or that you can't find a place for, consider selling or donating it. Donating it will give you the satisfaction of knowing that someone else can enjoy it as you have. If the item is useless to everyone but you, remember that letting go of it doesn't erase it from memory. The memory will always be there. The clutter resulting from that item (and all the other items) is something you truly don't need.

Step 7. Pace Yourself

Don't overdo it. This is a marathon, not a sprint. Don't wear yourself out. Try the "30-30 system": First, identify a small area that you would like to work on—for instance, the sofa seats, the corner of a room, or the kitchen table. Set a kitchen timer for thirty minutes, and then work on the area for that period of time. At the end of the thirty minutes, do something fun or relaxing for the next thirty minutes. Play games on the computer, cross-stitch, play with your children, or enjoy a cup of coffee and read a magazine.

Then set your timer and continue uncluttering for another thirty minutes. Continue in this way until the area is uncluttered. Your on again, off again time frame need not be 30-30, but any ratio that works well for you. You might unclutter for fifteen minutes then take a five-minute break, unclutter for five minutes and take a five-minute break, or even unclutter for just five minutes before taking a thirty-minute break. Work at it daily, but plan to take a day off every few days so you have a break to look forward to. Reward yourself when you get over a big hurdle—but be sure that the reward doesn't involve obtaining a new possession!

Step 8. When an Area Is Cleared, Decide How the Space Is to Be Used

Once you've cleared an area, use the plan you developed in step 4 to decide the best use for the space. Is it to be used for work? Relaxation? Sleep? Entertainment? Storage? Decoration? Then set up the area for its intended use. If you can't decide how to use it, it's fine to delay the decision until you know how you'd like to use it. But be sure to not clutter the area again! Establish a "no clutter" rule for this space in case you're tempted to clutter the area again, and stick to it!

Keys to Breaking Free from Hoarding

- During each uncluttering session, stay focused on one small area. Don't move into another area until you've completed the area you started. This way, you're more likely to see the positive effects of your efforts.
- If it isn't overly distracting, you can play soothing background music while uncluttering. This can make the job seem to go faster.
- Severe hoarding behavior is associated with a number of neurological and psychiatric disorders in addition to OCD (Damecour and Charron 1998). If you don't make progress with the self-directed program, obtain a thorough evaluation from a qualified neurologist or psychiatrist. Based on the results, a treatment program tailored to your specific hoarding problem can be developed.

UNCLUTTERING WILL HELP YOU MAXIMIZE USABLE LIVING SPACE

Set realistic goals, and then challenge yourself to go a step further each day. Discarding items will cause anxiety, but you'll find that the anxiety and distress will decrease a great deal over time. In the unlikely event that you find you need an item you've discarded, you'll probably discover that it can easily be replaced. This will increase your confidence. As you make progress in overcoming your hoarding, you'll be rewarded with more space where you can enjoy living. You may even be rewarded by knowing that others are now using things you only kept on a pile on the floor.

HELP FOR FAMILY AND FRIENDS

All decisions about saving, discarding, and organizing are to be made only by the person with the hoarding problem. You will be most helpful if you let your loved one make these decisions. Family members should involve themselves only to the extent that they are invited to do so by the person with the hoarding problem.

You will probably be frustrated at the pace and sometimes find it difficult to understand why it's so hard to discard seemingly meaningless items. Remember that there are many times when your loved one also doesn't understand the mysterious nature of hoarding OCD. Think of it as a battle you're fighting together. Your loved one is on the front lines and you're standing by, ready to provide support when asked to do so. Be ready to help with sorting, calling the thrift store, holding a garage sale, laughing, or crying—but only when called upon. This is a much more difficult task than stepping in and doing the sorting and discarding yourself. However, this way is less likely to cause tensions between you and your loved one that could interfere with slow, steady progress.

CHAPTER 15

Two Steps Forward, One Step Back: Maintaining Your Gains for the Long Haul

If you're trying to achieve, there will be roadblocks. I've had them; everybody has had them. But obstacles don't have to stop you. If you run into a wall, don't turn around and give up. Figure out how to climb it, go through it, or work around it.

—Michael Jordan

As you work through the self-directed program, you will have good days and bad days. As time goes on, you will have more and more good days. But what about the bad days? And what about those persistent OCD symptoms that seem to linger despite your efforts?

IT'S NOT WORKING: COMMON PROBLEMS

If you aren't making progress with your OCD problem, various factors could be involved. Among the most common are overvalued ideas, "compulsion creep" (substituting or modifying compulsions, rather than blocking them altogether), protecting yourself from exposures with distraction, continuing to avoid triggering situations, minimizing the importance of compulsions, denial and its cousin righteous denial, not taking medication or taking a less effective medication, family problems and life stress, lack of social support, lack of motivation, complicating illnesses, and alcohol or drug abuse. In the following sections, we'll help you identify what may be impeding your progress and discuss how to overcome these roadblocks.

Overvalued Ideas

Do you typically believe your obsessions are reasonable? Do you truly believe your compulsions are necessary to prevent misfortune or tragedy? If so, you've attached too much importance to your obsessions and compulsions. These faulty beliefs fall into the category of overvalued ideas, discussed in chapter 8. Overvalued ideas indicate a greater level of impairment from OCD and predict a poorer response to cognitive behavioral therapy. Loosening the grip of these unrealistic beliefs, even just a little, can make a difference in your progress. In the following space or in your journal, list any overvalued ideas or faulty beliefs you still hold. Then reread the relevant sections of chapter 8 to help you confront these thoughts and develop realistic appraisals and coping self-talk to counter them.

____

____

____

____

People with overvalued ideas almost always need to consider taking medication for OCD as an important component of their recovery. Review chapter 3 for a more in-depth discussion of medication options for OCD. It may take patience and persistence, but getting on the right medication or combination of medications can help people with overvalued ideas make significant progress. This is because a positive response to the medication can help you participate in and benefit from the cognitive behavioral strategies discussed throughout this book.

Compulsion Creep

OCD can be sneaky and persistent in reinvading your life. Sometimes people accommodate their OCD by substituting a new compulsion for an older one or change a compulsion by speeding it up or performing it differently. The new compulsion is likely to be less obvious than the old one was. For example, instead of checking the locked door a second time, you may tap the door, wiggle the doorknob, or cautiously stare at the door as you lock it. Or maybe you avoid checking the door altogether as long as you know your spouse is responsible for doing it. While shortening or altering compulsive behaviors can be a way of lessening their impact on your daily functioning, be aware that even less intrusive compulsions have the potential to grow more disruptive over time. Catch new, small compulsions before they grow into big ones. In the following space, list any substitute or modified compulsions that you may still be performing. Those that could potentially pose a bigger problem later should be added to your list of symptoms to be addressed using the ERP strategy you devised in your self-directed program.

____

____

____

____

Protective Distraction

You may be distracting yourself or unwittingly avoiding the full impact of exposure exercises so you won't feel too uncomfortable. This is self-defeating. Perhaps you're holding on to unrealistic beliefs about the dangerousness of anxiety and aren't willing to fully challenge those appraisals. As much as possible, try to hold the most horrific consequences of the fear-provoking situation vividly in your mind while doing an exposure. Be sure to allow the anxiety to rise and then wait for it to fall *on its own*. Try on an attitude of acceptance and tolerance of the anxiety. The faulty belief that the practice of exposure should eliminate all of your anxiety is the surest way to ensure that it will persist.

Think of handling the anxiety as similar to allowing yourself to be lifted by a wave. Picture yourself in the water at the seashore. In the distance you see a big wave coming your way. It looks scary, and you feel tempted to rush out of the water—it's that big. But you decide to stay and ride it out. You can feel the butterflies in your stomach as it approaches. You can handle the wave in two ways: You can tense up, hold your arms close, and make your body very tight and compact, like a deadweight. If you do that, when the wave hits you it will slam into you, tumble you over, and spin you around dizzyingly. A better way to handle it is to loosen your muscles and relax, making your body light. Spread your arms, and when the wave comes, allow it to lift you up off the ground. Then, as it passes by, gently descend back down and plant your feet firmly on the ocean floor. This is an apt metaphor for how you can get through anxious OCD moments.

Remember, the anxiety always passes eventually. How much you allow it to disrupt your life at any one moment is up to you. In the following space, list the ways you may be distracting yourself or resisting anxiety during ERP:

____

____

____

____

Avoidance

Be on the alert for any forms of avoidance that may persist. After working with your self-directed program, do you still avoid touching objects most people wouldn't usually consider dangerous? Do you avoid leaving the house so you won't be faced with having to lock the door without checking it? Do you still avoid being around young children? Do you continue to avoid driving near elementary schools for fear of running someone over? Remember that the situations that you continue to avoid for OCD-related reasons are like a tinderbox and may cause more severe OCD symptoms to flare up when you're under increased stress from life circumstances.

Getting to the next step in your recovery from OCD requires a high degree of courage—the courage to do the very things that your OCD brain screams you must not do! Treat these feelings and sensations as false alarms and do your best to ignore them. Treat the situations you avoid as you do all compulsions: with ERP. In the following space, list all of the situations that you still avoid. Use this list as a reminder of the ERP work you still need to do:

____

____

____

____

Minimizing the Importance of Compulsions

A compulsion is a compulsion. Don't fool yourself or thwart your progress by minimizing the importance of any compulsion, no matter how seemingly small, with statements such as these:

- That's not really a compulsion.
- I can stop it whenever I want.
- I just don't think I need to stop doing it.

Once you've overcome your major OCD compulsions, go after smaller ones. You may feel satisfied with only partial improvement of your OCD. If you've gotten rid of the major problems, you may feel ready to stop following the program. Don't do it! This will increase the likelihood that your next lapse will be more severe. If you were able to break free from major symptoms, chances are good that you can break free from minor symptoms too.

Denial: "Maybe It's Not OCD"

One of the most common barriers to progress in overcoming OCD is the idea that maybe this time, it isn't your OCD. This thought often occurs after people have made significant progress. You can hit a brick wall if you buy into the nagging thought that by not doing compulsions, somehow you or someone you love will be punished for your "negligence." This leaves you vulnerable to all of the irrational catastrophic thinking that generated the compulsions in the first place. Here are some examples of these sorts of ideas:

- If I touch the doorknob and don't wash this time, maybe I really will die of AIDS. Maybe I just dodged a bullet all of those other hundreds of times when I didn't wash.
- By not undoing this bad thought just this one time, I probably will cause harm to come to my loved one. I've been testing fate by not doing my compulsions, and now it's payback time.
- By not getting just this one extra medical test, I will pay for my flippant attitude and die of some dreaded disease.
- If I don't check the stove just one more time, in this particular instance fate will surely punish me for my inattention and cause a horrific accident.
- Just this one time, maybe having this thought of harming my loved one means I'll really do it. I could be the one in a billion who doesn't fit the standard profile.

No wonder OCD is called the doubting disease! Don't be fooled by this type of thinking. The OCD wants to pull you back into its grasp. Don't let up now. Continue to practice response prevention in triggering situations.

Righteous Denial, or the "Martyr Complex"

Righteous denial is a form of self-deception that enables those with OCD to avoid change by rationalizing their symptoms to themselves and others with the notion that they perform their rituals for everyone's good. This faulty belief shields them from the painful impact of their OCD on themselves and those around them. Their OCD becomes a secret source of pride and provides feelings of uniqueness and superiority. The rationale goes something like this: "How noble and wonderful I am! I'll gladly sacrifice my life doing endless compulsions (washing, counting, checking, and so on) all day long as a small price to pay to protect those I love from danger and harm. And since no one close to me yet died or suffered inordinately, I must be doing something right!"

Not Using Medication or Using a Less Effective Medication

If you find that, despite your best efforts to help yourself using ERP, your OCD is still quite disabling, it may be time to consider taking medication or asking your doctor to change your current medication regimen. For information on finding a qualified physician to prescribe or manage the medications you take, refer to chapter 19. Discuss with your physician the possibility of changing the type or dosage of your present medications or augmenting them with additional medications. There are a number of medication strategies that can help significantly decrease the severity of OCD symptoms.

Many people with OCD have fears about taking medication. Their fear may be due to overall discouragement, a previous negative experience with side effects, a particular physician, or just plain old what-ifs. Here are some common what-ifs, along with information to help combat them:

- **What if the medication doesn't help?** If one doesn't help or helps only minimally, another one or a new combination probably will help.
- **What if I have to take it the rest of my life?** Not a bad trade-off if it gives you greater freedom from OCD.
- **What if I get addicted to it?** OCD medications, specifically the SSRIs, aren't addictive. You can stop taking them anytime you and your doctor decide it's advisable to do so. To avoid withdrawal effects, it may be necessary to taper the dosage, rather than stopping all at once.
- **What if I take medication and don't get to the root cause?** That's okay. The root cause of OCD is unknown at present, and medication can help you feel a lot better as you search for it!

Don't give up on medication. Take a chance and keep trying. Use the knowledge you've gained from this book to locate a qualified medical professional who can help you find the right medication for your problem. It's worth it!

Family Problems and Life Stress

Family conflict, distress, and divisiveness can seriously interfere with your ability to maintain your progress. Likewise, economic distress and instability can topple even the most successful treatment efforts. An additional complication is that family members may unconsciously sabotage your progress. If your family has organized itself around your OCD, when you get better your family must reorganize itself. For example, you and your family members may find yourselves with spare time on your hands once you stop participating in OCD rituals. What then? Most families are elated by the added freedom that recovery from OCD brings. In some cases, however, family members may resent you because they feel unneeded now that you're breaking free from OCD.

Together, you must develop a new way of life within the family that isn't dependent on OCD symptoms. Chapter 18 provides more specifics on how to go about this. If problems persist, you may want to consider seeking family therapy from a qualified mental health professional who's familiar with OCD. Chapter 19 can help you make decisions in getting professional help.

Lack of Social Support

Often, the discouragement and isolation that accompany OCD can significantly interfere with making progress with your self-directed program. It can be so difficult to find people in your life who understand. Attending an OCD support group can be very helpful in this regard. When you share openly with other kindred spirits about the daily struggles and dilemmas of the disorder, their acceptance and understanding can make a huge difference in your recovery from OCD. Many groups welcome immediate family members as well, in which case the group can serve as a valuable resource for the entire family as all of you attempt to cope with the presence of OCD. Chapter 19 provides suggestions on how to locate an OCD support group. If there isn't one in your area, consider starting one yourself. Guidelines for starting a support group can be obtained from the Anxiety Disorders Association of America (see the resources section for contact information).

Lack of Motivation

Breaking free from OCD is hard work, and it takes time. You may sometimes find your motivation weakening. Here's a tip to help with that: In the following space, write several statements about how your life would be different, and better, without OCD—in your family life, relationships, job or career, and other aspects of life. Be very specific. Then, write these statements on small pieces of paper and post them in various places in your home, such as the refrigerator door or the bathroom mirror, to serve as reminders. When your enthusiasm wanes and you're tempted to give up, read what you've written. It will provide a quick boost and help you stay on track.

____

____

____

____

Here's another tip. Compose a short, five- to ten-minute self-motivational narrative, then make an audio recording of your script. We've provided guidelines for composing your narrative. Fill in the blanks using your particular symptoms and situation. Then read it as one complete narrative, using lots of expression to make it believable. You may want to ask your spouse, parent, or therapist to record it for you to make it more believable. Or you may want to record it in your own voice. The choice is yours.

Hello _______________, this is _______________ speaking. I've (you've) had OCD for years (months). My (your) problem is _______________ (washing, checking, repeating, ordering, intrusive thoughts, or whatever). This problem has prevented me (you) from living life freely. It has affected my (your) life in the following ways: (list several ways that OCD has negatively impacted your life in the areas of family and work, goals, hopes, and dreams). While neither I (you) nor anyone else is responsible for the fact that I (you) have OCD, I am (you are) responsible for taking every possible step to overcome it. I (you) have reached a point in my (your) life where I am (you are) unwilling to tolerate OCD symptoms anymore. I am (you are) committed to achieving a life in which OCD is, at most, a small, insignificant inconvenience.

To achieve this, I (you) must change my (your) attitude from one of hopelessness and defeat to one of hope and possibility. I am (you are) no longer willing to hide in shame in a dark corner with my (your) OCD. I am (you are) a whole person. I (you) have many great qualities. I am (you are) ____________________________ *(list at least five positive qualities or strengths in yourself).*

I am (you are) not just my (your) OCD symptoms!

Despite feeling alone with this disease much of the time, I (you) now realize I am (you are) not alone. There are literally thousands who understand what I am (you are) going through. I can (you can) reach out to these people for help and understanding. And regarding those who don't understand, I (you) must give up my (your) anger, cynicism, and negativity. I (you) must learn patience. With proper information and education, many others will someday see the light and understand what OCD is, one person at a time. I (you) must give up my (your) insistence that the world change just for me (you). I (you) can promote change when I (you) begin to change myself (yourself), my (your) attitude, and my (your) OCD.

To live life free of OCD, I (you) must strive to change my (your) attitude from mistrust to trust. Though I've (you've) been disappointed and discouraged before, I (you) must wipe the slate clean. I (you) may need to put my (your) faith in a doctor, expert, group, person, or program that will help me (you) confront and face the things I (you) fear, and guide me (you) toward the light of recovery. Though it's extremely scary, I'm (you're) ready and willing to do whatever it takes. I'm (you are) committed wholeheartedly to this.

I am (you are) committed to following through with medication—to take it religiously and only according to the directions of my (your) physician. I'm (you're) now ready to live a clean life, without any abuse of medication, which will only negatively affect the delicate balance of my (your) brain chemistry.

I'm (you're) willing to confront my (your) fears daily using the principles of cognitive behavioral therapy. I am (you are) working to recognize the differences between my (your) logical brain and my OCD. I (you) realize that the irrational messages from my (your) OCD brain are false and the compulsions only a waste of time. The obsessive thoughts are mere "ghosts and goblins," like a bad B-grade movie—they may look real for a moment, but they are not.

If I (you) let the OCD trick me (you) into reacting to the images and messages as if they were real, the OCD wins and it gains more and more control over me (you). I (you) win when I (you) resist the magnetic pull of the compulsive urge. And although there is great discomfort in not giving in to it, if I (you) wait and hang on through the discomfort, the urge will eventually diminish on its own. I am (you are) now willing to fight the battle of my (your) life to be victorious against this monster! I (you) hate this OCD so much, and my (your) commitment to recovery is so very strong, that I'm (you're) willing to put everything on the line and withstand the urge to perform a compulsion. Daily, I am (you are) gaining the strength and courage to begin to take charge of my (your) OCD.

Complicating Illnesses

Depression, other anxiety disorders, attention deficit disorder (ADD), Tourette syndrome, body dysmorphic disorder (BDD), trichotillomania, eating disorders, and substance abuse are just a few of the disorders that can complicate breaking free from OCD. See chapter 16 for a discussion of some of these complicating illnesses. As mentioned early on in the book, an important first step before starting the self-directed program is obtaining an accurate medical diagnosis from a qualified mental health professional. This will also determine whether other conditions are present that could complicate the process of recovery from OCD. Once these conditions are identified, a mental health professional can help you create a program that's tailored to your specific problems.

Alcohol or Drug Abuse

Excessive use of alcohol or drugs greatly complicates OCD treatment. If substance abuse is an issue for you, chances are good that you're self-medicating to relieve anxiety symptoms caused by the OCD. Be aware that these substances can cause adverse interactions with medications, unwanted side effects, and toxic reactions. In addition, illegal drugs and alcohol can neutralize the therapeutic effects of a prescribed medication. The health risks of mixing illegal drugs or alcohol with OCD medications are significant, so the obvious first step is detoxification and treatment from mental health professionals who specialize in dual-diagnosis psychiatric disorders. Once these conditions are under control, you have a much greater chance of success in breaking free from OCD.

MANAGING LAPSES AND PREVENTING RELAPSE

Expect lapses and beware of relapse—especially upon making progress. What's the difference between a lapse and relapse? There's a world of difference. Lapses are accompanied by a relatively minor increase in OCD symptoms, are usually short or limited in duration, and almost always occur during a period of short-term life stress or transition. Both happy and unhappy events—getting married or divorced, changing jobs, the birth of a child, a move to a new location or community, illness in the family, and so on—can be associated with a short-term lapse in your recovery from OCD. Lapses are completely normal and to be expected as part of the normal waxing and waning of OCD symptoms throughout your life. When life stresses subside, you should find that your recovery rebounds to its previous level.

Relapse, on the other hand, is much rarer and involves severe regression back to pretreatment levels of symptoms. It's usually associated with a significant life stressor or disruption in social support, plus additional factors such as alcohol or drug abuse and, in many cases, quitting a prescribed OCD medication.

In either case, lapse or relapse, the sooner you face the issues, the better. It's also a good idea to learn techniques to both prevent them and manage them when they occur. Here are some suggestions that will help you.

- Several weeks or months after successful treatment, you may feel you have it made. You may even think that you're cured. Don't be fooled! OCD is sneaky and persistent. It will give you a sucker punch when you least suspect it. In fact, we believe that recovery without having experienced and successfully endured a lapse in OCD symptoms is only partial recovery. Successfully managing lapses is a skill that will help you throughout your life with OCD.

- Lapses and relapses are not signs of failure; they're opportunities to further refine the skills you've learned in the self-directed program and strengthen your recovery from OCD. Be honest with yourself. When you slip up and perform a compulsion, admit it and make plans for how you can resist the compulsion in the future. Get back on track and don't get down on yourself. This can be challenging, as people with OCD are often very self-critical. If possible, immediately expose yourself to the feared situation again, and then move on.

- Don't compare yourself with others—with or without OCD. Your OCD problem is uniquely your own, and therefore your path to recovery will be uniquely your own.

- It isn't uncommon for those who make significant progress with their OCD in a relatively short time to go through a phase of feeling depressed. It's almost a state of bereavement: mourning for the years that were lost to OCD and the devastating toll it has taken. There may be a period of deep sadness and regret about what your life might have looked like had you recovered sooner. Forgive yourself and others for mistakes of the past. No life is ever perfect. Remember that without all of those blind alleys, you would never have gotten to the point you are at today. They were an inevitable part of your recovery. Use the painful past to further safeguard and solidify the recovery you've achieved now.

- The goal of this book is progress with your OCD, not a perfect cure. Be realistic in your expectations about recovery from OCD. Recovery is a lifelong process with many ups and downs—and with your OCD under good control, hopefully, many more ups!

- Sometimes it will be just plain difficult. When you're working hard at maintaining your previous gains, you may become discouraged and frustrated, as if you've accomplished nothing at all. At these times, don't lose sight of the progress you've made. Even at difficult times, find compassion for yourself, realize your self-worth, and give yourself a pat on the back for how far you've come. Then keep moving forward!

- Appreciate your small victories against OCD. Over time, even minor improvements eventually add up to larger gains.

- *Never, and we repeat, never* go off your medications without first consulting your physician. Many people make the mistake of discontinuing medications when they're feeling well only to discover later that they were feeling well only because they were taking the medication.

- While medication can make a big difference in your OCD symptoms, don't overly rely on medication to help you. The fact is, you can't medicate away all of your OCD symptoms. Sometimes the best "medicine" for nagging, residual OCD symptoms is a stronger effort with ERP.

Even when you're doing very well, you'll get spikes of anxiety on occasion. Don't be alarmed, and be aware that this is normal. How you engage with your OCD in those moments has a lot to do with whether those symptom remain fleeting or stick around. The following metaphor illustrates the optimum stance to take when unwanted thoughts return. You can use this metaphor to help you view the OCD-related discomfort like an unwanted houseguest and manage it more effectively. (This approach is similar to the metaphor of Joe the bum, from the literature on acceptance and commitment therapy; Hayes, Strosahl, and Wilson 1999.)

This feeling is just like a houseguest, a family member who you feel sorry for who thinks he can drop by any time he wants, when you least expect him, and at the most inconvenient times. He's ugly, stinky, scary, and intimidating—he can be nasty and he's much bigger than you are. When he visits, he plops himself down in your living room, takes off his smelly shoes, watches your TV, eats all of your food, reads your magazines, and takes up a lot of your precious time. Before you began treatment, he'd scare the daylights out of you and you'd do anything to get rid of him. You used to get awfully upset, even terrified by these visits. You'd scream at him to leave, pound your fists, stamp your feet, and agonize through every minute that went by until the moment he decided to leave on his own. Yet all of your commotion only caused him to stay even longer, entrenching himself ever more stubbornly in your living room. He gained enormous strength and power by feeding off of your desire to get rid of him. And when he finally did leave, you lived in constant fear and dread of his next visit.

Now that you've been helped by medication and CBT, this houseguest still looks really scary, but you know that he's just annoying, and essentially safe and harmless. And you've learned that how you react to him is what determines how long he stays. So now you take the attitude of calm, tolerant acceptance of his presence. You know that trying to get rid of him doesn't work and only makes things worse. So you just go about your business around the house without paying much, if any, attention to him. With none of your commotion to feed off of, he gets bored and after a while decides to leave on his own. Over time, his stays get shorter and shorter, and eventually he decides your home isn't even worth a visit, though he may decide to drop in on you by surprise sometime in the future, when you least expect it.

STAYING WELL AND LIVING AN OCD-FREE LIFESTYLE

Make ERP and the other elements of your self-directed program a major part of your lifestyle. Find ways to fit CBT approaches into your everyday life. For example, resist repeatedly checking the door every time you leave the house, or refuse to give in to washing after touching "dirty" money. In addition, a healthy lifestyle will help you stick with your program.

Fill the Empty Time

You may find yourself with huge chunks of free time that once were filled with compulsions. To keep OCD symptoms from sneaking back into your life, it's best to try to fill this time with meaningful, productive activity. Remember, "an idle mind is the devil's playground." In the following space, list several activities in which you'd like to participate. These activities could include hobbies, volunteer work, paid employment, drawing, journaling—the possibilities are endless. Then make plans to use these activities to fill the time you once dedicated to OCD.

____

____

____

Eat Right

A healthy, well-balanced diet will help you get the most out of your self-directed program. Good nutrition is essential if your body is to have sufficient levels of neurotransmitters, hormones, enzymes, and other substances that must work together for your brain to function properly. There is no magic formula to ensure that your brain functions at its best except this: Eat a healthy, well-balanced diet.

There are, however, a few dietary changes that can help you control particular symptoms. Avoiding alcohol will not only help reduce anxiety, it will also have a positive effect on depression, because alcohol is a central nervous system depressant. Many people with OCD feel anxious or overstimulated at times, and on top of this, some of the medications used to treat OCD can have overstimulation and anxiety as side effects. Staying away from foods with caffeine, such as coffee, many sodas, and chocolate, can help.

One of the most important dietary changes you can make is to avoid refined carbohydrates, such as candy and pastries. Stay away from anything with sugar in it. Replace refined sugar with fruits and complex carbohydrates, such as whole grain breads and pasta. This will help even out your moods and counteract two common side effects of OCD medications: weight gain and carbohydrate cravings. If you're susceptible to these side effects, knowing that they may occur and anticipating them will help you to control the weight gain.

Get Adequate Exercise

Adequate exercise is important, but there's no need to go overboard. You probably don't need heavy-duty exercise to get positive results. Regular moderate exercise has many benefits, including weight loss as a result of burning calories, increasing your metabolism, and decreasing your appetite. Exercise can reduce muscle tension, enhance concentration and memory, improve sleep, and reduce depression, anxiety, and stress—not to mention that as you begin to look better, you'll feel better about yourself and your confidence and self-esteem will improve. This can only help improve your OCD. Some exercise situations, such as being around sweaty people at a gym or jogging on "dirty" city streets, may offer the additional benefit of providing opportunities to practice ERP in real-life environments. Check with your doctor before beginning an exercise plan.

Reduce Stress

Many different life events can cause stress. Some particularly stressful times include periods of change and transition, such as moving, illness, birth, and death. Even something as simple as out-of-town visitors can provoke considerable stress. Since OCD tends to act up more during stressful times, you'll have more difficulty sticking with your self-directed program during these times. Expect this and give yourself a break. Be extra tolerant of yourself when life gets in the way of your program and just do your best. Make plans for reducing the amount of stress in your everyday life and find new ways to cope with stress. For example, you might take time to relax by listening to music, talking with a friend, or participating in a hobby.

Also, note that excessive fatigue tends to make OCD symptoms worse, so getting adequate sleep and rest is vitally important. If your OCD medication interferes with your sleep, talk to your doctor about this.

Commit to a Healthy Lifestyle

There are countless books and other resources that can help you reduce stress, learn relaxation techniques, improve your diet, and develop a personal fitness program. Explore and find the resources and techniques that work well for you.

In the following space, write your plans for stress reduction, relaxation, diet, exercise, and general lifestyle changes:

____

____

____

____

____

WELCOME LAPSES AS OPPORTUNITIES FOR GROWTH

The goal of recovery from OCD is to do a great job of managing this disease for the rest of your life. However, breaking free from OCD doesn't occur in a smooth, straight path. Rather, it's a bumpy, winding path with lots of ups and downs. OCD often waxes and wanes. Expect that sometimes your progress will be two steps forward and one step back. Persistence will definitely yield significant benefits.

At times the road will be smooth. Enjoy these times to their fullest. When life gets rocky, your OCD will unceremoniously remind you that it's still there. Rather than letting the OCD gain a greater foothold in your life at these times, see them as an opportunity to beat back your OCD and progress even further in your journey toward breaking free. And in the months and years to come, review this chapter frequently. It will help you renew your efforts to make the things you've learned in this book a major part of your lifestyle.

HELP FOR FAMILY AND FRIENDS

Read this chapter carefully. You and your loved one will find that the process of recovery from OCD is challenging and there will be setbacks. Don't let that discourage you. Remind yourself that this is to be expected. In fact, there is no real progress with OCD without an occasional setback. And when progress seems to be stalled, review this chapter with your loved one.

Also consider whether there are things that you're doing, or not doing, that could be contributing to the setback or stalled recovery:

- Are you assisting with rituals?
- When progress is slow, are you directing criticism or sarcasm toward your loved one? Do you perhaps have an attitude of "Get over it already!"
- Are you sabotaging your loved one's progress by not complying with or supporting therapy or medication recommendations?
- Are you providing verbal reassurance to your loved one in response to compulsive requests?
- Are you doing things your loved one is able to do so that he or she can avoid something? Even if you're doing this for your own convenience, ultimately it isn't helpful for either of you.
- Are you minimizing a ritual, perhaps by agreeing that it isn't really that important to stop that particular one?
- Are you and your loved one having difficulty filling free time that was once taken up by rituals? If so, talk about it, plan activities, and realign your daily plans.

It takes time to develop a new lifestyle to support breaking free from OCD. Be patient, and encourage your loved one to be patient. Even if lifestyle changes are rewarding, implementing them can be trying and frustrating. Build resilience in all family members by encouraging a healthy lifestyle that includes a well-balanced diet, adequate exercise, and stress reduction. Fill the free time that was once consumed by rituals with activities that will keep you active and bring you together as a family.

PART 4

Co-occurring Disorders, Family Issues, and Finding Help

CHAPTER 16

OCD and Company: Obsessive-Compulsive Spectrum Disorders

Even if you're on the right track, you'll get run over if you just sit there.

—Will Rogers

Certain other psychiatric disorders resemble OCD. Like OCD, they include symptoms such as intrusive thoughts, obsessions, and repetitive behaviors. Known as *obsessive-compulsive spectrum disorders* (OCSDs), these disorders include trichotillomania and body dysmorphic disorder (both discussed in this chapter), as well as hypochondriasis (discussed in chapter 13). The compulsive overpreoccupation with food and thinness found in such disorders as anorexia, bulimia, and obesity have features in common with OCD. Because many people with anorexia also have clear OCD symptoms, a strong relationship between these two disorders is suspected (Hecht, Fichter, and Postpischil 1983). Other disorders that commonly co-occur with OCD, such as depression, are called *comorbid disorders*. (Depression is discussed in chapter 2.)

Treatment of obsessive-compulsive spectrum disorders and comorbid disorders is challenging. The more comorbid disorders and symptoms the person appears to have, the more likely it is that treatment will require consultation and participation of a specialized team of mental health professionals.

BODY DYSMORPHIC DISORDER

People with body dysmorphic disorder (BDD) have a preoccupation with a minor bodily defect or imagined defect that they believe is conspicuous to others, and this concern causes significant distress or impairment in functioning. The name is derived from the Greek word *dismorfia*: *dis* meaning "abnormal" or "apart," and *morpho* meaning "shape." Before 1987, BDD was referred to as dysmorphobia, so named in the 1880s by Italian psychiatrist Enrique Morselli (Phillips 1996).

People with BDD typically aren't "ugly" at all, and the "flaw" they're concerned with is likely to go unnoticed by others. They are usually shy, seldom make eye contact, and have low self-esteem. They often go to extremes to camouflage their imagined defects by wearing sunglasses, hats, or bulky clothing.

Most BDD obsessions are related to the face: a specific part of the face, such as the nose, lips, or ears, or facial aspects such as wrinkles, color, blemishes, scars, veins, pore size, or texture. However, any body part can be the focus of attention, such as hair and hairline or the size and shape of arms, legs, buttocks, breasts, or genitals. Some have concerns involving body symmetry. Others have muscle dysmorphia, a type of BDD in which people worry that their bodies are too small and puny. Usually just the opposite is true; typically, they are large and muscular. People with facial and skin dysmorphia often pick and dig at their skin.

People with BDD are frequently unaware that their worries are excessive and unfounded. They often seek cosmetic surgery or dermatologic treatment for their perceived physical defects, but rarely do these treatments relieve their worries. They are highly unlikely to seek help from a mental health professional voluntarily until depression becomes a significant factor in their distress.

People with BDD often have a high degree of overvalued ideas or even delusional thinking. They often believe strongly in the reality of their perceived defect, despite assurances from others that no defect exists, or that if it does, it's largely unnoticeable. In addition to the obsessional nature of BDD, one study found that 90 percent of people with the disorder performed one or more repetitive and time-consuming behaviors (Phillips 1998) involving examining or attempting to improve or hide imagined defects, such as grooming, shaving, washing, skin picking, weight lifting, checking their appearance in mirrors, and comparing themselves with others. People with BDD either may seek reassurance from others or try to convince others of their defect.

Body dysmorphic disorder usually begins in adolescence, though it can start in childhood. Obsessive-compulsive disorder is common in people with BDD, occurring in over 30 percent of those with BDD (Phillips 1998).

People with BDD are prone to major depression and are at much higher risk of suicide than the general population, so this must be monitored closely. One study indicated a 60 percent rate of depression among those with BDD (Phillips 1998). About 80 percent of people with BDD have had thoughts of suicide (Phillips 1996), and a 2006 study (Phillips and Menard 2006) found people with BDD to be forty-five times more likely to die of suicide than the general population. It has also been suggested that the higher-than-average suicide rate among those who have undergone cosmetic surgery is due to undiagnosed BDD (Nowak 2006).

Selective serotonin reuptake inhibitors (SSRIs) are the medications of choice for treating BDD. Although most people with BDD are reluctant to take medication, it can help decrease the amount of time the person spends preoccupied with the imagined defect and engaging in associated compulsive behavior, and can also reduce anxiety and depressive symptoms. Successful medication therapy often helps people gain improved insight into their BDD. As with OCD, relapse is usually a problem when medication is discontinued.

Preliminary studies suggest that cognitive behavioral therapy can be helpful for people with BDD. Exposure and response prevention combined with cognitive techniques was an effective approach for 77 percent of people with BDD in one study (Phillips 1998). Often the challenge is in getting people with BDD to accept psychiatric treatment rather than dermatological, surgical, or other medical treatments intended to fix the perceived flaw. More research into BDD is needed, but there is hope. There are good treatments available for BDD. For further help, we recommend *The BDD Workbook* (Claiborn and Pedrick 2002). It's formatted much like *The OCD Workbook* and uses a cognitive behavioral approach, which is considered the most effective for BDD. You can use it alone or, in more severe cases, with the help of a therapist.

TRICHOTILLOMANIA

Trichotillomania (TTM) is characterized by chronic, repetitive pulling of hair. The sites of hair pulling include the scalp, eyelashes, eyebrows, armpits, and pubic area. Hair pulling tends to occur in episodes that are exacerbated by stress, or sometimes by relaxation (when reading a book or watching television, for example). All other causes of hair loss, including medical and dermatological problems, must be considered and ruled out before a diagnosis of TTM is confirmed. People with TTM experience an increasing sense of tension immediately before pulling out a hair or when attempting to resist hair pulling. When the hair is pulled, they experience immediate feelings of pleasure, gratification, and relief.

Although TTM was once thought to be rare, with a prevalence of only 0.05 to 0.6 percent, studies estimate a prevalence of 2 to 3 percent of the U.S. population (Keuthen, O'Sullivan, and Jeffrey 1998). As with OCD, people with TTM are often highly secretive about their symptoms. They may hide their symptoms by pulling hair from parts of the body that aren't easily visible, or they may wear wigs or style their hair in a way that conceals areas where hair has been pulled.

In children, trichotillomania has approximately the same prevalence rate in both genders. By adulthood, more women are diagnosed. The onset usually occurs in childhood or adolescence, although it can begin before the age of one or as late as middle age. There appears to be a subgroup of TTM with an onset before the age of five (Keuthen, O'Sullivan, and Jeffrey 1998).

Trichotillomania often co-occurs with other psychiatric disorders, including anxiety disorders, depression, eating disorders, attention deficit disorder, Tourette syndrome, and body dysmorphic disorder. Interestingly, one study found a significantly higher rate of hair pulling in people with both Tourette syndrome and OCD than in people with either Tourette syndrome or OCD alone (Keuthen, O'Sullivan, and Jeffrey 1998).

Complications of trichotillomania are alopecia (baldness), infection and scarring at hair extraction sites, slowed or stopped hair growth, and changes of hair texture or color. Some people eat the hair they've pulled, putting them at risk for stomach pain, gastrointestinal obstruction, peritonitis, and, in rare cases, even death (Keuthen, O'Sullivan, and Jeffrey 1998). The repetitive arm and hand movements involved in hair pulling can cause carpal tunnel syndrome and other neuromuscular problems (Keuthen, O'Sullivan, and Jeffrey 1998).

What causes trichotillomania? No one knows for sure, but there's growing evidence that brain function and structure may be involved. Abnormalities found in the brain structures and circuitry of people with trichotillomania overlap with those found in OCD and Tourette syndrome. Behavioral pediatrician Susan Swedo and her colleagues at the National Institute of Mental Health have proposed that streptococcus infections may be involved in some cases of early-onset hair pulling (Swedo et al. 1988; Keuthen, O'Sullivan, and Jeffrey 1998).

Self-Help for Trichotillomania

Trichotillomania is considered a challenging condition to treat. The treatments of choice over the past thirty years have included the use of medications, specifically SSRIs, and a behavioral treatment known as habit reversal training (Azrin, Nunn, and Franz 1980; Mouton and Stanley 1996). Habit reversal training involves the following components, carried out on your own or, better, with the help of a therapist familiar with the cognitive behavioral treatment of trichotillomania:

- **Awareness training:** For one week, monitor all urges to pull, actual occurrences of pulling, when and where they occur, the emotions you experience just prior to pulling, and feelings you have immediately after pulling.

- **Identifying response precursors:** What do you do with your arms and hands just before starting to pull? Do you touch or stroke your hair? Do you touch your face or eyelashes?

- **Relaxation training:** Practice relaxation techniques that work for you. Two recommended skills are progressive muscle relaxation and deep breathing exercises such as diaphragmatic breathing. If you'd like to learn these techniques, you can find instructions online or in many books. Relaxation skills can help you achieve awareness of and a release from the tension often associated with hair pulling. Practice your relaxation skills two to three times per day for one week.

- **Competing response training:** Choose an incompatible behavior—a simple, inconspicuous activity using the hand you use for pulling. This activity should both prevent hair pulling and help reduce the urge to pull. A commonly used strategy involves lightly tightening the arm muscles for ten seconds at a time with the arm in three different positions. Here's the sequence: With the arm extended straight out from your body, lightly tighten the arm muscles and hold for ten seconds, then release for five seconds. Repeat three times. Then, with the elbow bent 90 degrees, lightly tighten the arm muscles for ten seconds, release for five seconds, and repeat three times. Then, with the elbow bent 45 degrees, hold for ten seconds, release for five seconds, and repeat three times. Repeat the entire sequence until the urge to pull subsides. Practice this for one week before moving on to situational competing response training.

- **Situational competing response training:** Practice light muscle tightening in situations where the urge to pull is likely. For example, press your hand against your body when standing around in social situations, grasp your nonpulling hand with the pulling hand, or clasp or clench an object such as a belt buckle, a cell phone, or the sides of a chair. When driving, grip the steering wheel more tightly. Practice competing responses in varieties of situations by tightening for ten seconds and then releasing for ten seconds, especially when the urge to pull is strong. Continue to practice alternating tensing and releasing for one week, and notice its effects upon your urge to pull.

- **Combine relaxation training with competing response training:** Next, whenever you notice the urge to pull, relax by doing deep breathing for one minute. Then repeatedly do the competing response you've come up with until the urge subsides. If you find yourself already in a hair-pulling episode, use this procedure to interrupt the episode. Practice your combined habit reversal sequence daily, even in situations where no urges happen.

Habit reversal training has been the mainstay for helping people with trichotillomania and related disorders, such as skin picking and tic disorders. However, advances in the understanding of trichotillomania have pointed to the need for additional techniques for battling hair pulling. To address this, psychologist Charles Mansueto, director of the Behavior Therapy Center of Greater Washington, has pioneered an innovative self-help program called ComB, short for the comprehensive behavioral model (Mansueto et al. 1999). ComB addresses the wide variations in what drives hair-pulling behavior and offers an array of measures to address the individual needs of each hair puller (Mansueto et al. 1999).

Within the ComB model, compulsive hair pulling is seen as a way of regulating internally experienced states of either overstimulation or understimulation (Penzel 2002). This idea is supported by the common observation that people tend to pull their hair most often when either bored or overly stressed. By figuring out your hair-pulling profile, you can determine the best strategy to use to regulate your level of internal stimulation without the need for hair pulling. Another aspect of the model is the identification of the emotional, cognitive, and environmental cues that trigger hair pulling.

The ComB approach uses the acronym Fiddle SHEEP to help you isolate the individual components of your hair-pulling problem and understand your unique hair-pulling profile so that you can develop an appropriate strategy to address the problem:

- **Fiddle** refers to the state of needing to do something with your hands or mouth for stimulation. Remedies may involve grabbing textured children's toys such as a squishy ball or silly putty or objects such as twine, sandpaper, a swatch of silk, a piece of soft fabric, or worry beads.

- **S**ensory involves engaging in stimulating sensory activities such washing your face with a textured sponge, brushing your hair with a wide-toothed comb, brushing your eyebrows, using a tingly shampoo, putting an ice pack on your head or face, splashing your face with cold water, chewing gum, or eating sunflower seeds.

- "**H**ands have a mind of their own" addresses the needs of people who report that they sometimes pull hair without even being aware of it or in spite of strong efforts to resist. Remedies include putting band-aids on the fingertips, wearing light gloves or rubber fingertips, wrapping an elastic bandage around the elbow to inhibit bending, wrapping the hair in a towel, wearing a hat, and putting Vaseline on the eyelids.

- Environmental addresses pulling that seems tied to specific locations in the home, work environment, or elsewhere. Perhaps you tend to pull most when watching TV, in the bathroom, or when you're at school. Put sticky notes in locations where you tend to pull hair to remind yourself not to pull.
- Emotional addresses pulling due to feeling angry, depressed, or frustrated. You can address these emotional states through journaling, doing art, playing video games, engaging in a relaxing activity such as cooking, practicing relaxation techniques, or working on a hobby, like building model airplanes.
- Perfectionism refers to intolerance of hair feeling imperfect, uneven, or out of place. To counter perfectionism, you need to learn to treat yourself with compassion and acceptance and without judgment.

To use this approach successfully, it's important to employ multiple strategies simultaneously in any given triggering situation. Build your skills by creating a weekly schedule for practicing your strategies on a daily basis, choosing strategies appropriate for your profile. For example, say you tend to pull hair while watching TV in the evening and your hair pulling seems to be due to your hands having "a mind of their own," a need to do something with your hands, and a need for sensory stimulation. In this case, you could wear band-aids on your fingertips, play with silly putty, and put a cold compress on the back of your neck while watching TV.

Remember that trichotillomania requires a multifaceted approach. You must be persistent and patient with yourself. Don't expect instant results, but if you work on your problem daily, you will experience benefits over a period of weeks or months. A good source for the latest information on treatment is the Trichotillomania Learning Center. Their contact information and some excellent self-help books are listed in the resources section.

Skin Picking

Closely related to TTM is chronic self-injurious skin-picking, sometimes called neurotic excoriation, dermatillomania, or self-inflicted dermatosis. It is often found among people with OCD. Some people pick their skin primarily to soothe an internal feeling of tension and anxiety, while others do so in order to quell feelings of boredom from inactivity, similar to the urge to pull hair in trichotillomania. Many pick in both situations. Sometime an intolerance of imperfection results in attempts to even out blemishes or skin that appears uneven or imperfect. The preoccupation with imagined skin defects is much like the preoccupations that characterize people with body dysmorphic disorder, and, at times, skin picking can be a part of a broader problem with BDD. People with skin-picking problems can benefit from approaches similar to those described for trichotillomania, including habit reversal training (Teng, Woods, and Twohig 2006). For people who pick their skin as a result of BDD, exposure and response prevention combined with habit reversal yields the best results.

WHEN OCD ISN'T THE ONLY PROBLEM

The presence of obsessive-compulsive spectrum disorders or comorbid disorders such as major clinical depression can complicate the treatment of OCD. If you suspect your OCD is complicated by another disorder, consult a mental health professional. A comprehensive treatment strategy that addresses each diagnosis will be more successful than focusing only on your OCD. We've listed books and resources for people struggling with body dysmorphic disorder, trichotillomania, and depression in the resources section.

HELP FOR FAMILY AND FRIENDS

If your loved one has another mental health disorder in addition to OCD, recovery is likely to be more challenging, and perhaps more elusive. Having a physical illness such as diabetes, heart disease, or asthma can also complicate matters. In either of these cases, it's likely that a team of health professionals will be involved in your loved one's care.

Obsessive-compulsive disorder and depression both appear to be partly caused by problems with the regulation of the neurotransmitter serotonin, and both respond to the same medications, suggesting a possible link between the two disorders. The hopelessness about the future and lack of energy to carry out plans that so frequently accompany depression make it difficult to learn and remember details. They can also make people uninterested in treatment and its goals. If your loved one appears to be depressed, find a good time to discuss this and encourage him or her to seek treatment from a mental health professional. Also seek help for any other family members who appear to be depressed, yourself included. This way you'll all be better equipped to fight the OCD. Take any talk about thoughts about suicide seriously, especially if your loved one has severe symptoms of body dysmorphic disorder (described earlier in this chapter). If your loved one talks about thoughts of suicide or threatens to commit suicide, seek help from a mental health professional *immediately* or call a suicide hotline.

Obsessive-compulsive disorder tends to run in families. People with OCD are more likely to have first-generation family members with OCD and are also more likely to have obsessive-compulsive spectrum disorders, other anxiety disorders, and depression. If this is true in your family, think of it as having a naturally occurring support group. You can understand each other in ways that people who haven't been touched by fears and anxieties cannot. Even if other family members have physical illnesses, offering support for one another and each of you reaching out beyond yourself will be good for everyone, including your loved one with OCD.

CHAPTER 17

It Happens to Children Too: Helping Your Child with OCD

Avoiding danger is no safer in the long run than outright exposure. The fearful are caught as often as the bold.

—Helen Keller

Research studies have shown that one-third to one-half of OCD cases identified in adults began during childhood. The disorder may develop in childhood, adolescence, or young adulthood (March and Mulle 1998). About 1 percent of children, have OCD (Yaryura-Tobias and Neziroglu 1997b). A family history of OCD is more frequent in childhood OCD than in adult-onset OCD, indicating that genetic factors may play more of a role in childhood OCD (Geller 1998).

Children have a strong need to feel accepted by others and fit into their peer group. The strange behaviors and senseless compulsions of OCD are embarrassing to them, so they try to suppress their symptoms until they're alone, or at least until they get home from school. Because children often hide their obsessions and compulsive behaviors, months or years may pass before parents become aware that their child has a problem. This is unfortunate, as it's best to treat OCD early. The longer it goes untreated, the more entrenched the symptoms become, invading more and more of the child's everyday life and making the OCD more difficult to treat (Yaryura-Tobias and Neziroglu 1997b).

With treatment, OCD may or may not follow the child into adulthood. Some children may have minimal symptoms as adults, or no symptoms at all. Others go into remission; their symptoms disappear but return during adulthood. OCD often changes over time. People may experience different symptoms as adults than they did as children. Why do symptoms sometimes disappear with treatment and then reappear later in life? No one knows for sure, but hormones and stress may cause changes in biological makeup, and thus affect the expression of OCD symptoms (Yaryura-Tobias and Neziroglu 1997b).

CHILDREN AND RITUALS: COULD IT BE OCD?

The official diagnostic criteria for adult OCD include that "at some point during the course of the disorder, the person has recognized that the obsessions or compulsions are excessive or unreasonable" (American Psychiatric Association 2000, 457). This requirement for diagnosis doesn't apply to children, as they may lack adequate cognitive awareness to make this judgment (March and Mulle 1998). And when adults with OCD are anxious and obsessing, even they may not realize they are being unreasonable.

Most children go through developmental stages characterized by compulsive behaviors and rituals that are quite normal. These behaviors are common between the ages of two and eight and seem to be a response to children's needs to control their environment and master childhood fears and anxieties. They may demand a very specific bedtime routine. For example, a child may require that the parent pull down the shades a certain way, kiss the child, and utter a specially worded "good night." If the routine is disturbed, a temper tantrum might result. If a single detail is forgotten or not done properly, the parent may be asked to do it over.

Dr. Henrietta Leonard, who studied the relationship between children's developmental rituals, superstitions, and OCD, wrote that developmental rituals are usually most intense between the ages of four and eight (Leonard 1989). Children express their belief that certain kids have "cooties," a form of imagined contamination. As a result, they may vehemently avoid being touched by those children. By age seven, collecting things (hoarding in OCD) becomes common. Sports cards, comic books, toy figures, jewelry, and dolls are among the most popular collectibles. Between the ages of seven and eleven, children's play becomes highly ritualized and rule bound. Breaking the rules of a game is likely to be met with cries of "No fair!" In adolescence rituals may subside, but obsessive preoccupation with an activity or a music or sports idol is common.

Superstitions often lead to ritual-like behaviors in normal children. These are forms of magical thinking in which children believe their thoughts or trivial actions have the power to control events in the world. Lucky numbers and rhymes, such as "Step on a crack, break your Momma's back," help bring about a sense of control and mastery.

These normal childhood rituals advance development, enhance socialization, and help children deal with separation anxiety. Young children's rituals help them develop new abilities and define their environment. As children mature and develop into adulthood, most of these ritualistic behaviors disappear on their own. In contrast, the rituals of the child with OCD often persist well into adulthood. For children with OCD, their rituals are painful and disabling and result in feelings of shame and isolation. Attempts to stop doing the rituals result in extreme anxiety.

Parents of a child with OCD are frequently frightened, confused, and frustrated by their child's preoccupation with cleanliness, orderliness, or checking rituals. Often, parents react at the extremes, either trying to intimidate the child or passively enabling the behavior. If parents overreact and attempt to interrupt the behaviors, the child may become hostile and extremely anxious. So, out of frustration, many parents give in to the child and may even reluctantly assist in the rituals, for example, doing repeated loads of the child's laundry because the child insists the clothes are contaminated. Yet when parents give in to or enable the rituals, the child never learns to confront his or her fears.

Wanda's Story

Art is usually a favorite subject of third-graders. But not for Wanda. Sticky glue and paste, wet paint, powdery chalk, smelly clay—it was a nightmare. Her only escape was the bathroom. She breathed a sigh of relief, jumped up, and flew to the door each time her teacher let her go. She would hurry to the bathroom down the hall. Fifty steps. She counted them and knew exactly how many: fifty steps every time.

Then the ritual would begin. It was always the same routine. After turning on the hot water, she'd spread her fingers out and rinse them. Then she pumped soap into the middle of her left hand. She felt relief as she washed each finger over and over. Twenty times for each finger. After washing, Wanda would get a paper towel and carefully turn off the water, making sure she didn't touch the faucet with her hands. If she did, she washed again. More and more often, she had to wash several times.

Bathroom breaks became more frequent, not just during art class, but all day. Unwanted thoughts seemed to pop into Wanda's head without warning. At first, washing her hands helped for a few hours, maybe even for the whole day. But with time the thoughts came more and more often, while washing her hands relieved her anxiety for increasingly shorter periods of time.

Mrs. Chester, Wanda's teacher, became concerned about Wanda's frequent trips to the bathroom and her red, chapped hands. Daydreaming was a problem too. The other children were starting to snicker when Wanda didn't seem to hear directions or failed to answer a question when she was called upon. Wanda's mother was worried about Wanda's behavior too. She had tried several lotions to treat Wanda's red, chapped hands. None of them helped.

"If you'd just stop washing your hands so much, they would heal," she told Wanda. "Just stop!" Wanda's mother didn't realize that Wanda couldn't just stop. She had never heard of OCD and assumed that the constant hand washing was a habit Wanda could overcome with determination and willpower. She thought Wanda might grow out of it—that it was just one of those stages kids go through. Eventually, Mrs. Chester recommended a psychiatric evaluation, and Wanda's mother immediately took Wanda to her pediatrician. He referred Wanda to a psychiatrist, who diagnosed OCD.

Tom's Story

Once an A student, Tom started getting Cs and Ds, and an occasional F. He knew the material, but he rarely handed in his homework. When he did, it was late. He failed tests because he couldn't finish them. There just wasn't enough time. Was he lazy? Rebellious? No, he had OCD.

Tom feared making mistakes. He checked his homework papers repeatedly until they were past due. Then he figured there was no use turning the homework in. Tests were nightmares. He answered two questions, then checked his work, then answered two more questions, and then checked again. His writing had to be just right: neat, orderly printing with none of the letters or numbers touching each other. His papers were filled with eraser marks, sometimes to the point of wearing holes in the paper.

Tom didn't check just schoolwork. His bedtime checking often took a whole hour. First he had to check the door, then the stoves, appliances, windows, closets, and under the beds. His parents told him he didn't have to check these things, but he persisted. Tom's parents tried to talk him out of his checking rituals. What would happen if he didn't check? His answers were vague. Someone could be hurt. He wouldn't be able to sleep. Most often the answer was "I don't know, I just have to check." When they argued with him about it, he started over, so they learned to leave him alone while he checked. Like Wanda's mom, they thought he would outgrow it.

His mother, Charlotte, took Tom to the doctor, who referred them to a psychiatrist. After a thorough examination, the psychiatrist explained that Tom had a neurobehavioral disorder called obsessive-compulsive disorder. As the psychiatrist explained OCD, Charlotte began to cry. "Doctor, I gave Tom OCD! He learned it from me. I don't check, but I worry about things and I arrange everything in a certain order. Everything in all the drawers and cupboards has a specific place."

The psychiatrist explained that she hadn't given Tom OCD—that obsessive-compulsive disorder isn't learned. He went on to say that it's a neurobehavioral disorder, and that sometimes several people in a family have OCD because it seems to have a genetic basis. After that first visit, Tom and Charlotte both began to work on cognitive behavioral therapy together.

CLEANING, CHECKING, COUNTING, AND CHILDREN

Obsessions that focus on contamination are the most commonly reported obsessions in children (Piacentini and Graae 1997). Fears of contamination by dirt and germs lead to avoidance of the suspected contaminants and excessive washing. Children may wash themselves in a self-prescribed manner, frequently, or for excessive lengths of time.

An obsession with contamination sometimes produces the opposite effect. In these cases, fear of touching "contaminated" body parts, personal objects, or both leads to a reluctance or outright refusal to touch those parts or items. Watch for untied shoes, unbrushed teeth, sloppy clothing, or uncombed, dirty hair, especially in a child who was previously neat and well-groomed.

Checking compulsions are also common in children and adolescents with OCD. These compulsions are often precipitated by fear of harm to themselves or others, or by extreme doubt. Checking such things as doors, light switches, windows, electrical outlets, and appliances may take up hours of time every day. The child also may spend an inordinate amount of time on school assignments or feel compelled to check and recheck answers on assignments to the point that the checking interferes with completing the homework. Numerous worn-down pencil erasers may signal an obsession that homework must be "perfect." Repetitive questioning may signal an obsession with getting the perfect response from a teacher.

Some children with OCD have obsessions with numbers. They may have "safe" and "unsafe" numbers, repeat actions a certain number of times, or repeatedly count to a given number. They may also repeat actions, such as walking through a doorway, until it "feels right" or in a self-prescribed manner, or they may get in and out of chairs a certain way, or touch certain things a fixed number of times. This behavior may be disguised as forgetfulness or boredom.

Children with OCD may display a variety of other symptoms or characteristics. "Just right" obsessions may manifest in tying and retying shoes, or constantly rearranging objects until they are even or appear symmetrical to the child. Fear of harming others or self, excessive moralization, and religiosity are also often seen in children with OCD. Children and teenagers with OCD frequently have a tendency toward perfectionism and rigidity or stubbornness.

Many children with OCD have difficulty wearing certain clothes. Hypersensitivities to touch, taste, smell, and sound are also common. They are likely to have above-normal intelligence, a more adultlike moral code, more anger and guilt, and a more active fantasy life, and to be disruptive.

If any of the symptoms described above seem to fit your child, keep in mind that, by definition, OCD symptoms must be time-consuming, cause marked distress, or significantly interfere with the child's life in school and at home. The behaviors described above are simply signals that there may be a problem. If you notice such signs, discuss them with your child in a nonthreatening way. If you suspect that your child has OCD, consult a mental health professional who specializes in treating OCD.

TREATMENT FOR CHILDREN WITH OCD

Adults usually seek treatment because OCD is interfering with their lives. Children don't always recognize that they have a problem. They are often brought to the doctor when they exhibit unacceptable behavior and difficulty in school. Young people and their parents need to know that there is hope and help for children with OCD.

The combined use of medication and cognitive behavioral therapy is widely recognized as the best treatment for childhood OCD (March and Mulle 1998), just as it is for adults. Discuss your options with your child's medical team. You may want to try CBT alone first or combine CBT with medication. In severe cases, you will probably want to start medication before beginning CBT. Together, CBT and medication are powerful tools in the struggle against OCD.

Medication

We'll summarize medication treatment for children. However, a detailed discussion of medication treatment of OCD is beyond the scope of this book. Remember, this is only a review.

Medication has long been an important tool in the effective management of OCD in children. However, some question whether psychotropic medications are safe for children with psychiatric disorders, including OCD. While the safety and efficacy of many psychotropic medications has yet to be studied in young children, medications may be prescribed, especially when the potential benefits of treatment outweigh the risks.

When might this be the case? Some children are simply unable to benefit from cognitive behavioral therapy alone, and some problems are so severe and persistent that they would have serious negative consequences for the child if left untreated. As a parent, you will want to ask many questions and evaluate with your doctor the risks of having your child take these medications. Learn everything you can, including potential side effects, which side effects are tolerable, and which are worrisome. In any case, it's best to avoid combining multiple psychotropic medications in very young children unless considered absolutely necessary.

As with adults, seven medications make up the first line of defense in medication therapy for children with OCD: fluoxetine (Prozac), sertraline (Zoloft), paroxetine (Paxil), fluvoxamine (Luvox), citalopram (Celexa), escitalopram (Lexapro), and clomipramine (Anafranil). With the exception of clomipramine, all are selective serotonin reuptake inhibitors (SSRIs). It takes up to twelve weeks at the proper dose to determine whether a medication is going to work. If one medication doesn't work, there's a good chance that another will. If adequate symptom relief isn't achieved, other medications can be added to one of the SSRIs listed above. Medications sometimes added to SSRIs are buspirone (Buspar), clonazepam (Klonopin), and so-called antipsychotic medications taken in extremely low dosages. Clomipramine may also be combined with one of the SSRIs to achieve symptom relief.

Behavioral side effects, including irritability, impulsiveness, and hyperactivity, are sometimes a problem with OCD medications. If these side effects occur, the medication dosage can be adjusted, or another medication may be tried. Adjusting dosages in kids is tricky when one medication is withdrawn and another is introduced. Erratic changes in the child's behavior may occur during this time.

Many children treated with OCD medications have problems with bedtime and sleep. It's important to determine whether this is due to the medication or related to OCD symptoms. If the medication is interfering with sleep, moving the dose earlier in the day or decreasing the dose may help, but this should be done only with the advice of the prescribing doctor. Occasionally, the doctor will add another medication temporarily to aid sleep. On the other hand, the problem may simply be that obsessions and compulsions are worse at bedtime, as is often the case. Intrusive thoughts may make it difficult for the child to get to sleep. In this case, adjusting the medication and focusing cognitive behavioral therapy on these issues can help.

Children metabolize medications quickly, so it is especially important that they take the medication at regular intervals, as prescribed by their physician. This helps to maintain even blood levels of the medication and reduces the possibility of side effects.

Adolescence is a turbulent time for anyone, and teens with OCD are no different. Rebelliousness, acting-out behavior, and lack of compliance can interfere with OCD treatment. Agitation and hyperactivity can be exacerbated by OCD medications. Including cognitive behavioral therapy in the treatment regimen may make it possible to reduce side effects by decreasing medication dosages.

Cognitive Behavioral Therapy

Children can benefit from the self-directed program in parts 2 and 3 of this book, with the additional instructions discussed in this chapter. You may also find *Helping Your Child with OCD* (2003), by Lee Fitzgibbons and Cherry Pedrick, helpful. The first step toward recovery is recognizing that the struggle with OCD is a team effort. Parents, siblings, other family members, therapists, doctors, and school personnel all play important roles, including supporting the child in exposure and response prevention. We've listed books for parents, children, and teens in the resources section. They can be valuable tools as you help your child come to grips with and better manage the OCD.

We strongly advise a thorough evaluation by a mental health professional who specializes in childhood OCD before beginning the self-directed program with children. For help in finding a specialist, read chapter 19 and consult the website of the International OCD Foundation (see the resources section). It is advisable to have a therapist help guide your child through this program, but you may assist your child if you follow the program carefully. Either way, it's extremely important that you approach your role enthusiastically and with a positive attitude. Enthusiasm is contagious and will help your child develop a stronger desire to get better.

The next step is educating yourself and your child about OCD and its treatment, keeping in mind what sort of information and approach is most fitting for your child's age. Knowledge and understanding will make your collaboration with your child's doctor much more productive. Understand that going to the doctor is scary for children, especially if they are baffled by their symptoms or think they might be crazy or have a serious illness that can't be remedied. Learning the truth—that effective treatments are available—greatly reduces this anxiety.

It is important at the outset to clearly establish that OCD is the problem, *not* the child. Defining OCD as a medical problem involving brain chemistry and circuitry rightfully relieves the child and the family of the guilt that goes along with having a psychiatric diagnosis. This will help all of you direct energy where it belongs: toward treatment and effective management of the OCD.

Explain OCD and cognitive behavioral therapy to children in words they can understand. Depict OCD as a brain chemistry problem with terms such as "computer glitch," "a brain circuit that's shorting out," or "brain hiccups." You can use a car alarm as an example of how exposure and response prevention works. Talk about how you remember the first time you heard a car alarm, and how you were concerned that someone's car was being stolen. But after checking out a few cars when their alarms went off, you realized that they were usually false alarms and started ignoring them. So now when you hear a car alarm, you notice it, but you go on with whatever you're doing. Explain that with exposure and response prevention, you notice the obsessions and get to the point where you can effectively ignore the thoughts and their threatening content.

PEDIATRIC AUTOIMMUNE NEUROPSYCHIATRIC DISORDER ASSOCIATED WITH STREPTOCOCCI (PANDAS)

Childhood-onset OCD has been linked to group A beta-hemolytic streptococci, the bacteria that causes strep throat. In response to the presence of the bacteria, the body forms antibodies to fight these bacteria. These antibodies then attack neurons in the basal ganglia area of the brain. In other words, the same antibodies that combat the streptococci also attack brain tissue in areas of the brain related to OCD. It is believed that this leads to OCD symptoms or intensifies existing symptoms.

Children whose OCD is the result of this relatively rare autoimmune reaction of the body experience significant improvement or even the elimination of OCD symptoms when the streptococcus infection is treated with antibiotics (March and Mulle 1998). It is important to get prompt treatment for strep infections. A sudden onset or worsening of OCD symptoms accompanied by upper respiratory distress warrants a trip to the doctor to check for signs of strep infection.

OCD AND RELATED DISORDERS

More often than not, children and teenagers with OCD have more than one neurobehavioral disorder—a phenomenon sometimes referred to as "alphabet soup." Tourette syndrome (TS), attention deficit/hyperactivity disorder (ADHD), oppositional defiant disorder (ODD), major depressive disorder (MDD), tic disorders, learning disorders, Asperger's disorder, and other anxiety disorders are the common co-occurring disorders in children and teens with OCD. Depression can co-occur with OCD on its own, or as secondary to the OCD (Piacentini and Graae 1997; March and Mulle 1998).

When children have one or more other disorders, it's important to coordinate cognitive behavioral therapy for OCD with treatment for the other disorders. Doctors, therapists, teachers, counselors, and parents need to work as a team with the child to gain the upper hand over OCD and any related disorders. Because Tourette syndrome and ADHD are among the most common co-occurring disorders, we'll take a closer look at them in the following sections.

Tourette Syndrome

Tourette syndrome is an inherited neurological disorder that affects about 200,000 people in the United States (Koplewicz 1996). It is characterized by repeated and involuntary body movements and vocalizations. These are called tics. Symptoms begin before the age of twenty-one and last at least one year. Boys are three to five times more likely to have Tourette syndrome. It occurs in only one out of every two thousand children, but as many as 15 percent of children have transient tics (Koplewicz 1996). These are tics that come and go. In a minority of cases, the vocalizations can include socially inappropriate words and phrases. This is called coprolalia. These vocal outbursts are neither intentional nor purposeful. Tics can be described as sudden and repetitive urges to make virtually any movement or sound, including the following:

- Eye blinking
- Squinting
- Lip smacking
- Neck jerking
- Shoulder shrugging
- Throat clearing
- Blowing air through the mouth
- Coughing
- Sniffing
- Hissing

- Arm flailing or thrusting
- Nail biting
- Foot stomping
- Kicking
- Jumping
- Barking
- Humming
- Stuttering
- Sudden changes of voice tone, tempo, or volume
- Short, often meaningless phrases
- Swearing

Many children with Tourette syndrome or tic disorders also have another neuropsychiatric disorder, such as ADHD or OCD (McDougle and Goodman 1997). When a child has both Tourette syndrome and OCD, it's important to distinguish between tics and OCD symptoms because the treatments differ, yet it can be difficult to tell if a symptom is a tic or an OCD ritual. The major difference is that a tic is preceded by a sensory feeling, whereas an OCD compulsion is preceded by a thought.

However, this clinical distinction between Tourette syndrome and OCD has its limits, especially in children with compulsions such as counting, symmetry, repeating, and ordering that are not preceded by catastrophic ideas about harm or danger to themselves or others. This has led some clinicians to the idea that there's a form of OCD that seems to arise from a blend of OCD and Tourette syndrome. This has been termed "Tourettic OCD" (Mansueto and Keuler 2005). In this case, compulsions are typically preceded by feelings of internal tension or a sense of generalized physical discomfort, rather than intrusive thoughts. The resulting compulsions must be performed "just right" to relieve this state of internal tension.

In light of this newly described form of OCD, parents should be alert to the need for modified, more flexible approaches to the use of medications and CBT for their children. For example, the standard SSRIs for OCD may be combined with low dosages of atypical antipsychotics such ziprasidone (Geodon) or risperidone (Risperdal). Some hypertensive drugs, known as alpha-2 agonists, such as clonidine (Catapres) or guanfacine (Tenex) may be added, as they have been found useful in reducing tics in people with Tourette syndrome. The typical CBT approaches for OCD described in other chapters of this book may need to be modified. For example, many more repetitions of ERP may be necessary to achieve a significant reduction in body tension and anxiety. It may also be advisable to augment traditional ERP with muscle relaxation techniques and diaphragmatic breathing to reduce anxiety due to resisting rituals.

Attention Deficit/Hyperactivity Disorder

Attention deficit/hyperactivity disorder (ADHD) is the most common neuropsychiatric disorder in children. It affects 3 to 5 percent of children and occurs four to nine times more often in boys (Koplewicz 1996). Attention deficit disorder (ADD) and ADHD are characterized by inattention and impulsivity; that is, difficulty keeping attention focused on one thing and being susceptible to a broad range of distractions. Hyperactivity is excessive uncontrollable fidgetiness and inability to sit still to the point of interference at home and at school. When this symptom isn't present, the term "attention deficit disorder" is used. For either to be diagnosed, the symptoms must have all of the following characteristics:

- Present before the age of seven
- Chronic (of greater than six months duration)
- Present at home and at school
- Causing significant problems for the child
- Present more often than not

Other disorders can cause inattention, impulsivity, and hyperactivity. These include anxiety disorders, depression, and PANDAS. These disorders should be considered when symptoms begin after the age of seven (Swedo and Leonard 1998).

Most neuropsychiatric disorders can cause problems with attention and concentration similar to ADD symptoms. Children with OCD who appear preoccupied with obsessive thoughts and are performing compulsive rituals are often misdiagnosed with ADD and ADHD. However, some children with OCD also have ADHD or ADD.

Stevie's Story

Until he reached fourth grade, Stevie was a good student. But in fourth grade he became more and more inattentive. He seemed to be daydreaming much of the time, and when he wasn't daydreaming, he was out of his seat. "Sit down, Stevie!" became his teacher's constant refrain. He rarely turned in his homework, and he failed tests because he never finished them.

At first glance, it might seem that Stevie had ADHD. But careful evaluation showed that he had OCD. What were the clues to this diagnosis?

- Stevie's symptoms didn't start until he was nine years old.
- Further evaluation revealed that when Stevie was "daydreaming," he was actually focusing on obsessive thoughts.
- When Stevie left his seat in class, there was a purpose to his movements. His obsessive thoughts involved fear of harm coming to his mother. He felt temporary relief by touching the door, wall, or window. He disguised his touching rituals in what looked like aimless wandering.
- His problems with tests and homework were due to repeated checking. He spent hours on homework, checking and rechecking his answers, only to often throw it out rather than turn in something "imperfect."

FAMILY HELP FOR CHILDREN WITH OCD

By now, you undoubtedly realize the importance of proper diagnosis for children with neuropsychiatric disorders. Which medications and therapies to use depends on the disorder. So the first step is getting the right diagnosis.

If your child does have OCD, family support will be important, just as it is for anyone struggling with OCD. Family involvement is especially important for children. The rest of this chapter will discuss specific areas where you can help your child. We'll offer practical, concrete suggestions in all of these areas. Also read chapter 18 closely; it will help your family work as a team to fight the OCD.

Acceptance and Fairness

Obsessive-compulsive disorder isn't fair. It isn't fair for the child with OCD, and it isn't fair for the child's siblings, who may feel that the child with OCD gets away with misbehavior because of the disorder. They're probably right. Education will help your entire family understand the child's behavior. Giving OCD a name helps. Instead of blaming the child, siblings can blame OCD.

Help everyone in the family understand the difference between fairness and equality. We're all different. We all have different abilities, needs, and problems. The child with OCD just happens to have OCD as a problem. All children need to be treated according to their individual needs. This may not be equal, but it is fair.

Use examples from everyday life to illustrate this difference between equality and fairness. Tommy may be in Boy Scouts. Would you buy a Boy Scout uniform for Sally too? Of course not—but if she's involved in soccer, you would buy her a soccer uniform. If Sally wears glasses, would you make Tommy wear glasses to make Sally feel better? Would you tell Sally she can't wear glasses because Tommy doesn't? Of course not; that wouldn't be fair. Point out that everyone is different. We don't treat everyone the same. Instead, we take each person's needs into account. You can also discuss how your children's friends are different and have varying interests. For example, it's likely that your kids play different games with different friends.

Take a moment now to think about each of your children and how they're different. Then list some of the different interests and needs of each of your children. (You may also use a journal or separate piece of paper to do the exercises in this chapter.)

____

____

____

____

____

Do you treat them differently? If so, how? And is that fair? ______________________________

____

____

Structure and Discipline

Structure is very important in any family. Children feel more secure when they know they can depend on a daily routine. Obsessive-compulsive symptoms tend to become more severe when routines are broken. Vacations are fun, but they can lead to a whole new set of obsessive thoughts and compulsive behaviors. A child with OCD does best in a structured environment, and such an environment will also benefit the rest of the family.

Set clear rules and expectations. Post them on the refrigerator. State them in a positive way. Say, "You will do your homework before watching TV," rather than, "No TV until your homework is done." Or say, "You may watch TV for two hours today," rather than, "No more than two hours of TV."

Create a fairly routine schedule. Try to have dinner, homework, and bedtime at the same time most days. Schedule other activities too, and let your child know what the schedule will be for each day. What if things get off schedule? People with OCD tend to dislike change, but this is a part of life, and they need to accept that. You can help your child with the inevitable changes in several ways. When possible, discuss changes before the occur. Try to give your child an opportunity to provide input on possible changes; this will help your child have a sense of control. Look for ways to make changes less disruptive. And with major changes, such as moving to a new city or changing schools, be aware that your child's symptoms may temporarily increase until new routines are established. Be tolerant at these high-stress times.

Stress exacerbates OCD, especially in the beginning of treatment. Try to maintain a nonstressful environment at home. A structured environment with consistent routines and maintaining a positive attitude can go a long way in reducing stress.

Sometimes children find it less frightening to be disciplined than to fight OCD. Misbehavior might be part of a compulsion, or it could be avoidance behavior. Of course, misbehavior may or may not have anything to do with OCD. What about discipline for disobedience that has nothing to do with OCD? You're likely to find that rewards for positive behavior can help reduce problem behavior. Almost any activity that the child values can be used as a reward for good behavior, including compliance with ERP. Rewards can also be computer, TV, or telephone time, or outings with family or friends. Computer-generated certificates can be used to reward reaching special milestones in the self-directed program. Rewards help the child remember that OCD is the enemy and bolster pride for winning in the battle with the disorder.

With young children, stickers are often a good reward. Set up a sticker chart for all of the children and reward positive behavior with a sticker. These behaviors may be different for each child, depending on age, temperament, and personality. Get the children involved in setting goals and choosing behaviors to be rewarded. Encourage the child with OCD to set goals that involve fighting the OCD. At the end of each week, give small rewards for the stickers. Accompany stickers and rewards with praise. Even when children don't earn a reward, give praise for trying.

What behaviors do you want to reward? ________________________________

____

____

List some activities that could be used as rewards: ________________________

____

____

Time-out is another great discipline technique. Choose a place for time-out. The child's bedroom probably isn't the best place. The time-out needs to be in a place you can monitor that is free of distractions. For example, an area where other children are playing video games probably isn't a good time-out area. One minute of time-out per year of age is a good rule of thumb; for example, time-out for a four-year-old would be four minutes. Be clear about what behaviors will earn a time-out. You may say, "But when I give my child a time-out, I'm in time-out too." Even if this is true, you can make good use of this time. Plan activities you can do during time-outs. For example, this would be a good time to read a magazine or go online.

Children with OCD may need reminders when their behavior is out of control. Prearrange a signal to be used when the child's behavior is inappropriate. This is effective for adults with OCD, too. Cherry's husband did this with her. When they were around other people and he noticed that she was engaging in compulsive behavior, he gave her a little nudge.

Children with OCD misbehave in the same ways that children without OCD misbehave, and they need discipline for misbehavior that they can control. As medication and cognitive behavioral therapy begin to help, you should raise your expectations. Don't let your child use OCD as an excuse for unrelated misbehavior. Again, this also applies to adults. Cherry admits she sometimes used her OCD as an excuse for inappropriate behavior: "People will just have to understand; I have OCD." Your child's therapist can help you decide which negative behaviors should be disciplined and which shouldn't.

Homework

Even with kids who don't have OCD, the home can turn into a battlefield at homework time. Homework can be extra frustrating for many children with OCD, but there are some things you can do to help.

To get an idea of what your child is facing, try doing a page of his or her homework with the obsessions and compulsions your child experiences. For example, write very neatly and erase anytime a "mistake" is made. Mistakes might be letters touching each other or writing that isn't neat enough. When you get halfway through, throw it away and start over. Or do a page of homework while repeating a worry your child might have. Repeat it over and over, at least every thirty seconds. This will help you see the challenge your child faces in doing homework, and understand why your child might avoid doing homework.

A big part of the solution is to schedule homework time. The time just before or just after dinner is a good time for many families. Then, plan quiet activities before homework. It can be hard for children to focus on homework after playing hard outside or engaging in highly stimulating activities like computer games. And because people with OCD often have difficulty leaving things before they are completed, try not to let your child get involved in activities that can't be finished before homework time.

Have a homework time every night—even when there's no homework. If your child doesn't have school assignments, encourage him or her to read a book, write a story, practice math, or do other learning activities. Or give your child "Mom's Assignments" or "Dad's Assignments." Try to have at least thirty minutes of homework time. Help your child break assignments into small tasks to make them seem less overwhelming. Breaks between tasks might help. Let your child get up and move around a bit—but without getting involved in another activity.

Homework should be done in the same place whenever possible. Let your child help choose this place. Provide good lighting and keep plenty of supplies nearby. Stock the area with paper, pencils, pens, crayons, scissors—whatever is frequently needed for homework. This reduces the need for your child to go searching for things. If homework can't be done in the same place every night, put the supplies in a box that can be moved from place to place.

Keep a log of how much time your child spends on homework. If it's excessive, maybe the teacher will reduce the amount of homework until the OCD improves a bit. Communicate with your child's teachers about other issues, too. For example, is your child turning in assignments?

Reward your child for completing homework without complaints and tantrums. Give praise, and incorporate homework rewards into your sticker chart. Completing homework could earn one sticker, and doing so without complaining could earn another.

Finally, we recommend that you turn off the TV and get the entire family involved in homework time. This can be challenging, but everyone will benefit. You can use this time to read or work on bills and paperwork. When your child sees you reading books, it sets a great example. If you have preschoolers, use this time to read a book to them or work on numbers, letters, and shapes.

School

Your child's teachers and school counselor are important team members in the fight against OCD, but they may lack knowledge about the disorder. As a parent, you can help by providing information to your child's school.

The booklet *School Personnel: A Critical Link in the Identification, Treatment, and Management of OCD in Children and Adolescents* (1998), by Gail Adams and Marcia Torchia, is an excellent resource for school personnel. It can be obtained through the Awareness Foundation for OCD and Related Disorders (see the resources section).

Teaching the Tiger (1995), by Marilyn Dornbush and Sheryl Pruitt, is an excellent handbook for school personnel involved in teaching children and adolescents with OCD, attention deficit disorder, and Tourette syndrome. Many of the principles can also be applied to family situations. It's available through the International OCD Foundation (see the resources section).

If you have a local International OCD Foundation affiliate or support group, request that a representative provide an in-service presentation at your child's school. This will help school personnel better understand OCD and its management. If this isn't possible, the video *The Touching Tree* (also available through the International OCD Foundation) can improve understanding. It's about a boy with OCD whose teacher recognizes that he has a problem and assists him in getting help.

Communicate with your child's teachers through visits, phone calls, and notes. Inform them of new symptoms, medication changes, side effects of medications, your child's progress with cognitive behavioral therapy, and behavior for which to praise your child.

HOPE FOR THE FUTURE

Today's treatments have made it possible for children to break free from the distress of OCD. If you suspect that your child has OCD, get help now, before the symptoms become more generalized and ingrained. Start with a thorough evaluation by a mental health professional who specializes in OCD. Enlist other family members and perhaps personnel from your child's school to build a support team for your child. If possible, include a therapist who has experience treating children with anxiety disorders as you work through the self-directed program.

KEYS FOR HELPING CHILDREN BREAK FREE FROM OCD

Explain OCD to your child in understandable ways. For example, compare obsessions to hiccups. Emphasize that your child is *not* the OCD. The horrible thoughts and persistent worries are not who the child is. They are only symptoms of OCD. Here are some specific tips that will help you best support your child:

- Try to understand exactly what obsessions and compulsions your child is experiencing. Often children and teens are horrified by their obsessive thoughts and compulsive behaviors, thinking they are bad or evil for having these thoughts. As a result, they try to keep their symptoms secret, even from their parents and therapists.
- Help your child distinguish between obsessions and compulsions, because each is treated differently: Obsessions are usually thoughts, and compulsions are actions performed in response to the thoughts. Exposure is used to address obsessions, and response prevention is used for compulsions. Trying to prevent or stop the obsessions is counterproductive. Children must learn that while they can't control their obsessions, they have choices whether to carry out their compulsions or not.
- Help your child to see that doing compulsions doesn't make the anxiety better. In fact, it feeds the OCD "monster" and makes everything much worse. You can use the example of a Chinese finger trap—the more you try to get out of it, the more stuck you are.

- Give OCD a name. Mr. Worry, Mrs. Clean, Washy, Mr. Gooey, Checkers, and the Count are a few suggestions, or it could simply be something like Fred, Sam, Pete, Molly, or Jane. Do this together with your child and have fun with it. Using a name for the OCD will help your child begin to externalize the OCD, reinforcing that OCD is the problem, *not* the child. OCD becomes an enemy rather than a bad habit. Teens may find this too childish and may prefer to use the term OCD. That's okay; it still helps externalize the disorder.
- Parents should strive to make the exposure work fun and challenging. Incorporating games into the exposures will help increase the child's motivation to succeed. An example would be playing a fun game of catch with a "contaminated" ball.
- Children handle OCD much better when they understand that it isn't their fault and that they are not alone. A support group for kids with OCD can be extremely beneficial in this regard. Contact the International OCD Foundation (www.ocfoundation.org) for information about parent-child support groups in your area.
- Note that following the self-directed program may simply be too overwhelming for many children and their parents. In this case, professional treatment is in order. For information on finding a qualified therapist for your child's OCD see chapter 19.
- Refer to the resources section for details on age-appropriate books about OCD. There are now a variety children's books that explain OCD well. We've written a book for teens that describes OCD in a concise way that even many adults might find helpful: *Obsessive-Compulsive Disorder* (Hyman and Pedrick 2008).

CHAPTER 18

OCD Is a Family Affair: Working Together to Overcome OCD

Alone we can do little; together we can do so much.

—Helen Keller

The family plays an important role in OCD treatment and recovery. Family stress and dysfunction, while not a direct cause of OCD, can powerfully affect the person with OCD and the severity of symptoms (March and Mulle 1998). Conversely, having a family member with OCD can contribute to disruption, discord, and serious misunderstandings within the family (Yaryura-Tobias and Neziroglu 1997b).

What often gets lost is that OCD is the enemy, *not the person with the disorder*. Fighting and managing OCD should be the focus, and doing so must be a team effort. This chapter will help family members understand what it takes to support a loved one in breaking free from OCD.

SUPPORT STARTS WITH EACH FAMILY MEMBER

How well each family member copes with the OCD is largely determined by each individual's ability to deal with discomfort, confusion, and conflicting emotions toward the disease and the person with OCD. Because OCD can be so taxing on the emotional resources of the family, at times family members may become overwhelmed and fall back on attitudes and behaviors that are harmful to the person with OCD, such as ridicule, neglect, or outright hostility. The following strategies will help the family come together to promote your loved one's recovery from OCD.

Get the Facts First

If a member of your family is exhibiting the signs and symptoms of OCD, you must first learn as much as you can about the disorder. Acquiring good, solid facts and information about OCD can help ease the anxiety you may feel about the disorder. There is more quality information about OCD available now than ever before. Learn as much as you can. The appendix contains a short introduction to OCD and its treatment. This is a good starting point for family members. Part 1 of this workbook builds on that basic information, and part 2 will help you understand what your loved one is experiencing in working through the self-directed program. In addition, talk frankly with trusted professionals and experts about your family's problem. Find an OCD support group in your community and start learning more about OCD.

Quit the Blame Game

Shame, guilt, and self-blame among family members can impede effective management of OCD and support of your loved one. For decades it was common to blame OCD on inadequate child rearing, a chaotic family environment, and the like. If only human behavior were so simply explained. The fact is, there isn't a shred of evidence that early family interactions directly cause OCD (March and Mulle 1998). As explained in chapter 2, genetics and biology are the likely culprits when someone has OCD. A family affected by OCD should feel no more shame about it than they would if someone in the family had thyroid disease, sickle-cell anemia, diabetes, or any other chronic medical condition.

Get OCD Out of the Closet

There's an old phrase used in Alcoholics Anonymous that may apply here: You are only as sick as your secrets. Often, family members feel a collective sense of shame about having OCD in the family. Due to the overall lack of understanding of mental disorders in the general population, these disorders are shrouded in fear, mystery, confusion, and stigma. Family members often fear others will regard them with scorn, seeing them as bad parents, brothers, sisters, or children. Don't allow the ignorance of others to dictate your feelings about having someone with OCD in your family.

Talk openly about it with people you believe to be capable of understanding and providing support. Share the information in the appendix with extended family members and others who are close to you or your loved one. It is clear and concise enough for those who just want to know the basics. Participating in a good support group is another way to help bring OCD out of the closet and start to normalize your experience.

Manage Your Negative Feelings

Once you've achieved some understanding of OCD, the next step is to manage negative feelings about having OCD in the family. Anger, resentment, and frustration won't help you cope with the situation or support your loved one. Here are some tips to help you manage your negative feelings:

- **Let go of anger.** Work on accepting the facts of your family as they are while finding the strength and wisdom to change what you can. Acceptance doesn't mean doing nothing. It means devoting your energy to finding effective solutions, not staying angry and resentful. These emotions only waste your valuable time and energy. Work on letting go of anger and finding forgiveness for the person with OCD and, most of all, for yourself. You did nothing to cause the OCD; you don't somehow deserve this. It just is.

- **Let go of any insistence that others should understand.** No one is obligated to feel as you feel or do as you do just because you want them to. Arm yourself with facts and solid information and bring these educational materials into your home. Share the information with interested family members in a gentle, nonthreatening way.

- **Expect and accept resistance.** Because of the lack of understanding about mental illness, other family members may have preconceived ideas about what causes OCD. Expect and anticipate resistance to even the best, most qualified sources of information. You can try to change entrenched attitudes, but don't expect to succeed. Resist viewing the most antagonistic and biased individuals as wrong and therefore bad; rather, see them as "yet to be enlightened." People usually adopt new ways of seeing things when it becomes clear to them that it's is in their best interests to do so. Over time, patience and persistence can change even the most deeply ingrained attitudes.

- **Be a good listener.** Don't lecture. Siblings of a child with OCD often have significant issues, such as unexpressed anger, guilt, or resentment. Dealing with these may require professional guidance. If they feel comfortable talking about these feelings and are open to learning more about OCD, they'll be less likely to criticize and make hurtful remarks.

Communicate with Your Loved One's Health Care Team and Each Other

If the person with OCD is a child, establish close communication with the child's health care team. If the person with OCD is an adult, you'll need to ask how much he or she wants you to be involved. If the person with OCD gives consent, contact any therapists treating your loved one. Ask about what role you can play in the treatment process.

Encourage everyone in the family to express their feelings about how the OCD is affecting the family. OCD symptoms tend to wax and wane. Keep this in mind when the OCD seems worse than usual. Lower your expectations for the time being and, together, remember other times when the OCD seemed especially bad but then things got better. Keep communication simple and clear.

HOW FAMILY MEMBERS CAN HELP THE PERSON IN THE SELF-DIRECTED PROGRAM

Once the person with OCD begins the self-directed program, family members can play important roles in progress and recovery. People with OCD often need a support person at home to assist them with the exposure tasks and homework assignments. However, before you take on the role of support person, learn what will be expected of you. This is a long-term project and requires that you set aside time on a regular basis to help with real-life practice. Are you prepared for such a serious commitment?

Regardless of whether you take on the role of support person, it's important to support your loved one's recovery by not participating in OCD rituals and not enabling the OCD. For example, don't give in to excessive requests for reassurance.

Don't Participate in OCD Rituals

One of the negative ways caregivers and family members deal with the disruption caused by OCD behaviors in the family is by participating in rituals. Participation, also called enabling or accommodating, can be the family's way of keeping the peace in the face of the sufferer's persistent demands for immediate relief from obsessive worries. Often, it's seen as a practical necessity for dealing with compulsions that are out of control and extremely disruptive to the family. However, the unfortunate result of enabling or participating in OCD rituals is that the OCD symptoms are reinforced and strengthened, and now the entire family is immersed within them.

Typical Ways Family Members Participate in OCD Behaviors

- Doing the laundry for the person with OCD, who treats unworn or briefly worn clothing as contaminated and therefore in need of unnecessary laundering.

- Repeatedly reassuring the person that he or she doesn't have a dreaded disease in response to excessive reassurance seeking.
- Reassuring the person with OCD that doors and windows are locked and that appliances are turned off or safe, or assisting with related checking rituals.
- Providing repeated reassurance that your loved one didn't harm anyone while driving.
- Helping a loved one with a hoarding problem by examining each piece of trash before throwing it away to ensure that nothing "important" is discarded.
- Changing clothes in the garage before coming into the home to mollify fears about "contaminating" the house.
- Avoiding the purchase of particular household products because the person with OCD believes they are dangerous or "contaminated."
- Giving in to persistent requests by the person with OCD for verbal reassurance that something is "right," "okay," "correct," or "not bad, harmful, or dangerous." Until the "right" response is provided, the request may be repeated over and over.
- Trying to deal with the OCD by reasoning. Offering endless reiterations about how unreasonable the particular obsessive concern is, or repeating the facts about how HIV is caught, for example, will be fruitless and will end up making both you and the person with OCD even more frustrated. This is because the person with OCD already knows that these fears are unreasonable but cannot shake the feeling that something is terribly wrong or potentially dangerous.

With the above-described behaviors in mind, take a close look at your family situation and your individual responses to the person with OCD. Use the following space to list the various ways in which you or other family members have participated in your loved one's OCD rituals. You can photocopy the exercises in this chapter or do them in a notebook if you prefer not to write in the book, or if multiple family members would like to do the exercises in this chapter.

1. ______________________________
2. ______________________________
3. ______________________________
4. ______________________________
5. ______________________________
6. ______________________________
7. ______________________________
8. ______________________________

Don't Give in to Compulsive Reassurance Seeking

Compulsive reassurance seeking is a particularly distressing and annoying symptom of OCD that family members tend to get entangled with. It usually occurs in the following sequence:

1. **An obsessive thought intrudes.** The person with OCD experiences an intrusive thought that could be about almost any frightening or uncomfortable idea or notion. Here are a few examples:

   - Maybe I'll get AIDS and die a slow death.
   - What if my parents die in an accident while away from the house?
   - What if the pantry isn't clean and I contaminate my child?
   - Maybe I didn't lock the door when I left the house today.

2. **The person feels a jolt of anxiety.** At the moment the thought strikes, the person experiences severe discomfort. People with untreated OCD have a limited capacity to manage their discomfort through productive, logical self-talk or self-reflection.

3. **The anxiety leads to a strong urge for relief.** The person experiences a seemingly uncontrollable urge to obtain immediate relief and therefore poses a question specifically to receive verbal reassurance from an authority figure or someone he or she trusts.

4. **The person gets the "fix."** A family member, sensing this severe anxiety, offers verbal reassurance intended to calm the person down such as, "No, you won't get AIDS," "Mommy will be right back," or "Don't worry, it's clean." However, the response often must be repeated, over and over again, until the anxiety of the thought is neutralized and the person with OCD feels better.

5. **The cycle repeats.** Then the cycle starts over. This annoying pattern persists because it provides immediate relief. However, it deprives the person with OCD of the opportunity to manage obsessive thoughts and anxiety in a healthier way.

Although this incessant reassurance seeking is no laughing matter, demands for reassurance are sometimes best met with a humorous remark to lighten the tension. Avoid an angry and critical tone. Here are some examples of how you might use humor:

Question: Did I check the door locks enough times?

Answer: I think Fort Knox could use your talents. Or maybe we should just donate everything we own to the Lonely Home-Invaders Society.

Question: Did I harm anyone?

Answer: You left a trail of death in your wake. You and Jack the Ripper should compare notes.

Question: Are you coming back?

Answer: No, I'm going to Hollywood to make it big.

Question: Will I get AIDS?

Answer: We might as well make funeral arrangements now.

Question: Did I hurt your feelings?

Answer: Yes, and I'll just never recover from it.

Using humor in these situations probably won't be welcomed by the person with OCD—at least not initially. If fact, your loved one is likely to find it somewhat threatening at first, then funny, and then annoying. However, stick with it to get a smile on your loved one's face. While the urge to ask for reassurance isn't likely to subside, your lightened response can help ease tension in the family and pave the way toward eventual disengagement from participation in the OCD.

Stop Enabling OCD

When you accommodate OCD symptoms, you strengthen the OCD. You may wonder whether you should just suddenly quit participating in rituals and giving reassurance. Probably not. Doing so without first explaining and enlisting the cooperation of the person with OCD is likely to cause tremendous anxiety and disruption. The best plan of action is to collaborate with the person with OCD and come up with a plan for disengaging from rituals. Ideally, this would be done when your loved one is ready to begin the self-directed program. We provide some guidelines for disengaging, but be aware that the assistance of a counselor or therapist familiar with OCD can be especially useful here.

Guidelines for Disengagement

- Anticipate that your loved one's anxiety will go up for a while when you begin to disengage. This heightened anxiety may be disruptive at first, but it's a sure sign of change, and it will eventually diminish. Stay cool.
- Decrease your participation gradually, though not too gradually. For example, cut your participation in half to start, and decrease by half every week or two thereafter. Use the Weekly Plan for Disengagement Worksheet, later in this chapter, to plan your strategy.
- Plan on completely stopping all participation in compulsive rituals after an agreed-upon period of time. Make this nonnegotiable.
- Discuss all disengagement plans openly with the person with OCD before implementing them. No surprises.

- Expect a certain amount of resistance to decreasing your participation in rituals. Resistance may range from mild discomfort to anger, rage, or even violence. However, violent behavior is rare and should never be tolerated.

- Explain your reasons for disengaging clearly and honestly. Remain calm yet firm and straightforward. It is very important to respond in a consistent manner.

- When demands to neutralize anxiety occur, family members should explain, in a calm, reasonable, and low-key manner, why they won't comply. Here are some examples of what you might say:

    - I must refuse to help you neutralize your anxiety because it's destructive to your health and the family's health in the long run.

    - Because I love you, I refuse to participate in harmful behavior.

    - While I might be helping you feel better in the short run, in the long run I'll only be harming you.

    - I know it's hard and may be upsetting to you, but it's best if I don't do that ritual for you.

    - Your doctor has instructed me to not participate. The doctor knows what he or she is talking about, and we decided to trust the doctor's judgment.

- If total nonresponse to requests for reassurance is unrealistic, start by agreeing to respond to requests only once per day. Use this agreement as a stepping-stone to stopping reassurance behaviors altogether.

- Prior to beginning to disengage, make a copy of the OCD Enabler's Declaration of Independence, fill it out, and sign it, and then post it in a prominent place in your home.

OCD Enabler's Declaration of Independence

Dear ______________________________,

I'm offering this to you from a deep and profound sense of respect, love, and acceptance that you have an illness that has caused you to be very difficult to be with. As someone who has been involved in your OCD symptoms, I have come to realize that by participating in your OCD, I have not only hurt myself, I have also contributed to your OCD problem without meaning to do that. Here are some of the ways that I've been enabling you:

- Assisting in or carrying out your compulsive behaviors in order to make you more "comfortable" or shield you from discomfort.
- Assisting in or carrying out your compulsive behaviors in order to keep the peace in the family.
- Assisting in or carrying out your compulsive behaviors because I was afraid you would ____.
- Lying to myself and others about your condition and about the pain your OCD symptoms have caused.
- Making my life into an unhealthy extension of your illness. In trying to help you and relieve your pain, I have gotten further and further from the person I really am, and I have unintentionally reinforced your illness and my entrenchment in it.

I hereby place you on notice that from this moment on, I will lovingly and respectfully refuse to assist in any of your compulsive rituals. I will lovingly decline to satisfy your compulsive requests for reassurance. This means that I love you more than I can describe. It means that my belief in you and your capacity for health and wellness is so great, so overwhelming, that I will hold to this with the greatest resolve. I believe in you!

Signed ______________________________

Date: ______________________________

Identify Emotions That Keep You Stuck in Enabling

If you've found yourself entangled in the vicious cycle of enabling or accommodating your loved one's OCD, you may have encountered some powerful feelings that keep you locked into this unhealthy pattern. It's typical to experience some or all of the following feelings:

- **Fear:** You may fear for the immediate health and well-being of your loved one, so you assist in a ritual or compulsion out of a sense of obligation to protect your loved one.
- **Guilt:** You may feel guilty that the OCD is somehow your fault, and therefore think you should do everything you can to help your loved one feel better by enabling the OCD. And even if you know the OCD isn't your fault, you may fear feeling guilty in the future if you don't intervene to reduce your loved one's discomfort.
- **Identification with your loved one:** You may find it difficult to see your loved one's emotional pain when he or she is deprived of the rituals or compulsions that temporarily relieve that pain. You feel the natural impulse to help alleviate the pain however you can, and not acting on that impulse brings up feelings of helplessness and powerlessness.
- **Keeping the peace:** The OCD rituals and compulsions have become integrated into the family's normal day-to-day routines. To stop participation in those rituals may disrupt this "unholy peace."

These kinds of feelings are natural; they occur in every family and aren't "abnormal" responses to the OCD. Perhaps this is why they can be so insidious in taking hold of the family. Be that as it may, these feelings can create patterns that keep the family locked in a pattern of enabling the OCD. Recognizing, acknowledging, and confronting these feelings is an important first step toward not reinforcing your loved one's OCD.

Create a Plan for Disengaging from Participation in the OCD

Now that you better understand that participation in your loved one's OCD is harmful, and may even make the situation worse, describe your personal plan to stop participating in and enabling OCD in the family.

Compulsive rituals my family members and I have been participating in: ______________________

____

Feelings that have kept me involved in enabling my loved one's OCD: ______________________

____

____

With what you've learned in this chapter and the information recorded above, use the following worksheet to make a plan for disengaging from your loved one's OCD. We've included a sample plan to provide you with an idea of how it might go. It's essential that your loved one collaborate in making the plan; otherwise he or she may be less likely to cooperate. For this reason, we've included a space for you to record whether your loved one participated in drafting the plan.

Disengagement Planning Worksheet

	Participation in rituals I will disengage from	**How much will I reduce involvement? (Be specific)**	**Did the person with OCD collaborate?**	**Did you achieve your goals? If no, why not**
Week 1	*Buying paper towels and wet wipes. Doing three extra loads of laundry per day, and using excessive detergent.*	*Reduce the number of paper towels and wipes purchased by a third. I will do three extra loads of laundry but use half the detergent.*	*No at first, but after a heart-to-heart talk at the end of the week, she agreed to the plan.*	*Reduced purchases by one-fourth and reduced wipes used a bit. Used less detergent.*
Week 2	*Buying paper towels and wet wipes. Doing three extra loads of laundry per day, and using excessive detergent.*	*Reduce the number of paper towels and wipes purchased by half. I will do two extra loads of laundry and keep using half the detergent*	*Yes, but very uncomfortable with change. Wanted to quit, but offered a gift card to a favorite store if she cooperates*	*No. Will try again next week.*
Week 3	*Buying paper towels and wet wipes. Doing three extra loads of laundry per day, and using excessive detergent.*	*Reduce paper the number of paper towels purchased towels by half, and restrict wet wipes to essential cleaning only. I will do two extra loads of laundry for the week and further reduce detergent to a normal amount.*	*Yes. Doing ERP while I reduce my involvement.*	*Good week! She's catching on to the program, but still using too many wipes. Did much less laundry this week—only one extra load.*
Week 4	*Buying paper towels and wet wipes Doing three extra loads of laundry per day, and using excessive detergent*	*Reduce the number of paper towels purchased by three-fourths. I won't do any extra loads of laundry this week, and I'll keep using a normal amount of detergent.*	*Yes. Doing well.*	*Yes. Washing and cleaning down to normal levels Laundry at normal levels!*

Disengagement Planning Worksheet

	Participation in rituals I will disengage from	How much will I reduce involvement? (Be specific)	Did the person with OCD collaborate?	Did you achieve your goals? If no, why not
Week 1				
Week 2				
Week 3				
Week 4				

Cultivating More Helpful Responses

People often express a fear of failing and disappointing others. Yet in the initial stages of exposure and response prevention, your loved one's progress may be somewhat slow. Be patient, and help your loved one cultivate patience and celebrate small successes. Here are some examples of statements you might hear from your loved one during this time, along with examples of two types of responses: helpful and unhelpful. Use these examples as guidelines for how to support and encourage your loved one.

Person with OCD: "This treatment really freaks me out. I'm scared to death! Maybe I shouldn't do this!"

> **Helpful response:** "I understand this really scares you. Change is hard. But hang in there! Take one step at a time, and things can get better. I believe in you."
>
> **Unhelpful response:** "There you go again, wimping out as usual! You're just wasting my time and money!"

Person with OCD: "I did something today that I haven't done in years! I actually got through an entire day without doing a ritual!"

> **Helpful response:** "It's great that you feel so good about what you accomplished. Keep working at it and you're bound to be successful. We're really proud of you!"
>
> **Unhelpful response:** "It's about time. Isn't that what we've been trying to get you to do all along? Big deal! Now do that every day."

Person with OCD: "I worked with my therapist on not checking my blood pressure. Don't you think a visit to the ER for a checkup is needed even though my therapist advised against it?"

> **Helpful response:** "Your best bet is to follow your therapist's advice. She knows what's best in this situation. Hang in there."
>
> **Unhelpful response:** "If I've told you once, I've told you a thousand times: There's nothing wrong with you! Are you just plain stupid?"

Person with primarily obsessional OCD: "Did I molest that child?" What if I did and didn't realize that I did it?"

> **Helpful response:** "I don't know for sure exactly what happened. But what is for sure is that you have OCD, and as long as you rely on me to tell you whether things are okay or not your disease will continue to flourish."
>
> **Unhelpful response:** "No, for the umpteenth time, I'm sure you didn't! Why would that child want to keep playing with you if you harmed her in any way?"

Person with OCD: "I slipped up and washed my hands when I shouldn't have. Don't tell my therapist. He'll fire me as a client!"

Helpful response: "I think your therapist would want to know how you're doing—the good and the bad. It's best for you to report everything related to your progress or lack of progress."

Unhelpful response: "I won't tell him. We'll keep that between you and me."

Person with OCD: "I touched a red spot today that could be hep-C. Do you think I've contracted a serious disease?"

Helpful response: "I guess anything is possible. I don't want to feed your OCD problem."

Unhelpful response: "I'm absolutely sure you didn't. But just in case, I think your therapist should let you check it out at the local walk-in clinic just to be safe."

Person with OCD: "I really slipped up today, and I was doing so well. I know you're deeply disappointed in me. I'm such a screwup! I'll never get well."

Helpful response: "Don't give up now! Tomorrow's another day. This OCD is a tough foe. Hang in there and remember, it's a fifteen-round fight. The OCD may have won this round, but you don't have to let it win tomorrow. We're proud of you."

Unhelpful response: "Why do I even waste my time with a screwup like you? You'll never get better."

Person with OCD: I've worked hard on ERP and I'm much better, but I still have OCD. I must be a hopeless loser."

Helpful response: "You've really worked hard and you can see the payoff in how much you've progressed. Ask your therapist how you can improve even more."

Unhelpful response: "You've obviously failed to achieve your goals. Just give up. I'm tired of this OCD crap. You just need to get over it and get a life!"

Person with OCD: "I'm doing just great with my OCD. This treatment has given me my life back!"

Helpful response: "That's great! You deserve all the credit for taking on your OCD and succeeding."

Unhelpful response: "Why didn't you do this ten years ago when we literally begged you to get help and you insisted you could overcome OCD on your own? We always knew what was best for you, but you never listened to us."

ADDITIONAL TIPS FOR DEALING WITH OCD IN THE FAMILY

Here are some tips, some obvious, some not so obvious, to assist the family in moving toward recovering from OCD in a healthy way.

Encourage compliance with medication and cognitive behavioral therapy. Taking OCD medication requires patience and persistence to achieve the maximum benefits. People with OCD, especially children or young adults, occasionally need encouragement and reminders to take their medications as prescribed. Sometimes this means hanging in there with the medication even when side effects are bothersome and symptoms haven't yet begun to abate. If compliance is a problem, discuss this issue openly and directly. If forgetfulness is a problem, use a weekly pillbox to avoid missed or extra doses. Also provide plenty of encouragement as the person with OCD works through the self-directed program. Familiarize yourself with the program so you can be an effective cheerleader. It's hard work, and sometimes discouraging, but it will eventually lead to a better quality of life—for your loved one and for the whole family.

Be supportive and encouraging. Setting expectations too high sets people up for disappointment. However, not progressing fast enough can also be discouraging. Help your loved one set reasonable goals. Recognize, encourage, and reward even small signs of success. Avoid comparisons with others who have OCD or with family members who don't have the disorder. The person with OCD probably already has a rather low self-image. OCD is demoralizing, and people with OCD are often ashamed of their behavior. They know it's irrational, and shame about the behavior can lead to more generalized shame. The thought "OCD makes me do weird things" turns into "I'm weird." People need to know that they aren't weird or crazy because of their OCD behavior. They are not their OCD. Separating their wonderful selves, with their many positive attributes, from the OCD is important.

Minimize family stress. Keeping stress in the family under control is especially important during the early stages of treatment. Keep the family routine as normal and consistent as possible. For those with OCD, change and uncertainty promotes stress, and stress exacerbates OCD symptoms. Even happy, satisfying events, such as vacations, can cause an increase of symptoms.

Become familiar with signs of lapse and relapse—and know the difference. Read chapter 15. It will help you recognize the signs of worsening OCD symptoms. It explains reasons why this might occur and offers suggestions for maintaining and building on the gains your loved one makes in the self-directed program.

Turn off the TV! Television, with its great potential to entertain and inform, has become a breeding ground for fear and worry in people with OCD. Bad news tends to dominate, and it travels faster than good news. Plus, tabloid TV, news programs, and so-called human interest shows purposely highlight harm or potential danger to attract viewers and keep them glued to the program. People with OCD tend to be hypersensitive to images of potential harm and danger and overestimate risk. Such programs can trigger fresh, new obsessions or exacerbate existing obsessive worries and compulsions. Be much more selective in the programming your family views, and consider doing what you can to reduce your family's TV time.

Commit to change. Sometimes it helps to put commitments in writing. If you haven't already done so, review the OCD Enabler's Declaration of Independence with your loved one. Discuss it together and make any changes you agree upon. Then sign it. Commit to changing the way you respond to OCD, and to helping your family member break free from OCD.

Take care of *yourself*. Taking good care of yourself is perhaps the most important guideline. OCD tends to take over the afflicted person's entire life, then proceeds to dominate family life. Work hard to not let OCD rule every aspect of your life. Find a sense of balance between family responsibilities and personal time to recharge your battery. Attend to your needs for health and well-being. Pursue a hobby or take an exercise or meditation class to manage stress.

ASSISTING SOMEONE WHO WON'T ACKNOWLEDGE HAVING OCD AND REFUSES HELP

In some cases, family members or friends may recognize signs of OCD years before the person with OCD acknowledges and accepts it. In spite of serious impairment, the person may deny the illness and refuse to seek help, extending and deepening his or her own pain and also causing a great deal of pain and hardship for the entire family. Feelings of depression, hopelessness, and helplessness may prevail among family members who are at a loss as to how to help the person who is in denial.

If all efforts to convince the person to get help have failed, you need to address the issue head-on. Here are some guidelines that will enhance your chances of success:

- Plan a family intervention. Since there's strength in numbers, it's helpful to confront the person with OCD as a unified group.
- It is essential to obtain the help of a trained family therapist or a counselor familiar with OCD, who can assist in facilitating communication between family members and the person with OCD.
- During a family intervention, all family members must firmly yet compassionately explain specifically how the OCD behavior is affecting them individually and how the situation is intolerable. They must also stress their commitment to helping. Acknowledge that the

person is in pain, and that gaining support, knowledge, and tools to face the disorder can help. Emphasize that the OCD and its behaviors are what is intolerable, and not the person with OCD.

- If your loved one persists in denial, say that this too is a symptom of the illness. Offer to help, and explain that doing nothing is not an acceptable option. Have each family member state what he or she is willing to do or not do to help change the present situation. Give a time frame for obtaining appropriate professional help and state clear contingencies if the plan isn't followed within the specified time frame, such as moving the person to a group home, hospital, or other supervised living situation.
- Be firm yet flexible and realistic. If change appears unlikely, what is most important is to take whatever measures are necessary to ensure that your loved one lives independently and with dignity, and has ample opportunities to improve his or her standing in life.
- If the person with OCD threatens to harm himself or herself during the process of intervention, it is important to take such threats seriously. Consider such threats as further evidence that professional help is needed. An active suicidal gesture requires immediate inpatient hospitalization to protect the life of the person with OCD.

FAMILY MEMBERS PLAY AN IMPORTANT ROLE

Breaking free from OCD goes more smoothly and is more successful when it's viewed as a family effort. The right support can make a tremendous difference. If you have a loved one with OCD, your first step is to learn as much as you can about OCD and how you can support your loved one's recovery. You are an important part of the team. Communicate openly about the struggle with OCD and work together to define the role you can play in recovery. We've listed books for family members in the resources section. They can be helpful as you support your loved one in breaking free from OCD.

CHAPTER 19

Where to Get Help: How to Find a Good Therapist and Other Sources of Support

Talk doesn't cook rice.

—Chinese proverb

From the beginning of this workbook, we've recommended that you consult a mental health professional before starting the self-directed program. This helpful step can make a significant contribution to your progress in recovering from OCD. Perhaps you've put off discussing your OCD problem with a mental health professional, or maybe you're seeing a professional for other problems. Whatever your situation, this chapter will help you find a mental health professional to help you break free from OCD. We'll also briefly discuss support groups and how to find more information and support online.

PROFESSIONAL HELP FOR OCD

The best professional to help you with your OCD is someone who knows a great deal about OCD and how it is treated. Usually this will be a psychiatrist, psychologist, or therapist. Psychiatrists are medical doctors who specialize in treating disorders of the brain and mind. Their primary role is to prescribe medications for OCD. They usually aren't trained to do cognitive behavioral therapy, but they should be aware of this approach. On the other hand, psychologists, therapists, and counselors who treat OCD cannot prescribe medication, but they are usually trained in cognitive behavioral therapy. It is rare for one doctor to do both, so you'll probably need two separate professionals on your treatment team, one for medication and one for CBT.

Whether you begin treatment with medications or CBT usually doesn't matter, though if your OCD is severe you may benefit from starting with medication (see chapter 3 for more on this topic). As we've stressed throughout this workbook, the optimum treatment is the combined use of medications and CBT. Both play important roles in recovery. The person with OCD who chooses one and ignores or avoids the other is receiving only partial treatment and therefore will experience only partial results.

Remember, too, that different people respond differently to medications and CBT. Some people who have broken free from OCD consider medication the key factor in their recovery and see CBT as less important. Conversely, others feel that CBT was the key ingredient in their recovery. And still others contend that both were equally important. Everyone responds differently to different treatments. What is right for you can only be determined by trying combined treatment.

Again, it's very important that the psychiatrist and therapist you consult are experienced in treating OCD. Although any licensed physician can prescribe medication for OCD, consulting a board-certified psychiatrist who understands treatment of the disorder is by far the best choice. The International OCD Foundation maintains a listing of psychiatrists and therapists who claim to have knowledge and experience in the treatment of OCD (see the resources section for contact information). Because the International OCD Foundation doesn't specifically research the credentials and qualifications of every doctor and therapist on their referral list (which would be an overwhelming and expensive process), you must still be cautious. However, consulting their website would be a useful first step toward identifying a qualified professional in your area. Then, be sure to use the questions a little later in this chapter to ensure a prospective therapist is a good choice for you. The Anxiety Disorders Association of America (ADAA) and the Association for Behavioral and Cognitive Therapies (ABCT) also maintain listings of therapists who have indicated an interest in treating OCD and related disorders. (See the resources section for contact information for these groups.)

If an experienced therapist isn't available locally, you may choose to travel to one of a number of centers where OCD is treated. Contact the International OCD Foundation for a current list of inpatient and outpatient programs. You could stay in a motel or with friends and attend an outpatient clinic for evaluation and intensive therapy. Afterward, telephone sessions may be a possibility. Inpatient treatment may be necessary if you have a substantial risk of self-harm as a result of your OCD symptoms.

Because treatment can be expensive and time-consuming, select your therapist carefully. Use the Counselor Selection Interview Worksheet that appears later in this chapter as a guide in evaluating therapists. Consider asking other professionals for their opinion of the therapist in question. If possible, get feedback from current and former patients of the professional you're considering. Beware, however, of any tendency to obsess about making the "perfect" decision. This can delay getting the help you need. If this is a problem, just go with your gut feelings about what is best.

Questions to Ask Prospective Therapists

Interviewing therapists prior to choosing a mental health professional may feel intimidating. However, most therapists don't mind taking a few minutes over the phone to answer questions about their practice and qualifications to treat your problem. If you detect a defensive or dismissive attitude from the professional, move on. If you feel you need more time than a few minutes over the phone, consider making an appointment and paying for the therapist's time to answer the questions to your satisfaction.

What techniques or methods do you generally use to treat OCD?

Either "cognitive behavioral therapy" or "behavior therapy" is a good answer. Cognitive behavioral therapy means that the principles of cognitive restructuring (changing beliefs and attitudes) are used alongside the principles for behavioral change (targeting compulsive behaviors and rituals). Go a step further and ask therapists what kind of behavior therapy they use. If the reply doesn't include exposure and response prevention or exposure and ritual prevention (both terms are used), you may want to look for a different therapist. After reading through this book, you should have a pretty good understanding of what exposure and response prevention is. If you don't, review chapters 3 through 6.

Are you licensed by the state?

Every state in the United States now requires mental health professionals to be licensed, which can only occur once certain educational and experience requirements are met. Most therapists' credentials can be verified online through the website of the state agency responsible for licensing. While just having a state license to practice is no indicator of competence, it is the minimum essential requirement you should screen for. Plus, choosing a state-licensed professional gives you legal recourse in the unlikely event that you become a victim of grossly incompetent care or improper behavior.

What are your credentials?

In seeking cognitive behavioral treatment, be aware that a master's degree in a mental health discipline is the minimal acceptable training. Don't be overly impressed by credentials, however. A talented, skilled master's level therapist with significant experience with OCD can be much more helpful than a Ph.D. with lots of education but little real knowledge of OCD. Look for membership in the International OCD Foundation, the Anxiety Disorders Association of America (ADAA), or the Association for Behavioral and Cognitive Therapies (ABCT). If you're seeking medication for your OCD, it must be prescribed by an MD or DO, preferably with a specialty in psychiatry. For MD psychiatrists, certification by the American Board of Psychiatry and Neurology (www.abpn.com) is essential.

Do you have OCD or personally know anyone who has it?

This is an excellent question, if a little brazen. Though few qualified mental health professionals are likely to have OCD, a number do have personal experience with family members or others who have the disorder. This may be a sign that the doctor understands OCD well.

Where did you learn about OCD treatment?

Training is important, as is experience. A single weekend professional workshop on OCD is insufficient. Look for a background that includes intensive training in cognitive behavioral therapy for anxiety disorders and ongoing case supervision. Psychiatrists should have received continuing education specifically about the pharmacology of OCD treatment.

How many patients or clients have you actually treated for OCD?

There is no magic number, but it is important that the therapist has experience in treating clients with OCD *for their OCD*. Many nonspecialists help people with OCD with all kinds of general life-stress issues. Although this contributes somewhat to their knowledge of OCD, it doesn't provide sufficient background and experience to treat people for OCD.

What are the most important factors for helping people with OCD get better?

Look for a therapist who endorses and practices within a neurobehavioral framework of understanding OCD. This means the therapist recognizes the need for a multimodal approach, combining the use of both medications and cognitive behavioral therapy to help people with OCD. The therapist must have significant knowledge of what it's like to have OCD from the client's point of view and convey a deep sense of empathy for the client's struggle. Walk away from any therapist who minimizes the impact of OCD or views it simply as a dysfunctional lifestyle choice. It is vital that you have a sense that the therapist cares.

How many of your current clients have OCD?

The more the therapist's practice focuses on treating OCD and anxiety disorders—and using cognitive behavioral therapy to do so—the better. However, be aware that only therapists who specialize in OCD or anxiety disorders are likely to have more than just a few clients currently being seen specifically for OCD.

Would you be willing to leave your office to do exposure and response prevention if needed?

Flexibility is key here. If exposure work requires a home visit or a series of visits to public areas such as malls, stores, or hospitals, is the therapist willing to accompany you in carrying out those exposures? And if not, can provisions be made for someone such as an assistant therapist or family member to supervise exposures outside of the office?

During exposure and response prevention, are you available between sessions if I get stuck or need support while doing exposures?

Again, flexibility is key. The therapist must fully understand the stress that exposure work may initially entail and must be willing to be available between sessions for brief telephone support and monitoring of progress.

Do you support the use of appropriate medication for OCD when needed?

Avoid therapists who dogmatically object to the use of medication for OCD or, for that matter, medical doctors who dismiss cognitive behavioral approaches to OCD.

How cured will I be by the end of treatment?

Walk out if the therapist offers you a "cure" for OCD or boasts a long list of "cured" clients. Most qualified, competent therapists won't promise a cure, but they will offer hope for significant relief from symptoms, as well as assistance with learning to live a more satisfying life, despite the OCD.

Other Considerations in Choosing a Therapist

In addition to asking a prospective therapist all of the questions above, it's also important to ask yourself a few questions. After meeting a prospective therapist, consider whether you feel you'll get along with this person. It's vital that you feel comfortable talking openly with your therapist. Do you get the feeling that the therapist cares about you and your problem? Also consider whether you feel you can trust this person's knowledge and expertise. You must be willing to do whatever he or she says is necessary to make progress, so trust is key.

In the event that you feel a therapist is a good fit but he or she isn't experienced with OCD, does the therapist indicate a willingness to learn more about it? Therapists experienced in the treatment of OCD may not be available in your area. If that's the case, a therapist who is willing to learn and help you work through the self-directed program is the next best choice.

The following form provides a place where you can record the most important information you learn when interviewing therapists. You may also record this information in your journal.

Counselor Selection Interview Form

Therapist Name: ______________________ Date ________

Office Hours: (evening and/or weekend appointments?) ________________

How much do services cost? ______________________

Do you participate in any insurance panels, or Medicare/Medicaid? ____________

What are your credentials?

Are you licensed as a therapist? (psychologist, social worker, counselor, or marriage and family therapist) ______________________

What year did you get your license? ______________________

Where did you receive your professional training? ________________

What is you primary professional activity? (clinical practice, teaching, research) ________

How long have you been in practice? ______________________

Are you a member of any professional organizations related to OCD? ________

____

Do you have advanced training in CBT for OCD? (e.g., Behavior Therapy Institute of the International OCD Foundation) ______________________

What do you consider your practice specialty? ______________________

What is your primary practice orientation? (cognitive-behavioral, psychodynamic, family systems, etc.) ______________________

Do you see families in addition to individuals? ______________________

How many patients with OCD do you see in an average week? ____________________

Do you do exposure and response prevention (ERP)? ____________________

Do you ever leave the office to conduct "exposure in vivo"? ____________________

Do you have a qualified psychiatrist to refer to if it is determined that I need medication?

____

Additional Question(s): ____________________

____

____

____

Overall Impression: ____________________

____

____

____

____

____

SUPPORT GROUPS

If there is a good OCD support group in your area, it can help you reach your goal of breaking free from OCD. It can be an enormous relief to realize that you are not alone, and that others have similar symptoms and challenges. Support groups also can be helpful for the families of people with OCD, especially parents who have children with OCD who are still living at home.

Support groups for OCD are conducted in a variety of formats, depending upon the approach taken by organizers and leaders. For example, Obsessive Compulsive Anonymous (OCA) is a support group founded in 1988 that utilizes principles similar to other 12-step programs, such as Alcoholics Anonymous, Narcotics Anonymous, Gamblers Anonymous, and Alanon. The program is described in the book *Obsessive Compulsive Anonymous: Recovering from Obsessive Compulsive Disorder* (1999), by Roy C. A list of local groups is available on their website or by phone (see the resources section).

GOAL (Giving Obsessive-Compulsives Another Lifestyle) is a support group format begun by members of the Philadelphia affiliate of the International OCD Foundation. Their emphasis is on choosing behavioral goals to work on between meetings. Dr. Jonathan Grayson, Ph.D., one of GOAL's founders, advises having a mental health professional who is experienced with OCD assist the group. This person answers questions, helps keep the meetings on track, and gives individual assistance when needed.

Local support groups may use one of these formats, or they may use another that works for them. A list of OCD support groups throughout the United States and abroad is available through the International OCD Foundation (see the resources section).

HELP IN CYBERSPACE

A vast range of support and information for people with OCD and their families is available on the Internet. Many discussion groups exist for people with OCD and their families. Among the best for adults with OCD is OCD-Support (health.groups.yahoo.com/group/OCD-Support). This is an e-mail-based online discussion group with thousands of members. It brings people with OCD together through e-mail and is skillfully moderated by Wendy Mueller, who has experienced OCD and recovered. Expert advice is provided by Michael Jenike, MD (a Harvard professor who heads the Scientific Advisory Board of the International OCD Foundation), and James Claiborn, Ph.D. and Dr. Jon Grayson, both specialists in the treatment of OCD. In addition to this general list for discussion of the effects of OCD and its treatment, there are smaller support lists for family members, parents, teens, children, and people with specific symptoms. Stuck in a Doorway (www.stuckinadoorway.org) is another excellent moderated online message board for people with OCD. It's based in the United Kingdom and focuses on people with horrific thoughts, but all forms of OCD are represented.

There are many websites dedicated to providing information about OCD. Many of them, including the website of the International OCD Foundation (www.ocfoundation.org), have message boards, chat rooms, and resources for finding help in dealing with OCD. They may also have a page or resource dedicated to seeking information from experts. We've listed some of our favorite OCD websites in the resources section.

HELP FOR FAMILY AND FRIENDS

Your loved one may ask you for assistance in finding professional treatment for OCD. If so, read this chapter to help equip yourself. We also recommend that you take advantage of any support groups available to you. Some regions have groups for parents, other family members, and friends. If not, you can participate in an online group; there are many e-mail groups devoted to family members of people with OCD. If so, read the information in this chapter about seeking support in cyberspace. You need to know that you aren't alone. Countless other families are going through similar struggles. They can share strategies for coping and give you hope that your loved one will indeed break free from OCD.

THIS IS ONLY THE BEGINNING

As we end *The OCD Workbook*, it is our hope that you are well on your way to breaking free from obsessive-compulsive disorder. For many people with OCD, breaking free is a lifelong challenge, as symptoms tend to wax and wane. The resources section is filled with more avenues for help and hope. Besides providing information on organizations, websites, and support groups, we've listed many books that can help you or your loved one on your journey toward recovery.

Appendix

A BRIEF INTRODUCTION TO OBSESSIVE-COMPULSIVE DISORDER FOR FAMILY AND FRIENDS

Obsessive-compulsive disorder is characterized by obsessions and/or compulsions that are time-consuming, distressing, and/or interfere with normal routines, relationships, or daily functioning. *Obsessions* are persistent impulses, ideas, images, thoughts, or urges that intrude into a person's thinking and cause excessive worry and anxiety. *Compulsions* are covert mental acts or overt behaviors performed repetitively in response to obsessions to relieve or prevent the worry and/or anxiety generated by the obsession. They often have the intention of magically preventing or avoiding some dreaded event, such as death, illness, or some other perceived misfortune.

A diagnosis of OCD is made on the basis of a psychiatric or psychological examination, a history of the person's symptoms and complaints, and the degree to which the symptoms interfere with daily functioning. Based on the nature, length, and frequency of the symptoms presented, the mental health professional will differentiate OCD from other conditions with similar symptoms.

Studies have shown that 80 to 99 percent of all people experience unwanted thoughts (Niehous and Stein 1997). But most people can hold unpleasant thoughts in their mind without too much discomfort, or they can easily dismiss the thoughts entirely. Their thoughts are shorter in duration, less intense, and less frequent than the intrusive thoughts of those who suffer from OCD. The obsessive thoughts of

OCD, on the other hand, usually have a specific onset, produce significant discomfort, and result in a powerful, overwhelming urge to neutralize or lessen them.

People with OCD frequently suffer from various degrees of clinical depression. Approximately one-third are depressed at the time they seek treatment. About two-thirds of people with OCD have had at least one episode of major clinical depression in their lifetime (Jenike 1996). Many others suffer from lesser forms of depression. It's very important to watch for warning signs of depression.

What Causes OCD?

No one knows exactly what causes OCD, but researchers are piecing together the puzzle. It appears that OCD results from a combination of genetically inherited tendencies or predispositions, together with significant environmental factors. Inherited tendencies include subtle variations in brain structure, neurochemistry, and circuitry. Environmental factors include psychological and physical trauma, childhood neglect, abuse, family stress, illness, death, and divorce, plus major life transitions, such as adolescence, moving out to live on one's own, marriage, parenthood, and retirement. Inherited biological predispositions serve as a kind of tinderbox, which, when combined with environmental lightning bolts, can ignite and activate OCD symptoms.

How Is OCD Treated?

Medication and cognitive behavioral therapy (CBT) are the most effective treatments for OCD. They can be used alone for significant benefit, but some people require a combination of medication and CBT for best results. The medications most effective for treating OCD belong to the family of drugs known as selective serotonin reuptake inhibitors (SSRIs). They include fluvoxamine (Luvox), fluoxetine (Prozac), sertraline (Zoloft), paroxetine (Paxil), citalopram (Celexa), and escitalopram (Lexapro). They help correct neurochemical imbalances and thereby help relieve OCD symptoms. Some people will have to try more than one of these medications to find the one that works best for them. Others may need to take a combination of medications.

Cognitive behavioral therapy helps by giving the person with OCD tools to manage the obsessions and compulsions. Exposure and response prevention (ERP) is the principal cognitive behavioral technique for treating OCD. It involves prolonged exposure to real-life situations that provoke obsessive worries and typically trigger compulsive behavior. For example, the person with OCD may have to touch or directly contact some feared object, such as an empty garbage pail or other "contaminated" object, without relieving the resulting anxiety by washing his or her hands. Through repeated practice, the person realizes that the feared disastrous consequences do not and will not occur, and that the severe anxiety initially associated with that situation decreases. This is the process of *habituation*. Exposure is best done in stages, taking baby steps toward the ultimate goal of complete habituation to feared objects or situations.

The purpose of response prevention is to decrease the frequency of rituals. The person with OCD faces feared stimuli, experiences the urge to do rituals, and simultaneously blocks ritual behaviors, such as hand washing or excessive checking. If this is too hard to do all at once, the person may first delay performing a ritual and then gradually work toward totally resisting the compulsion.

Initially, cognitive behavior techniques can appear quite challenging and even scary, but obtaining relief from OCD symptoms makes it highly worthwhile. When used together, medication and cognitive behavioral therapy complement each other. Medication improves the regulation of serotonin in the brain, while cognitive behavioral therapy helps to temper obsessive thoughts by modifying the habitual, faulty responses to those thoughts. Medication can reduce the anxiety associated with obsessions, making it easier to implement cognitive and behavioral techniques.

The OCD Workbook leads people with OCD through a self-directed program for breaking free from OCD. The primary tool is exposure and response prevention. The program also uses cognitive therapy techniques to help the person to identify his or her faulty beliefs and attitudes and challenge them with healthier, more accurate appraisals.

How to Give Support to a Loved One

Your family member or friend has decided to use cognitive behavioral techniques, especially exposure and response prevention, to break free from OCD. Exposure and response prevention can be highly challenging and will inevitably impact family members. You may wonder how you can be helpful in supporting your loved one's goals of overcoming OCD. For a detailed answer, please read chapter 18 of *The OCD Workbook*, as well as the "Help for Family and Friends" sections at the end of most of the chapters.

In brief, we'll say that, over the years, Dr. Hyman has observed many family members interacting with a loved one who is engaging in exposure and response prevention. He believes that the best attributes a family member can display include remaining calm; being positive (seeing the glass half full, rather than half empty); not being negative, critical, or blaming and instead encouraging the person's best efforts; and offering praise and verbal reinforcement for positive steps taken in treatment, no matter what the size of those steps.

Don't shrink from addressing the problems that your loved one encounters while doing exposure and response prevention. Emphasize being in the here and now and moving forward without looking back. If a therapist is involved, family members shouldn't interfere with treatment and should follow the therapist's instructions faithfully.

It is extremely important that you have a solid understanding of OCD derived from extensive reading about OCD and its treatment, and from interacting with other people with OCD who aren't family members, as in an OCD support group. Read the first few chapters of *The OCD Workbook* to get a better understanding of OCD, then read the chapters that have the greatest bearing on your loved one's OCD. Judgmental attitudes based on gut feelings rather than solid experience, knowledge, and information about OCD will probably be detrimental. If you think you really "get" OCD without having spent a lot of time educating yourself and seeing OCD through the eyes of someone with the disorder, you're probably fooling yourself. Check guilt and blame at the door and suppress your judgments and attitudes, especially while your loved one is working on exposure and response prevention.

YALE-BROWN OBSESSIVE COMPULSIVE SCALE (Y-BOCS)

The Y-BOCS is the scale most widely used by OCD clinicians and researchers to determine the severity of OCD symptoms. Your score can help you determine the severity of your OCD problem before starting the self-help program. You can take the test again a time or two during the program and again at the end of the program to get a sense of your progress.

Questions 1 through 5 are about your obsessive thoughts.

Obsessions are unwelcome and distressing ideas, thoughts, images, or impulses that repeatedly enter your mind. They may seem to occur against your will. They may be repugnant to you, and you may recognize them as senseless, and they may not fit your personality.

Please think about the *last seven days* (including today), and check one answer for each question.

1. Over the last seven days, how much of your time was occupied by obsessive thoughts? How frequently did the obsessive thoughts occur?

____ 0 = None (If you checked this answer, also check 0 for questions 2, 3, 4 and 5 and proceed to question 6)

____ 1 = Less than 1 hour per day, or occasional intrusions (occurred no more than 8 times a day)

____ 2 = 1 to 3 hours per day, or frequent intrusions (occurred more than 8 times a day, but most hours of the day were free of obsessions)

____ 3 = More than 3 hours and up to 8 hours per day, or very frequent intrusions (occurred more than 8 times a day and during most hours of the day)

____ 4 = More than 8 hours per day, or near-constant intrusions (too numerous to count, and an hour rarely passed without several obsessions occurring)

2. Over the last seven days, how much did your obsessive thoughts interfere with your social or work functioning? (If you are currently not working, please think about how much the obsessions interfered with your everyday activities.) (In answering this question, please consider whether there was anything that you didn't do, or that you did less, because of the obsessions.)

____ 0 = No interference

____ 1 = Mild, slight interference with social or occupational activities, but overall performance not impaired

____ 2 = Moderate, definite interference with social or occupational performance, but still manageable

____ 3 = Severe interference, caused substantial impairment in social or occupational performance

____ 4 = Extreme, incapacitating interference

3. **Over the last seven days, how much distress did your obsessive thoughts cause you?**

____ 0 = No distress

____ 1 = Mild, infrequent, and not too disturbing distress

____ 2 = Moderate, frequent, and disturbing distress, but still manageable

____ 3 = Severe, very frequent, and very disturbing distress

____ 4 = Extreme, near-constant, and disabling distress

4. **Over the last seven days, how often did you try to disregard or ignore these obsessive thoughts and let them pass naturally through your mind? (Here we are *not* interested in how successful you were in disregarding your thoughts but only in how much or how often you *tried* to do so.)**

0 = I always tred to let the obsession pass naturally through my mind

1 = I tried to ignore or disregard them most of the time (i.e., more than half the time)

2 = I made some effort to ignore or disregard them

3 = I rarely tried to ignore or disregard them

4 = I never tried to ignore or disregard them

5. **Over the last seven days, how *successful* were you at ignoring or disregarding your obsessive thinking? (*Note*: Do not include here obsessions stopped by avoidance or doing *compulsions*.)**

0 = I was always successful in ignoring or disregarding the obsessions

1 = I was usually successful in ignoring or disregarding them (i.e., more than half the time)

2 = I was sometimes successful in ignoring or disregarding them

3 = I was rarely successful in ignoring or disregarding them

4 = I was rarely able to disregard them even momentarily

Questions 6 through 10 are about your compulsive behaviors.

Compulsions are behaviors or acts that you feel driven to perform although you may recognize them as senseless or excessive. At times, you may try to resist doing them, but this may prove difficult. You may experience anxiety that does not diminish until the behavior is completed.

Please think about the *last seven days* (including today), and check one answer for each question.

6. Over the last seven days, how much time did you spend performing compulsive behavior? How frequently did you perform compulsions? (If your rituals involve daily living activities, please consider how much longer it took you to complete routine activities because of your rituals.)

____ 0 = None (If you checked this answer, also check 0 for questions 7, 8, 9, and 10)

____ 1 = Less than 1 hour per day was spent performing compulsions, or occasional performance of compulsive behaviors (no more than 8 times a day)

____ 2 = 1 to 3 hours per day were spent performing compulsions, or frequent performance of compulsive behaviors (more than 8 times a day, but most hours of the day were free of compulsions)

____ 3 = More than 3 hours and up to 8 hours per day were spent performing compulsions, or very frequent performance of compulsive behaviors (more than 8 times a day and during most hours of the day)

____ 4 = More than 8 hours per day were spent performing compulsions, or near-constant performance of compulsive behaviors (too numerous to count, and an hour rarely passed without several compulsions being performed)

7. Over the last seven days, how much did your compulsive behaviors interfere with your social or work functioning? (If you are currently not working, please think about your everyday activities.)

____ 0 = No interference

____ 1 = Mild, slight interference with social or occupational activities, but overall performance not impaired

____ 2 = Moderate, definite interference with social or occupational performance, but still manageable

____ 3 = Severe interference, caused substantial impairment in social or occupational performance

____ 4 = Extreme, incapacitating interference

8. Over the last seven days, how did you feel or would you have felt if prevented from performing your compulsion(s)? How anxious did you become or would you have become?

____ 0 = Not at all anxious

____ 1 = Only slightly anxious if compulsions prevented

____ 2 = Anxiety would mount but remain manageable if compulsions prevented

____ 3 = Prominent and very disturbing increase in anxiety if compulsions prevented

____ 4 = Extreme, incapacitating anxiety from any intervention aimed at reducing the compulsions

9. Over the last seven days, how much of an effort did you make to resist the compulsions? Or how often did you try to stop the compulsion? (Rate only how often or how much you *tried* to resist your compulsions, not how successful you actually were in stopping them.)

____ 0 = I always made an effort to resist (or the symptoms were so minimal that there was no need to actively resist them)

____ 1 = I tried to resist most of the time (i.e., more than half the time)

____ 2 = I made some effort to resist them

____ 3 = I yielded to almost all compulsions without attempting to control them, but I did so with some reluctance

____ 4 = I completely and willingly yielded to all compulsions.

10. Over the last seven days, how much control did you have over the compulsive behavior? How successful were you in stopping the ritual(s)? (If you rarely tried to resist, please think about those rare occasions on which you *did try* to stop the compulsions, in order to answer this question.)

____ 0 = I had complete control over the compulsive behavior

____ 1 = Usually I could stop compulsions or rituals with some effort and willpower

____ 2 = Sometimes I could stop the compulsive behavior, but only with difficulty

____ 3 = I could only delay the compulsive behavior, but eventually it had to be carried to completion

____ 4 = I was rarely able to delay performing the compulsive behavior even momentarily

_______ TOTAL

Scoring

0 to 7:	non-significant
8 to 15:	mild OCD
16 to 23:	moderate OCD
24 to 31:	severe OCD
32 to 40:	extreme, disabling OCD

Y-BOCS is printed with the permission of Wayne Goodman, Department of Psychiary, Mount Sinai School of Medicine, New York, New York. The original version was published in "Yale-Brown Obsessive Compulsive Scale I: Development, Use and Reliability," by W. K. Goodman, L. H. Price, S. A. Rasmussen, C. Mazure, R. L. Fleischmann, C. L. Hill, et al. *Archives of General Psychiatry* (1989) 46(11):1006-1011. This version includes modifications made in 2002, with permission, by Bruce Mansbridge, Ph.D.

Resources

SELF-HELP BOOKS

Baer, L. 2001. *Getting Control: Overcoming Your Obsessions and Compulsions*. New York: Plume.

Baer, L. 2002. *The Imp of the Mind: Exploring the Silent Epidemic of Obsessive Bad Thoughts*. New York: Plume.

Bell, J., and M. Jenike. 2009. *When in Doubt, Make Belief: An OCD-Inspired Approach to Living with Uncertainty*. Novato, CA: New World Library.

C., Roy. 1999. *Obsessive Compulsive Anonymous: Recovering from Obsessive Compulsive Disorder*. New Hyde Park, NY: Obsessive Compulsive Anonymous.

De Silva, P., and S. Rachman. 2009. *Obsessive-Compulsive Disorder: The Facts*. New York: Oxford University Press.

Dumont, R. 1996. *The Sky Is Falling: Understanding and Coping with Phobias, Panic, and Obsessive-Compulsive Disorders*. New York: W. W. Norton.

Foa, E. B., and R. Wilson. 2001. *Stop Obsessing! How to Overcome Your Obsessions and Compulsions*. New York: Bantam Books.

Grayson, J. 2003. *Freedom from Obsessive-Compulsive Disorder: A Personalized Recovery Program for Living with Uncertainty*. New York: Tarcher/Penguin Putnam.

Hyman, B. and DuFrene, T. 2008. *Coping with OCD-Practical Strategies for Living Well with OCD.* Oakland, CA: New Harbinger Publications.

Munford, P. R. 2004. *Overcoming Compulsive Checking: Free Your Mind from OCD.* Oakland, CA: New Harbinger Publications.

Neziroglu, F., J. Bubrick, and J. Yaryura-Tobias. 2004. *Overcoming Compulsive Hoarding: Why You Save and How You Can Stop.* Oakland, CA: New Harbinger Publications.

Penzel, F. 2000. *Obsessive-Compulsive Disorders: A Complete Guide to Getting Well and Staying Well.* New York: Oxford University Press.

Rapoport, J. L. 1997. *The Boy Who Couldn't Stop Washing: The Experience and Treatment of Obsessive-Compulsive Disorder.* New York: Signet Books.

Schwartz, J., with B. Beyette. 1997. *Brain Lock: Free Yourself from Obsessive-Compulsive Behavior.* New York: Harper Perennial.

Tolin, D., R. Frost, and G. S. Steketee. 2007. *Buried in Treasures: Help for Compulsive Acquiring, Saving, and Hoarding.* New York: Oxford University Press.

BOOKS ON SCRUPULOSITY

Ciarrocchi, J. W. 1995. *The Doubting Disease: Help for Scrupulosity and Religious Compulsions.* Mahwah, NJ: Paulist Press.

Crawford, M. 2004. *The Obsessive-Compulsive Trap.* Ventura, CA: Regal Books.

Osborn, I. 2008. *Can Christianity Cure Obsessive-Compulsive Disorder? A Psychiatrist Explores the Role of Faith in Treatment.* Grand Rapids, MI: Brazos Press.

Osborn, I. 1999. *Tormenting Thoughts and Secret Rituals: The Hidden Epidemic of Obsessive-Compulsive Disorder.* New York: Dell Publishing Company.

Santa, T. 2007. *Understanding Scrupulosity: Questions, Helps, and Encouragement.* Liguori, MO: Liguori Publications.

MEMOIRS AND NOVELS

Murphy, T. W., M. A. Jenike, and E. E. Zine. 2009. *Life in Rewind: The Story of a Young Courageous Man Who Persevered Over OCD and the Harvard Doctor Who Broke All the Rules to Help Him.* New York: HarperCollins.

Wilensky, A. 2000. *Passing for Normal: A Memoir of Compulsion.* New York: Broadway Books.

BOOKS FOR FAMILIES

Landsman, K., K. Ruppertus, and C. Pedrick. 2004. *Loving Someone with OCD: Help for You and Your Family*. Oakland, CA: New Harbinger Publications.

BOOKS FOR CHILDREN AND TEENS

Hyman, B. M., and C. Pedrick. 2008. *Obsessive-Compulsive Disorder.* Brookfield, CT: Twenty-First Century Books.

March, J. 2007. *Talking Back to OCD: The Program That Helps Kids and Teens Say "No Way"—and Parents Say "Way to Go."* New York: Guilford Press.

Talley, L. 2004. *A Thought Is Just a Thought.* New York: Lantern Books.

Wagner, A. P. 2000. *Up and Down the Worry Hill: A Children's Book About Obsessive-Compulsive Disorder and Its Treatment.* Rochester, NY: Lighthouse Press.

BOOKS FOR PARENTS AND EDUCATORS

Chansky, T. E. 2001. *Freeing Your Child from Obsessive-Compulsive Disorder: A Powerful, Practical Program for Parents of Children and Adolescents.* New York: Three Rivers Press.

Chansky, T. E. 2004. *Freeing Your Child from Anxiety: Powerful, Practical Solutions to Overcome Your Child's Fears, Worries, and Phobias.* New York: Broadway Books.

Chansky, T. E. 2008. *Freeing Your Child from Negative Thinking: Powerful, Practical Strategies to Build a Lifetime of Resilience, Flexibility, and Happiness.* Cambridge, MA: Da Capo Press.

Dornbush, M., and S. Pruitt. 1995. *Teaching the Tiger: A Handbook for Individuals Involved in the Education of Students with Attention Deficit Disorders, Tourette's Syndrome or Obsessive-Compulsive Disorder.* Duarte, CA: Hope Press.

Fitzgibbons, L., and C. Pedrick. 2003. *Helping Your Child with OCD: A Workbook for Parents of Children with Obsessive-Compulsive Disorder.* Oakland, CA: New Harbinger Publications.

Wagner, A. P. 2002. *What to Do When Your Child Has Obsessive-Compulsive Disorder: Strategies and Solutions.* Rochester, NY: Lighthouse Press.

Wagner, A. P. 2002. *Worried No More: Help and Hope for Anxious Children.* Rochester, NY: Lighthouse Press.

BOOKS FOR MENTAL HEALTH PROFESSIONALS

Clark, D. A. 2006. *Cognitive-Behavioral Therapy for OCD.* New York: Guilford Press.

Eifert, G. H., and J. P. Forsyth. 2005. *Acceptance and Commitment Therapy for Anxiety Disorders: A Practitioner's Treatment Guide to Using Mindfulness, Acceptance, and Values-Based Behavior Change Strategies.* Oakland, CA: New Harbinger Publications.

Frost, R., and G. S. Steketee. 2002. *Cognitive Approaches to Obsessions and Compulsions: Theory, Assessment, and Treatment.* Cambridge, MA: Pergamon.

March, J. S., and K. Mulle. 1998. *OCD in Children and Adolescents: A Cognitive-Behavioral Treatment Manual.* New York: Guilford Press.

Steketee, G. S. 1993. *Treatment of Obsessive Compulsive Disorder.* New York: Guilford Press.

Steketee, G. S. 1999. *Overcoming Obsessive-Compulsive Disorder: Therapist Protocol.* Oakland, CA: New Harbinger Publications.

Taylor, S., and G. Asmundson. 2004. *Treating Health Anxiety: A Cognitive-Behavioral Approach.* New York: Guilford Press.

Wells, A. 2000. *Emotional Disorders and Metacognition: Innovative Cognitive Therapy.* New York: Wiley.

Wilhelm, S., and G. S. Steketee. 2006. *Cognitive Therapy for Obsessive-Compulsive Disorder: A Guide for Professionals.* Oakland, CA: New Harbinger Publications.

BODY DYSMORPHIC DISORDER

Claiborn, J., and C. Pedrick. 2002. *The BDD Workbook: Overcome Body Dysmorphic Disorder and End Body Image Obsessions.* Oakland, CA: New Harbinger Publications.

Phillips, K. A. 2005. *The Broken Mirror: Understanding and Treating Body Dysmorphic Disorder.* New York: Oxford University Press.

TRICHOTILLOMANIA

Claiborn, J., and C. Pedrick. 2000. *The Habit Change Workbook: How to Break Bad Habits and Form Good Ones.* Oakland, CA: New Harbinger Publications.

Keuthen, N. J., D. J. Stein, and G. A. Christensen. 2001. *Help for Hair Pullers: Understanding and Coping with Trichotillomania.* Oakland, CA: New Harbinger Publications.

Penzel, F. 2003. *The Hair-Pulling Problem: A Complete Guide to Trichotillomania.* New York: Oxford University Press.

Vavrichek, S., and R. G. Golomb. 2000. *The Hair Pulling "Habit" and You: How to Solve the Trichotillomania Puzzle.* Silver Spring, MD: Writers Cooperative of Greater Washington.

ACCEPTANCE AND COMMITMENT THERAPY AND MINDFULNESS

Eifert, G. H., and J. P. Forsyth. 2007. *The Mindfulness and Acceptance Workbook for Anxiety: A Guide to Breaking Free from Anxiety, Phobias, and Worry Using Acceptance and Commitment Therapy.* Oakland, CA: New Harbinger Publications.

Hayes, S. C., and S. Smith. 2005. *Get Out of Your Mind and Into Your Life: The New Acceptance and Commitment Therapy.* Oakland, CA: New Harbinger Publications.

Kabat-Zinn, J. 1990. *Full Catastrophe Living: Using the Wisdom of Your Body and Mind to Face Stress, Pain, and Illness.* New York: Delta.

Langer, E. J. 1990. *Mindfulness.* Cambridge, MA: Perseus Publishing.

MENTAL HEALTH ORGANIZATIONS AND WEBSITES

American Foundation for Suicide Prevention (AFSP): 888-333-2377; www.afsp.org

Anxiety Disorders Association of America (ADAA): 240-485-1001; www.adaa.org

Association for Behavioral and Cognitive Therapies (ABCT): 212-647-1890; www.abct.org

Association for Contextual Behavioral Science (ACBS): contextualpsychology.org. This website is dedicated to information on acceptance and commitment therapy and is mainly for therapists and academicians, but people with OCD can learn a great deal about ACT here as well.

Attention Deficit Disorder Association (ADDA): 800-939-1019; www.add.org

Awareness Foundation for OCD and Related Disorders (AFOCD): www.ocdawareness.com

Center for Psychiatric Rehabilitation, consumer website for living well with a psychiatric disability in work and school: 617-353-3549; www.bu.edu/cpr/jobschool

Cherry's website: cherrypedrick.com

Children and Adults with Attention-Deficit/Hyperactivity Disorder (CHADD): 800-233-4050; www.chadd.org

Depression and Bipolar Support Alliance (DBSA): 800-826-3632; www.dbsalliance.org

International OCD Foundation (IOCDF): 617-973-5801; www.ocfoundation.org

Internet Mental Health: www.mentalhealth.com

Mental Health America (MHA): 800-969-6642; www.nmha.org

National Alliance on Mental Illness (NAMI): 888-999-6264; www.nami.org

National Anxiety Foundation (NAF): 859-281-0003; www.lexington-on-line.com/naf.html

National Association of Anorexia Nervosa and Associated Eating Disorders (ANAD): 630-577-1330; www.anad.org

National Eating Disorders Association (NEDA): 800-931-2237; www.nationaleatingdisorders.org

National Institute of Mental Health (NIMH): 866-615-6464; www.nimh.nih.gov

National Mental Health Consumers' Self-Help Clearinghouse (NMHCSH Clearinghouse): 800-553-4539; www.mhselfhelp.org

Obsessive Compulsive Anonymous (OCA): 516-739-0662; obsessivecompulsiveanonymous.org

Obsessive Compulsive Information Center, Madison Institute of Medicine: 608-827-2470; www.miminc.org/aboutocic.asp

PsychCentral: 978-992-0008; www.psychcentral.com

Scrupulous Anonymous: 800-325-9521; mission.liguori.org/newsletters/scrupanon.htm

National Tourette Syndrome Association (TSA): 718-224-2999; www.tsa-usa.org

Trichotillomania Learning Center (TLC): 831-457-1004; www.trich.org

References

Abramowitz, J., S. Taylor, and D. McKay. 2009. Obsessive-compulsive disorder. *Lancet* 374(9688):491-499.

Adams, G. B., and M. Torchia. 1998. *School Personnel: A Critical Link in the Identification, Treatment, and Management of OCD in Children and Adolescents.* Milford, CT: OC Foundation.

Alsobrook, J. P., and D. L. Pauls. 1998. Genetics of obsessive-compulsive disorder. In *Obsessive-Compulsive Disorders: Practical Management*, 3rd edition, edited by M. Jenike, L. Baer, and W. Minichiello. St. Louis, MO: Mosby.

American Psychiatric Association. 2000. *Diagnostic and Statistical Manual of Mental Disorders*, 4th edition, text revision. Washington, DC: American Psychiatric Association.

Azrin, N., and R. G. Nunn. 1973. Habit reversal: A method of eliminating nervous habits and tics. *Behaviour Research and Therapy* 11(4):619-628.

Azrin, N. H., R. G. Nunn, and S. E. Franz. 1980. Treatment of hair pulling (trichotillomania): A comparative study of habit reversal and negative practice training. *Journal of Behavior Therapy and Experimental Psychiatry* 11(1):13-20.

Baer, L., and M. Jenike. 1998. Personality disorders in obsessive-compulsive disorder. In *Obsessive-Compulsive Disorders: Practical Management*, 3rd edition, edited by M. Jenike, L. Baer, and W. Minichiello. St. Louis, MO: Mosby.

Beck, A. T., G. Emery, and R. L. Greenberg. 1985. *Anxiety Disorders and Phobias: A Cognitive Perspective.* New York: Basic Books.

Benson, A. L. 2008. *To Buy or Not to Buy: Why We Overshop and How to Stop.* Boston: Shambhala Publications.

Billett, E. A., M. A. Richter, and J. L. Kennedy. 1998. Genetics of obsessive-compulsive disorder. In *Obsessive-Compulsive Disorder: Theory, Research, and Treatment*, edited by R. P. Swinson, M. M. Antony, S. Rachman, and M. A. Richter. New York: Guilford Press.

Burns, D. D. 1980. *Feeling Good: The New Mood Therapy.* New York: Avon.

C., Roy. 1999. *Obsessive Compulsive Anonymous: Recovering from Obsessive Compulsive Disorder.* New Hyde Park, NY: Obsessive Compulsive Anonymous.

Ciarrocchi, J. 1995. *The Doubting Disease: Help for Scrupulosity and Religious Compulsions.* Mahwah, NJ: Paulist Press.

Ciarrocchi, J. 1998. Religion, scrupulosity, and obsessive-compulsive disorder. In *Obsessive-Compulsive Disorders: Practical Management*, 3rd edition, edited by M. Jenike, L. Baer, and W. Minichiello. St. Louis, MO: Mosby.

Claiborn, J., and C. Pedrick. 2002. *The BDD Workbook: Overcome Body Dysmorphic Disorder and End Body Image Obsessions.* Oakland, CA: New Harbinger Publications.

Coric, V., S. Taskiran, C. Pittenger, S. Wasylink, D. H. Mathalon, G. Valentine, et al. 2005. Riluzole (Rilutek) augmentation in treatment-resistant obsessive-compulsive disorder: An open-label trial. *Biological Psychiatry* 58(5):424-428.

Cottraux, J., I. Note, S. Yao, S. Lafont, B. Note, E. Mollard, et al. 2001. A randomized controlled trial of cognitive therapy versus intensive behavior therapy in obsessive compulsive disorder. *Psychotherapy and Psychosomatics* 70(6):288-297.

Damecour, C. L., and M. Charron. 1998. Hoarding: A symptom, not a syndrome. *Journal of Clinical Psychiatry* 59(5):267-272.

Dornbush, M., and S. Pruitt. 1995. *Teaching the Tiger: A Handbook for Individuals Involved in the Education of Students with Attention Deficit Disorders, Tourette's Syndrome or Obsessive-Compulsive Disorder.* Duarte, CA: Hope Press.

Eifert, G. H., and J. P. Forsyth. 2007. *The Mindfulness and Acceptance Workbook for Anxiety: A Guide to Breaking Free from Anxiety, Phobias, and Worry Using Acceptance and Commitment Therapy*. Oakland, CA: New Harbinger Publications.

Eifert, G. H., J. Forsyth, J. Arch, E. Espejo, M. Keller, and D. Langer. 2009. Acceptance and commitment therapy for anxiety disorders: Three case studies exemplifying a unified treatment protocol. *Cognitive and Behavioral Practice* 16(4):368-385.

Ellis, A. 1962. *Reason and Emotion in Psychotherapy*. New York: Lyle Stuart.

Emmelkamp, P., and H. Beens. 1991. Cognitive therapy with obsessive-compulsive disorder: A comparative evaluation. *Behaviour Research and Therapy* 29(3):293-300.

Fitzgibbons, L., and C. Pedrick. 2003. *Helping Your Child with OCD: A Workbook for Parents of Children with Obsessive-Compulsive Disorder.* Oakland, CA: New Harbinger Publications.

Freeston, M. H., and R. Ladouceur. 1997. What do patients do with their obsessive thoughts? *Behaviour Research and Therapy* 35(4):335-348.

Freeston, M. H., R. Rheaume, and R. Ladouceur. 1996. Correcting faulty appraisals of obsessional thoughts. *Behaviour Research and Therapy* 34(5):433-446.

Frost, R. O., and R. Gross. 1993. The hoarding of possessions. *Behaviour Research and Therapy* 31(4): 367-381.

Frost, R. O., and G. S. Steketee. 1998. Hoarding: Clinical aspects and treatment strategies. In *Obsessive-Compulsive Disorders: Practical Management*, 3rd edition, edited by M. Jenike, L. Baer, and W. Minichiello. St. Louis, MO: Mosby.

Geller, D. A. 1998. Juvenile obsessive-compulsive disorder. In *Obsessive-Compulsive Disorders: Practical Management*, 3rd edition, edited by M. Jenike, L. Baer, and W. Minichiello. St. Louis, MO: Mosby.

Goodman, W. K., L. H. Price, S. A. Rasmussen, C. Mazure, R. L. Fleischmann, C. L. Hill, et al. 1989. Yale-Brown Obsessive Compulsive Scale I: Development, use and reliability. *Archives of General Psychiatry* 46(11):1006-1011.

Greenberg, D. 1984. Are religious compulsions religious or compulsive? A phenomenological study. *American Journal of Psychotherapy* 38(4):524-532.

Greenberg, D. 1987. Compulsive hoarding. *American Journal of Psychotherapy* 41(3):409-416.

Greist, J. H., and J. W. Jefferson. 1995. *Obsessive-Compulsive Disorder Casebook.* Washington, DC: American Psychiatric Press.

Harris, R. 2006. Embracing your demons: An overview of acceptance and commitment therapy. *Psychotherapy in Australia* 12(4):2-8.

Hayes, S. C., K. D. Strosahl, and K. G. Wilson. 1999. *Acceptance and Commitment Therapy: An experiential approach to behavior change.* New York: Guilford Press.

Hecht, A. M., M. Fichter, and P. Postpischil. 1983. Obsessive-compulsive neurosis and anorexia nervosa. *International Journal of Eating Disorders* 2(4):69-77.

Huey, E. D., R. Zahn, F. Krueger, J. Moll, D. Kapogiannis, E. M. Wassermann, and J. Grafman. 2008. A psychological and neuroanatomical model of obsessive-compulsive disorder. *Journal of Neuropsychiatry and Clinical Neuroscience* 20(4):390-408.

Husted, D., and N. Shapira. 2004. A review of the treatment for refractory obsessive-compulsive disorder: From medicine to deep brain stimulation. *CNS Spectrums* 9(11):833-847.

Hyman, B. M., and C. Pedrick. 2008. *Obsessive-Compulsive Disorder.* Brookfield, CT: Twenty-First Century Books.

Jenike, M. 1996. *Drug Treatment of OCD in Adults*. Milford, CT: Obsessive-Compulsive Foundation.

Jenike, M. 1998. Theories of etiology. In *Obsessive-Compulsive Disorders: Practical Management*, 3rd edition, edited by M. Jenike, L. Baer, and W. Minichiello. St. Louis, MO: Mosby.

Kabat-Zinn, J. 1990. *Full Catastrophe Living: Using the Wisdom of Your Body and Mind to Face Stress, Pain, and Illness*. New York: Delta.

Keuthen, N., R. L. O'Sullivan, and D. E. Jeffrey. 1998. Trichotillomania: Clinical concepts and treatment approaches. In *Obsessive-Compulsive Disorders: Practical Management*, 3rd edition, edited by M. Jenike, L. Baer, and W. Minichiello. St. Louis, MO: Mosby.

Koplewicz, H. S. 1996. *It's Nobody's Fault: New Hope and Help for Difficult Children and Their Parents*. New York: Times Books.

Lafleur, D. L., C. Pittenger, B. Kelmendi, T. Gardner, S. Wasylink, R. T. Malison, et al. 2005. N-acetylcysteine augmentation in serotonin reuptake inhibitor refractory obsessive-compulsive disorder. *Psychopharmacology* 184(2):254-256.

Leonard, H. 1989. Childhood rituals and superstitions: Developmental and cultural perspectives. In *Obsessive-Compulsive Disorder in Children and Adolescents*, edited by J. L. Rappoport. Washington, DC: American Psychiatric Press.

Linehan, M. M. 1993. *Cognitive-Behavioral Treatment of Borderline Personality Disorder*. New York: Guilford Press.

Mansueto, C. S., R. G. Golomb, A. M. Thomas, and R. M. Stemberger. 1999. A comprehensive model for behavioral treatment of trichotillomania. *Cognitive and Behavioral Practice* 6(1):23-43.

Mansueto, C. S., and D. J. Keuler. 2005. Tic or compulsion? It's Tourettic OCD. *Behavior Modification* 29(5):784-799.

March, J. S., and K. Mulle. 1998. *OCD in Children and Adolescents: A Cognitive-Behavioral Treatment Manual*. New York: Guilford Press.

McDougle, C. J., and W. K. Goodman. 1997. Combination pharmacological treatment strategies. In *Obsessive-Compulsive Disorders: Diagnosis, Etiology, Treatment*, edited by E. Hollander and D. J. Stein. New York: Marcel Dekker.

Mechanic, D. 1983. Adolescent health and illness behavior: Review of the literature and a new hypothesis for the study of stress. *Journal of Human Stress* 9(2):4-13.

Mell, L. K., R. L. Davis, and D. Owens. 2005. Association between streptococcal infection and obsessive-compulsive disorder, Tourette's syndrome, and tic disorder. *Pediatrics* 116(1):56-60.

Mouton, S. G., and M. A. Stanley. 1996. Habit reversal training for trichotillomania: A group approach. *Cognitive and Behavioral Practice* 3(1):159-182.

Nakatani, E., A. Nakagawa, Y. Ohara, S. Goto, N. Oozumi, M. Iwakiri, et al. 2003. Effects of behavior therapy on regional cerebral blood flow in obsessive-compulsive disorder. *Psychiatric Research: Neuroimaging* 124(2):113-120.

Niehous, D. J. H., and D. J. Stein. 1997. Obsessive-compulsive disorder: Diagnosis and assessment. In *Obsessive-Compulsive Disorders: Diagnosis, Etiology, Treatment*, edited by E. Hollander and D. J. Stein. New York: Marcel Dekker.

Nowak, R. 2006. Cosmetic surgery special: When looks can kill. *New Scientist* 192(2574):18-21.

Osborn, I. 2008. *Can Christianity Cure Obsessive-Compulsive Disorder? A Psychiatrist Explores the Role of Faith in Treatment.* Grand Rapids, MI: Brazos Press.

O'Sullivan, G., H. Noshirvani, and I. Marks. 1991. Six-year follow-up after exposure and clomipramine therapy for obsessive-compulsive disorder. *Journal of Clinical Psychiatry* 52(4):150-155.

Pavone, P., E. Parano, R. Rizzo, and R. R. Trifiletti. 2006. Autoimmune neuropsychiatric disorders associated with streptococcal infection: Sydenham chorea, PANDAS, and PANDAS variants. *Journal of Child Neurology* 21(9):727-736.

Pedrick, C. 1999. Taking medications safely. *Mature Years*, Fall, pp. 48-51.

Pennebaker, J. W. 1980. Perceptual and environmental determinants of coughing. *Basic and Applied Social Psychology* 1(1):83-91.

Penzel, F. 2002. A stimulus regulation model of trichotillomania. *In Touch* 3:12-14.

Phillips, K. A. 2005. *The Broken Mirror: Understanding and Treating Body Dysmorphic Disorder.* New York: Oxford University Press.

Phillips, K. A. 1998. Body dysmorphic disorder: Clinical aspects and treatment strategies. In *Obsessive-Compulsive Disorders: Practical Management*, 3rd edition, edited by M. Jenike, L. Baer, and W. Minichiello. St. Louis, MO: Mosby.

Phillips, K. A., and W. Menard. 2006. Suicidality in body dysmorphic disorder: A prospective study. *American Journal of Psychiatry* 163(7):1280-1282.

Piacentini, J., and F. Graae. 1997. Childhood OCD. In *Obsessive-Compulsive Disorders: Diagnosis, Etiology, Treatment*, edited by E. Hollander and D. J. Stein. New York: Marcel Dekker.

Rachman, S., and P. de Silva. 1978. Abnormal and normal obsessions. *Behaviour Research and Therapy* 16(4):233-248.

Salkovskis, P. M. 1985. Obsessional-compulsive problems: A cognitive-behavioural analysis. *Behaviour Research and Therapy* 23(5):571-583.

Salkovskis, P. M., and H. M. Warwick. 1986. Morbid preoccupations, health anxiety, and reassurance: A cognitive-behavioural approach to hypochondriasis. *Behaviour Research and Therapy* 24(5):597-602.

Salzman, L. 1973. *The Obsessive Personality: Origins, Dynamics and Therapy.* New York: Jason Aronson.

Schwartz, J. M., with B. Beyette. 1997. *Brain Lock: Free Yourself from Obsessive-Compulsive Disorder.* New York: Harper Perennial.

Segal, Z. V., J. M. G. Williams, and J. D. Teasdale. 2001. *Mindfulness-Based Cognitive Therapy for Depression: A New Approach for Preventing Relapse.* New York: Guilford Press.

Seuss, L., and M. S. Halpern. 1989. Obsessive-compulsive disorder: The religious perspective. In *Obsessive-Compulsive Disorder in Children and Adolescents*, edited by J. L. Rappoport. Washington, DC: American Psychiatric Press.

Slavney, P. R. 1987. The hypochondriacal patient and Murphy's "law." *General Hospital Psychiatry* 9(4):302-303.

Steketee, G. S. 1993. *Treatment of Obsessive-Compulsive Disorder.* New York: Guilford Press.

Swedo, S., and H. Leonard. 1998. *Is It "Just a Phase"? How to Tell Common Childhood Phases from More Serious Problems.* New York: Golden Books.

Swedo, S. H. L. Leonard, M. Garvey, B. Mittleman, A. J. Allen, S. Perlmutter, et al. 1988. Pediatric autoimmune neuropsychiatric disorders associated with streptococcal infections: Clinical descriptions of the first 50 cases. *American Journal of Psychiatry* 155(2):264-271.

Teng, E. J., D. W. Woods, and M. P. Twohig. 2006. Habit reversal as a treatment for chronic skin picking: A pilot investigation. *Behavior Modification* 30(4):411-422.

Twohig, M. P. 2009. The application of acceptance and commitment therapy to obsessive-compulsive disorder. *Cognitive and Behavioral Practice* 16(1):18-28.

Twohig, M. P., S. C. Hayes, and A. Masuda. 2006. A preliminary investigation of acceptance and commitment therapy as a treatment for chronic skin picking. *Behavior Research and Therapy* 44(10):1513-1522.

Twohig, M. P., J. C. Plumb, L. D. Pruitt, A. B. Collins, H. Hazlett-Stevens, M. R. Woidneck, et al. 2010. A randomized clinical trial of acceptance and commitment therapy vs. progressive relaxation training in the treatment of obsessive-compulsive disorder. Unpublished manuscript.

Van Oppen, P., E. de Haan, A. J. van Balkom, P. Spinhoven, K. Hoogduin, and R. van Dyck. 1995. Cognitive therapy and exposure in vivo in the treatment of obsessive compulsive disorder. *Behaviour Research and Therapy* 33(4):379-390.

Visser, S., and T. K. Bouman. 2001. The treatment of hypochondriasis: Exposure plus response prevention vs. cognitive therapy. *Behaviour Research and Therapy* 39(4):423-422.

Wegner, D. M. 1989. *White Bears and Other Unwanted Thoughts.* New York: Viking Penguin.

Wells, A. 1997. *Cognitive Therapy of Anxiety Disorders: A Practical Manual and Conceptual Guide.* New York: Wiley.

Wilhelm, S., and G. Steketee. 2006. *Cognitive Therapy for Obsessive-Compulsive Disorder: A Guide for Professionals.* Oakland, CA: New Harbinger Publications.

Wilhelm, S., G. S. Steketee, N. A. Reilly-Harrington, T. Deckersbach, U. Buhlmann, and L. Baer. 2005. Effectiveness of cognitive therapy for obsessive-compulsive disorder: An open trial. *Journal of Cognitive Psychotherapy* 19(2):173-179.

Yaryura-Tobias, J. A., and F. A. Neziroglu. 1997a. *Biobehavioral Treatment of Obsessive-Compulsive Spectrum Disorders.* New York: W. W. Norton.

Yaryura-Tobias, J. A., and F. A. Neziroglu. 1997b. *Obsessive-Compulsive Disorder Spectrum: Pathogenesis, Diagnosis, and Treatment.* Washington, DC: American Psychiatric Press.

Zung, W. W. K. 1965. A self-rating depression scale. *Archives of General Psychiatry* 12:63-70.

Photo by Robin Weinberger

Bruce M. Hyman, Ph.D., LCSW, is a cognitive behavioral therapist in private practice in Hollywood, FL, and has been the director of the OCD Resource Center of Florida (www.ocdhope.com) since 1991. He specializes in the cognitive behavioral treatment of adults and children with OCD, OCD spectrum disorders, and anxiety disorders, and is coauthor of *Coping with OCD*.

Cherry Pedrick, RN, is a registered nurse and freelance writer in the greater Seattle, WA, area. She is coauthor of *Loving Someone with OCD, Helping Your Child with OCD, The Habit Change Workbook, The BDD Workbook, Obsessive-Compulsive Disorder, and Anxiety Disorders.*